The Biblical Echo

Reflections on Bible, Jews and Judaism

by

EMANUEL FELDMAN

KTAV PUBLISHING HOUSE, INC.
HOBOKEN, NJ
1986

OTHER BOOKS BY EMANUEL FELDMAN

The Twenty-Eighth of Iyar

Biblical and Post-Biblical Defilement and Mourning:
Law as Theology.

Some of the material in this book originally appeared in the following publications: *Dor Le-Dor* (Jerusalem); *Emory University Quar-
terly; Jewish Observer Magazine;* "After Einstein," (Memphis State
University Press, 1981); *The New Republic; Saturday Review;
Sh'ma Magazine; Tradition Magazine.*

Library of Congress Cataloging-in-Publication Data

Feldman, Emanuel, 1927-
  The biblical echo.

  1. Jewish sermons—United States. 2. Sermons,
American—Jewish authors. 3. Bible. O.T.—Sermons.
I. Title.
BM740.2.F45   1986   296.4'2   86-10347
ISBN 0-88125-104-6

MANUFACTURED IN THE UNITED STATES OF AMERICA

In honor of my parents who are my teachers
Rabbi and Mrs. Joseph H. Feldman of Jerusalem

תפארת בנים אבותם (משלי י״ז:ו)

". . . and the glory of children are their parents."
(Proverbs 17:6)

Contents

Introduction

KING SOLOMON DID not say it, but he might have: "of the making of rabbis' books there is no end." "*Mah nishtanah*" is thus a legitimate question: How does this book differ from other books of this genre?

It is to be hoped that a perusal of these pages will provide its own answer and justification. But let it be said at the outset: this is not offered as a book of sermons. The selections presented here contain a variety of material: studies, essays, reviews, personal reminiscences, a bit of satire. Some are in fact formal pulpit sermons; but some were written for publication in journals, or were delivered as lectures to various non-synagogue audiences; still others were written as notes to myself. It is my hope that, in addition to the ideas and concepts he may find here, the reader will accept this volume as a kind of retrospective of some three decades in the American rabbinate.

It is a commentary of sorts that, after two thousand speeches and lectures and some one hundred published articles and reviews, I find that there are altogether less than one hundred pieces which can still be offered to a wider audience. Perhaps this is a function of false modesty. Or perhaps it is the silent intimidation of the printed page: a speech evaporates—sometimes blessedly—but the page of words refuses to disappear, and remains a mute, permanent, black-and-white testament either to the author's pedestrian mind or to his scintillating wit and wisdom. The fear posed by the former possibility far outweighs the fantasy of the latter.

Beneath all else there rests a painful truth: much of what a rabbi utters, declares, pronounces, writes, and pontificates upon during his career may be immediately useful and even occasionally uplifting for his audience; but very little is suitable for posterity. If ever a rabbi had any such illusions, the most effective way to discover that

1

he is really not a Moses is to have him prepare for publication a collection of his material. Among other benefits, this is an effective exercise in enforced humility.

In gathering this material, a serious question arose in my mind regarding the sermons and lectures: can a speech, designed for listening, be successfully transferred to the printed page? The spoken word depends heavily on the dynamic interaction between speaker and audience: on gesture, voice, inflection, eye contact, atmosphere—elements which simply cannot be replicated on paper. This is the classic "can/should" dilemma: *can* that which is created for a warm, living, personal dialogue between speaker and listener be transferred to cold print? And, since inevitably the original impact will be lost, *should* one attempt such a transition in the first place? After all, it was only at the theophany of Sinai that Israel saw that which was meant to be heard.

Rather than attempt to resolve the dilemma, I have simply ignored it, in the hope that the reader will nevertheless find some satisfaction and stimulation in the ideas that emerge from that portion of the material which was originally prepared for listening and not for reading, and which in any event applies to less than half of the offerings here presented.

I am struck anew, incidentally, by the differences between the genres of writing and speaking. In preparing for a speech, not every word need be written out, not every phrase carefully worded. Once the essential ideas are clear in the speaker's mind, once they are noted down in their proper sequence, once he knows how he will begin and how he will end, he is ready to speak. His use of particular words and phrases will depend on the mood of the moment. In fact, a written text can only hamper and stultify him, and make his presentation one of artifice rather than one of genuine spontaneity.

But the essay! Here the word, the nuance, the continuity, the phrasing, must be right on target—and must be so the first time. There are no second chances: the writer cannot clarify an idea by approaching it from a different angle if the first attempt is unsuccessful. He cannot rely upon the electricity which is generated between speaker and audience. Here it is the stark, lonely, empty page waiting to be filled; here it is the reader confronting black typeface on white paper. Each word must be precise: there is only one right word, not two. There can be no indulging in the luxury of repeating phrases, or the virtuoso and spontaneous shaping of thoughts. True, the writer has the opportunity to rewrite his words, to restructure, to rephrase, to revise tirelessly: he is not required to think on his feet. But once the final draft is completed, it stands alone on the printed page, isolated and vulnerable: it can be studied, read and reread. If the tone is unsteady or the words unfocused, the writer has no opportunity to recapture his audience. The reader will have exercised his prerogative: he will have closed the book.

Confession: although I spend much of my time speaking, I find writing far more demanding; the confrontation between writer and blank page, the careful search for precision, the ideational development, the lonely, silent struggle of the writer against himself—these represent major hurdles which, when overcome, offer major satisfactions. It is no wonder that Maimonides writes, in his *Iggeret ha-Shemad* ("Letter on Apostasy"), that a person should review "two or three or four times that which he desires to say, and should learn it exceedingly well" before he speaks in public. However, when it comes to writing, "it would be proper for the writer to go over his words one thousand times if at all possible."

At the same time, I do not take lightly the act of speaking, and am in the habit of preparing sermons carefully—even the simplest ones, even the ordinary ones. I have always envied those preachers who have the God-given ability to extemporize skillfully and eloquently, who can develop an idea in their minds a few moments before they mount the pulpit, and who are thus spared the nagging vexation of worrying, during the week, what to speak about on Shabbat. And while I do occasionally extemporize, and rarely bring a written speech to the platform, it is clear that the Biblical text and an intelligent audience require more thought than can be realized by a frenetic last-minute search for ideas.

It is my hope that in the small number of sermons, lectures, and essays presented in these pages, the reader will find, here and there, insights and ideas that are a bit beyond the conventional. If this turns out to be the case, then it is my congregation which deserves some acknowledgment. An ordinary congregation begets ordinary sermons, but an extraordinary congregation demands more of its rabbi. My congregation, intellectually and Jewishly sophisticated, demands ideas which are more than superficial, and which require planning and thinking on my part, and careful, attentive listening on their part. The series of sermons on Joseph, for example, or on the Biblical Echo, or the Isaac/Ishmael series, or the Eve/Serpent talks were not designed as entertainments: they presumed a listener who was perceptive and discerning.

There is no greater fulfillment for a rabbi than to alight upon an exciting idea, to think it through, agonize over it, develop it, clarify it, organize it, deliver it, and then to know that the words have struck home to the audience. In this regard, speaking offers a kind of instant gratification which is unavailable to the writer. But it also offers instant disappointment. For there is no deeper sense of frustration than to realize, five minutes into a sermon, that after all the labor and effort, one has given birth to nothingness, and that almost no one is listening. Suddenly, the rabbi finds himself in full sympathy with Ezekiel's moving words in 33:32: "thou art unto them as a love song of one that has a pleasant voice, and can play well on an instrument; so they hear thy words, but they do them not."

I am grateful to my congregation, which has so often created fulfillment and not disappointment for its rabbi. It is relatively easy to deliver a well-liked sermon: take a current headline, stir in a Biblical verse, mix in a light anecdote, blend quickly, and out pops a fluffy and frothy sermon which everyone "enjoys"—mental junk food. My listeners have by and large been dissatisfied with junk food and have insisted on a full, wholesome diet.

While the criteria by which these selections were finally chosen for inclusion are very subjective and personal, one central motif informs those selections which deal with Biblical matters. The idea of Torah as a living and infinitely profound wellspring of ideas and concepts is unknown to most American Jews, brought up as they often are on Sunday School banalities and superficialities. The sections on the Bible attempt, therefore, to plumb the depths of what seem on the surface to be merely arresting narratives. I have been concerned not so much to show the relevance of the text to contemporary times as to demonstrate that the Bible contains in it more than meets the superficial glance, and that it speaks with great urgency and immediacy not only to the mind but to the soul of contemporary man.

In addition, I have tried to show how one goes about reading a Biblical text, to illustrate how it contains layer upon layer of meaning, subtlety, and nuance which completely elude us if we treat it as ordinary, earth-bound literature. In brief (if not always briefly) this is an attempt to create, at the very least, *respect* for the Biblical text.

It is natural, I suppose, that most of the Biblical selections should be centered on Genesis. Perhaps this is because its narratives are so touching, containing in them elements that are universal and human and personal. Or perhaps it is a function of the long, winter Friday nights which coincide with the reading of Genesis: what greater pleasure can there be than to sit at the Friday-night table with one's family and friends and to spend the time with Joseph and his brothers, or with Jacob and his strange wrestling, or the silent Isaac, or the powerful Rebecca, or the mysterious twin trees of the Garden of Eden?

Of the material in this book which was not spoken, I have included those essays, articles, and reviews which best reflect the kind of Jewish life which a rabbi witnesses during his years of pulpit service. These years have been for the Jewish community a time of deepening Jewish awareness and self-discipline on the one hand, and of profoundly dangerous stirrings on the other. Renewed commitment to Judaism by the core group has been more than counterbalanced by a striking and alarming surge towards assimilation and intermarriage—inevitable products of the indifference and self-indulgence which have been the hallmarks of the larger society around us. A rabbi whose gaze has encompassed these two simultaneous forces will, it is hoped, be excused the occasional note of frustration which now and then may intrude themselves into these pages. While a rabbi who constantly carps and rebukes is ineffective, one who is wholly uncritical is either uncaring or unseeing.

I hereby express my gratitude to my brother, Rabbi Aaron Feldman of Jerusalem, who unstintingly took precious time from his duties as a scholar, teacher, and writer to read parts of the manuscript, to point out various source materials, and to make many helpful suggestions. It goes without saying that the errors and imperfections which may be found here are mine alone.

In describing the Torah, Moses, in his farewell address to the people Israel, states: "My doctrine shall drop as the rain" (Deut. 32:32). On which the Sifre comments: "Just as rain is one entity, and yet supplies each tree with that which it requires: to the grape according to its needs; to the olive according to its needs; to the fig according to its needs; so also are the words of the Torah: they are all one entity, but there is found in them Scripture, Mishnah, Law, and Lore."

It is my prayer that this modest volume will supply the reader with an occasional insight, or inspiration, or understanding, or perception, "according to his needs." At the very least, the reader will gain some insight into the thinking and aspirations, triumphs and trials, of a contemporary American rabbi.

Part I

The Jew and His Bible

Biblical Echoes

Sounds, resonance, reverberations: if we listen carefully and lovingly and attentively, we hear them on every Biblical page: echoes. The Book of the Torah is eternal and never-ending, as its Author is eternal and never-ending. Thus it comes as no surprise that what occurs in the Book is also never-ending, silently reverberating from one generation to the next. Silently: but if we listen, we can hear the still small voice of eternity as it resounds . . .

Of Eve and the Serpent

ESAU AND JACOB, the twin brothers, are diametrical opposites. One is primarily materialistic, the other is primarily spiritual; one is the hunter, the other is the dweller in tents; one is loud and boisterous, a hypocrite and a masquerader; the other is quiet, innocent, concerned with the relationship of God and man.

Their struggle within their mother's womb is a portent of things to come; the long struggle between them will go on until the end of days, for they are the prototypes of good and evil.

Good and evil have earlier roots in the Torah. At another time and in another place Adam and Eve are commanded, "From the tree of knowledge of good and evil ye shall not eat."

On the surface, there is no connection between Jacob and Esau, and the Garden of Eden. But on a deeper level, the Jacob-Esau narrative echoes those earlier events which took place in the Garden. God commands Adam: "From all the trees in the Garden you may eat, but from the tree of knowledge of good and evil you may not eat, else you will surely die" (Gen. 2:16). "But the serpent was the most sly of all the creatures" (3:1), and whispers into the ears of Eve and tempts her to proceed and take from the tree of good and evil. And by his guile and trickery and cleverness he sways her, induces her, cajoles her into violating the command of God. She and Adam eat, and suddenly their eyes open up: they are aware of the existence of good and evil. Where before they were innocent, they now realize that they are naked—in more ways than one. They cover themselves and they try to hide from God, and God finds them and banishes them from the Garden, because the Garden is only for innocents. To Eve God says: "In pain shalt thou bring forth children." And to Adam He says: "By the sweat of thy brow shalt thou eat bread all the days of your life."

Certain acts and events bear their own echoes which resonate down the corridors of time.

Many generations after Eve, another woman conceives. Her name is Rebecca. The Torah informs us that her pregnancy is so difficult that she cries out, *Lammah zeh anokhi*, "Wherefore do I live?" (Gen. 25:22). She is the only one of the matriarchs to do so. Is this a dim echo of what God once said to the first woman: "In pain shalt thou bring forth children"? Is there something of Eve in the person of Rebecca? Look further: whom does Rebecca finally bring forth? The twins, Esau and Jacob, the prototypes of good and evil. In brief, Rebecca brings into the world good and evil—just as Eve's act first brought into the world good and evil. Is Rebecca a kind of incarnation of Eve?

Esau and Jacob: luminous opposites. But their saintly father Isaac knows not the difference, and he loves Esau. The knowledge of good and evil which Rebecca—the echo of Eve—plainly sees in her two sons is completely hidden from Isaac. He does not know good and evil. Like Adam and Eve prior to their sin, Isaac is innocent. It is as if his experience at the Akedah has transformed him into an angelic, otherworldly creature who transcends the mundane, and lives once again in the Garden of Eden.

But innocence can have catastrophic consequences in a world where not everyone is innocent. For if Isaac persists in his ways, if he continues in his blindness towards the evil of Esau and gives his eternally effective blessing to him, then the destiny of the Jewish people, the spiritual purpose of Israel—and thus the entire divine plan for the world—is thwarted. If Esau and not Jacob receives the blessing, it can result in premature death for the people Israel.

We have here the inverse situation of Eden: there the innocents were to be protected from good and evil lest death be brought into the world. Here, the innocent one must learn good and evil lest death be brought to Israel. Thus it becomes necessary for Isaac to be given that which he lacks: the knowledge to distinguish between good and evil. But how can this knowledge, which has been hidden from him, now be restored to him?

It can be restored to him only through the identical means through which the knowledge of good and evil originally entered the world. The serpent had used the handmaidens of evil: guile, cleverness, trickery, falsehood, concealment. And now these very same qualities will have to be used once more, in order to present to Isaac that which he lacks.

And so the roles of the Eden story—the events and the actions—now begin to repeat themselves—but in reverse, like a mirror image, like the negative of a photograph, where the shadows are white, and the whites are shadows. And what we are about to see are acts of redemption, expiation, and correction of the sin of the Garden of Eden which utilize the same means to give the knowledge of good and evil to Isaac. This is a kind of reenactment of the sin of Adam and Eve, but now the instrument of sin (the loss of Isaac's innocence) will be utilized for the purpose of overcoming evil.

There is now a transferring of roles: the serpent once whispered into the innocent ears of Eve and told her to learn of good and evil. Now Rebecca, in a prophetic vision, whispers into Jacob's ear and tells him how to restore the knowledge of good and evil to his father Isaac. The guile of the serpent, which was used for evil, is now redeemed: Rebecca uses the same guile for good. They will deceive the blind old father: Jacob will disguise himself in goatskins, the father will touch him and be fooled, he will think it is Esau, and thus the rightful heir will receive the blessing.

The full tapestry begins to emerge. Once there was a woman, Eve, who was deceived into bringing good and evil into the world. And now, in Rebecca, the roles are reversed. Here is a woman who initiates the trickery against the deception by Esau, and thus Eve's act is corrected. The guile of the serpent who deceived Eve by masquerading as a righteous one is now turned back against him, and he who now once again masquerades as a righteous one— Esau—becomes the victim of the masquerade, as Jacob imitates him, dresses like him, poses as the evil one, and redeems the original wrong perpetrated by the serpent.

What the serpent (evil) once perpetrated upon the Woman is now perpetrated by a woman against Esau (evil).

And the role of Jacob in all this? Jacob is an unwilling accomplice, but cooperates with his mother—just as Adam was an unwilling accomplice who cooperated with Eve.

Note also the key role played by food in these two incidents. In the one, there are the prohibitions against eating certain fruits from certain trees, and the express permission to eat other fruits from other trees; in the other, there is the pottage and the venison. Nor can we overlook the theme of clothing: the coverings which God fashions from the leaves of the Garden for the naked Adam and Eve, and the coverings which Rebecca takes from the goatskins for her son Jacob.[1]

Are we only imagining that we hear faint echoes of the Garden

---

1. For more on the role of food and clothing in Genesis, see below, "On Completing Genesis."

story? Note this striking Midrash: "Esau was born with a sign of the serpent upon his thigh" (Midrash Yalkut Reuveni on Gen. 25:25). Esau is the embodiment of the serpent of the Garden. And note also the Zohar in sidrah *Toledot*, 143a, which states that the serpent in the Garden brought a curse into the world through his cunning, for by forcing Adam and Eve to sin, he prevented God's blessing from entering the world as God had originally intended. The Zohar continues that it is impossible to restore the blessing to the world unless one uses the methods of the serpent. Thus, Isaac tells Esau that Jacob came *be-mirmah* (Gen. 27:35), "in cunning," translated by the Targum as *be-ḥakhmeta*, "in wisdom." By fooling his father and taking the blessing from the embodiment of the serpent, Jacob restores the blessing to the world: it is measure for measure.

And what of Isaac? What is his relationship to the Eden story? Let us return to Isaac's Akedah. After the near-sacrifice, we hear nothing about Isaac. Why does the Torah simply say, after the Akedah, that "Abraham returned to his servant"? Abraham alone? What of Isaac? He disappears from the scene until many years later. Rebecca dies and is buried, and there is no Isaac. Eliezer searches for a wife for Isaac at the behest of Abraham; but there is no Isaac. Then, suddenly, in Genesis 24:62, we find that Isaac has been in *be'er lakhai ro'i*—and the rabbis say that he has returned "from the Garden of Eden" (Midrash Yalkut Reuveni).

Isaac, then, represents innocence, the innocence of the Garden into which good and evil were introduced by stealth, and to whom this same knowledge is now introduced by stealth.

But there are further echoes, and further resonances. For seminal acts and events do not take place in isolation; they echo throughout history, causing subsequent events to reverberate over and over again with their original sound.

Jacob deceived his father, taking advantage of the darkness of his eyes. Years later Jacob, too, will be deceived by Laban, and in the darkness of the wedding night Laban will substitute the older sister Leah for the beloved Rachel, for whom Jacob has labored so long. Surely Jacob will perceive a dim echo of his own act against his father: you fooled your father, and now you will be fooled. And, in fact, the Midrash informs us that when Jacob asked Leah why she had deceived him, she replied, "And you—were you permitted to deceive your father?"

And more: you deceived your father with the skin of a goat which you donned on your body to become a hairy Esau; now your own sons will deceive you through a goat, and when your beloved Joseph is sold into slavery by his brothers, your sons will come forward and show you his garment—which will have been dipped into the blood of a goat. And later, Judah himself will be entrapped by Tamar—also with a goat. Still later, in the Book of Numbers, the priest will sacrifice, as atonement for the sins of Israel, nothing other than two goats.

Echoes: actions and events engender other actions, other events. Nothing goes unanswered, nothing is left hanging in the air. There is a principle of *middah ke-neged middah*, "measure for measure." What you sow, you will reap, for the future is a continuation of the past; better, it is a result of the past. Each man creates his future by his present. In a very real way, the future, the present, the past are all one.

A Tale of Two Trees

A NUMBER OF questions occur as we read the magnificent Jacob/ Esau narrative.

How can it be that the wise Isaac does not know that his son Esau is evil, and almost gives him the blessing which might have altered the destiny of the Jewish people? How can it be that a man with prophetic power such as Isaac does not recognize the incarnation of evil which was his son Esau? Why is it that Leah's eyes are *rakkot* (Gen. 29:17), which the tradition interprets to mean that she has been weeping constantly? What is the real meaning behind her weeping? Why is it that after receiving the blessings from his father, Jacob's life changes from one of relative calm and tranquility to one of storm and struggle?

The narratives in Genesis form the richest tapestry of our people, and in this tapestry there are certain luminous threads which wind their way from one end of the book to the other and beyond, and which suggest some answers to these questions.

Let us go back to the Garden of Eden. The focal point in that Garden are the two major trees: the tree of life, from which Adam may eat and in fact is encouraged to eat; and the tree of knowledge of good and evil, which is strictly forbidden to him.

The Torah does not describe the tree of knowledge, but it uses very suggestive words like *da'at, tov,* and *ta'avah,* "knowledge," "good," and "desire." Thus, the tree is delightful, attractive, irresistible, apparently appealing to all the physical senses.

Why does God place the tree of knowledge in the Garden of Eden in the. first place? Is its designed purpose to attract Adam, to entice him, to test him, to entrap him?

Not at all. God does not play games with mankind. He is teaching Adam, and us, an important lesson. The two trees represent two paths to human perfection and completion. One path is that of

16

ḥayyim, "life," and all that is spiritual and good: kindness, compassion, sensitivity to others, morality, decency, ḥesed; mitzvot like tefillin, Shabbat, kashruth, mikveh, study of Torah: all those acts of outreach between man and man and man and God which sanctify life and which connect us ultimately with God, with others, and with our own selves.

The other tree also represents an aspect of human perfection. While the tree of life represents total purity and sanctity and spirituality, the tree of knowledge represents the mixture of good and evil in this world, the need to distinguish between them, and, by so doing, to withdraw from evil, from the merely physical for its own sake despite its attraction; to refrain from inhumanity, vulgarity, immorality, unethical acts, selfishness, dishonesty, the swift, impulsive satisfaction of the physical appetites.

On the path of life, man encounters two challenges: (a) the requirement to strive for a holy and caring life; (b) the requirement to refrain from evil.

The tree of life represents positive acts, "thou shalt"; the tree of knowledge represents the negative, refraining from doing wrong: "thou shalt not." Each is an aspect of *shelemut*, the completion of the human personality.

The two trees are a result of a tension within each individual: a pull upward towards good and spirituality, and a pull downward towards evil and physicality; a yearning for heaven, and an appetite for earth.

This polarity between good and evil is adumbrated in the Thirty-fourth Psalm: *sur me-ra, va-aseh tov,* "withdraw from evil and perform good, seek peace and pursue it." That is, the withdrawal from *ra*—evil—and the doing of *tov*—good—are the prerequisites for the pursuit of *shalom*, which is not merely "peace," but personal completion. *Sur me-ra* is the negative command: thou shalt not. There is here no positive, committed service of God. There is merely the refraining from evil. *Aseh tov* is the positive command: thou shalt. Here there is required a doing, an action. One can fulfill the *sur me-ra* simply by doing nothing, and thus withdraw from the evils of the world. But through this alone one cannot reach the higher levels of God's service. In order to reach higher, one must fulfill the *aseh tov*: active and committed pursuit of the way of God.

Which is the greater service of God, *sur me-ra* or *aseh tov*, the negative or the positive commandment? On the face of it, *aseh tov* is primary, because it can reach higher spheres. But a case can be made for *sur me-ra*: in Judaism one walks on God's path by physical means, by using the body, the flesh, material things. We are created with temptations and hungers, and the purpose of Torah is to teach us how to utilize the physical in the service of God. Thus, the flesh has to be encountered, understood for what it is—and ultimately bent into God's service. And by so doing the *aseh tov* comes into being. The negative thou-shalt-not is an integral part of thou-shalt, because the thou-shalt is only fulfilled through means of the thou-shalt-not.

Certain personalities are better suited to confront this world and to subjugate it. Others are better suited to reach upward to higher spheres.

In some souls, the *aseh tov* strain is dominant; for such a person, it is less difficult to overcome evil, to elevate it, to sanctify it, to convert it into good. Such a person is the *aseh tov* personality.

In others, the pull towards evil is dominant. Such a person must utilize and sanctify the physical in order to overcome the attraction towards evil. This is the *sur me-ra* personality. This individual is no less significant than the *aseh tov;* in fact, when one learns how to cope with the physical and with the attraction of immediate pleasure, he has the potential of becoming a great and noble human being, perhaps even greater than the *aseh tov* personality.

In the Jacob-Esau encounter, these two stark contrasts are present. Rebecca is told that she is "carrying two nations" in her womb (Gen. 25:23); that is to say, she is carrying within her the two prototypes, the two dominant aspects of the human personality: Jacob, the tree of life; and Esau, the tree of knowledge. Jacob, the *aseh tov*, the dweller in tents, in whom the pull towards good is dominant, and who will attain his personal completion through reaching for the good; and Esau, the *sur me-ra*, whose task it will be to understand his *sur me-ra* personality, to learn to elevate it, utilize it, and through this to grow spiritually. If Esau succeeds in his task, he can become even greater than Jacob, for by learning to sanctify the earthly and the physical, he can reach heights of spirituality unattainable to anyone else.

Isaac is not naive. He knows his son Esau has a natural pull towards immediate gratification. He knows that Esau and not Jacob is the one who is attracted to the hunt, to the field, to the kill, to fulfilling his every physical desire: he is the *sur me-ra* personality. But Isaac perceives—erroneously—that Esau is struggling and winning the battle, and that he will thus become the greater and more noble of his sons. And thus Isaac is willing to give Esau the blessing which is designed to imprint upon him and his seed for all time the ability to cope with the attractions of the now, the truly physical, and to utilize it to grow into spirituality. Note carefully the blessing which Isaac intends to give Esau:

> God will give thee of the dew of heaven, and of the fat places of the earth, and plenty of corn and wine. Let peoples serve thee, and nations bow down to thee. Be lord over thy brethren, and let thy mother's sons bow down to thee. Cursed be everyone that curseth thee, and blessed be everyone that blesseth thee (Gen. 27:28).

Such a blessing will endow the recipient with eternal power over the merely physical.

But Rebecca sees things as they really are: Esau, far from utilizing evil for holy purposes, has been overcome by evil. He willingly allows himself to eat of the forbidden tree because he is attracted to its tempting surface. Thus she knows that he is not worthy of representing that second way of human perfection, the *sur me-ra* way. She knows that Esau has forfeited it. The power to dominate the physical and to utilize it for God must now be given to Jacob. And so Rebecca does what has to be done. She sees to it that the blessing is given to Jacob.

The result is that Jacob is now not only the *aseh tov;* he also possesses a powerful new quality, the *sur me-ra.*

This has major implications in the life of Jacob. Until now, his life has been one of tranquility. Not for him the struggles of the world. He has been a "dweller in tents," the quintessential *aseh tov,* the tree of life, the "thou shalt." Temptations, forbidden things, "thou shalt nots," this-worldly gratifications—these have not been part of Jacob's life. But now that he has within him the quality of *sur me-ra* as well, he must leave the "tent" and begin to struggle within the world.

He leaves his father's house, encounters the cunning Laban, and then engages in the monumental wrestling with the strange creature of the night, the *ish*/man.

This wrestling prefigures Jacob's destiny: he will be able to vanquish the temptation of evil; he will be called *Yisrael,* the "conqueror" (Gen. 32:29). He and his progeny are destined to dominate physicality. His new name indicates that he will correct, sanctify, and elevate the world by teaching that it is possible for man to overcome evil, to utilize it, raise it.

But the life of a *sur me-ra* is a difficult one: he lives with Laban and is constantly cheated; his beloved Rachel is denied him; he emerges from the wrestling with a limp; there is distrust between

Joseph and the rest of Jacob's sons; Joseph disappears; Dinah is ravished; Judah falls from his lofty position of leadership; Simeon is imprisoned in Egypt; Rachel dies prematurely, and she will not be buried with him.

Small wonder that when Pharaoh, in Genesis 47:8, asks Jacob about the years of his life (apparently, Pharaoh is not inquiring merely about Jacob's age), Jacob replies that he is one hundred and thirty years old, and that the years have been *me'at ve-ra'im*, "few and evil."

In the midst of these crises, Jacob never forgets that, since his father blessed him, he is also now a *sur me-ra*, and he knows the hidden side of that which seems not good, and realizes that *ra* can be utilized to reach *tov*, goodness and perfection. Through all these tragedies he remains steadfast, continues to grow, and ultimately becomes what the tradition calls the *beḥir ha-avot*, the preeminent patriarch.

The concepts of *sur me-ra* and *aseh tov* are not limited to Jacob and Esau. They appear in two other siblings, in the persons of Leah and Rachel, the daughters of Laban, and granddaughters of Bethuel. "And the eyes of Leah were *rakkot*, and Rachel was beautiful of form and beautiful of visage" (Gen. 29:17). The tradition tells us that Leah had eyes which were *rakkot*—soft, pale—because of her weeping. Why was Leah weeping? As the older of the sisters, she had been told that she was destined to marry the other older sibling in her family, Esau—just as the younger Rachel would marry the younger Jacob.

But it is more than a matter of older and younger siblings. Leah is also the *sur me-ra* personality, destined for Esau, her opposite *sur me-ra*—while Rachel, the *aseh tov* personality, is destined for Jacob. But there is one difference: unlike her counterpart Esau, Leah has vanquished the physical and, realizing that Esau has failed in the struggle and has been vanquished by the physical, she weeps. She wants nothing to do with a man who is dominated by the physical.

However, when Jacob, through his father's blessing, becomes a *sur me-ra*, when he acquires the ability to reach perfection through the utilization of the physical, Leah too is now destined to become the wife of Jacob. Jacob wants Rachel because, like himself, Rachel is an *aseh tov*. Now that Jacob is both *sur me-ra* and *aseh tov*, he is to marry both Rachel and Leah. And perhaps this also explains why Rachel remains Jacob's most beloved: Jacob is the *aseh tov* in essence, as is Rachel. Leah is less beloved because the *sur me-ra* is what Jacob *acquires* later but is not really his own original essence.

But we are not done. The thread continues in the children of Jacob. Joseph, like his mother Rachel, is the *aseh tov*. The brothers, like their mother, Leah, represent the *sur me-ra* qualities: they are endowed with the power to subjugate and convert the physical. Thus, the conflict between Joseph and his brothers is at bottom a conflict between these two approaches to life: which way is the most pleasing to God, the *sur me-ra*, or the *aseh tov?* Each misunderstands the other, and each sees in the other a threat to the future of the people Israel.

The brothers in effect say: man cannot live withdrawn from the reality of life, above the strife. We must be involved with mankind, with the struggles of the body, with temptation, with the presence of evil, with the appetites, with the pull of the flesh. These are integral aspects of human life, and we must learn to convert them to good: the *lo ta'aseh*, the "thou shalt not," is a greater challenge than the *aseh*, the "thou shalt."

Joseph, child of Rachel, is the *aseh tov*. He embodies the positive commandment and recoils from the physical: allow the sacred acts of the Jew to elevate life, disengage from the affairs of the world, live a holy life, unencumbered by temptation. To such an approach— which turns away from this world—the way of the brothers is foolhardy, When Joseph reports the evil behavior of his brothers (Gen. 37:2), he is misreading them. He does not realize that they are the ideal *sur me-ra*. He thinks that they are new Esaus who allow the physical to conquer them, when in fact they, in the person of their leader Judah, are well on the way to converting the physical—as Leah, the mother of Judah, has done.

The brothers in turn view Joseph, resplendent in his many-colored cloak, as a threat to the destiny of Israel. He is unconcerned with the life around him, apparently concerned only with his personal growth, aloof from the affairs of the world. If Joseph is to be the leader, what will become of God's world?

Thus, the conflict between the brothers can be viewed in a new light: as part of that dual approach to the world which is first represented in the tree of life and the tree of knowledge; which reveals itself again in Jacob and Esau, and in Rachel and Leah; which is seen in the thou-shalt and the thou-shalt-not; and which finds its formulation in the psalmist's *sur me-ra* and *aseh tov*.

The physical by itself is not inherently evil. In dealing with it, we are presented with choices. We can turn our back on it, flee from it, and approach God through our minds and souls and not our bodies. Or we can confront the physical, wrestle with it, and convert its innate energy into spiritual power.

The Ram of Isaac

OF ALL THE narratives in the Torah, none has had a greater impact on the Jewish soul than the story of father Abraham, granted a child with Sarah his wife in their old age, who suddenly hears the commanding voice of God bidding him to take his son, his only son, and offer him up as a sacrifice.

In this supreme act of faith—the three-day journey to Moriah; the brief, halting dialogue between father and son along the way; the scene on that mountaintop which is destined to become the site of the great Temple—Abraham raises the knife to slaughter his son, the voice from on high stays his hand, and Abraham sees a ram caught in the thicket by its horns and offers the ram up as a sacrifice instead of his son Isaac.

We know what happened to Abraham and to Isaac, but one question remains: what ultimately happened to the ram which was actually sacrificed in Isaac's place? The Torah only tells us that it was caught in a thicket by its horns. But the ram is, after all, a major figure in the story. It is from that ram that we derive the focal point of Rosh Hashanah, the shofar. And it is the ram who is the surrogate Isaac. Without it there would have been no Isaac, no Jacob, no children of Israel, and God's covenant would have come to an end. Surely we cannot ignore the ram.

The sages of our history certainly do not ignore it. There is an ancient tradition that the ram was no accident: God had created it on the eve of the Shabbat of Creation, together with several other of His miraculous creations (see Avot 5:6; Pesaḥim 54a). And that ram was set aside, some say in the Garden of Eden, destined to be used specifically for the *Akedah* sacrifice.

Fine, the ram is no accident: it was part of God's plan that it be sacrificed. But is that the end of the ram? Evidently not. The sages

22

tell us (Yalkut 101, and on Isa. 27:13, #436) that not one part of the ram went to waste:

> The tendons of the ram, what happened to them? They became the ten strings of King David's harp a thousand years later. Its skin, what happened to that? The skin became the leather belt around the loins of Elijah the prophet a thousand years later. And what happened to the horns? The left horn, God sounded the shofar with it at Mount Sinai. And the right horn? The right horn will form the shofar at the ingathering of the exiles at the final redemption.

In order to understand this Midrash, we must shed the literal-mindedness of our lives and move into a realm where our hearts and not our minds function, where the poetic and imaginative faculties within us take over from the merely cognitive and literal.

Nothing was lost from this prototypical sacrifice. Part of it went into the ten-stringed harp of David. Who is David, and what does he represent? David represents man reaching up towards God. *Ne'im zemirot yisrael*, he is called: "the sweet singer of Israel," the teacher of Israel, teaching us how to pray. David's words are the words of the Psalms, which form the bulk of our prayerbook, man's most eloquent expression of upreach to God. And David's harp is an integral element in his prayers: it is the harp which brings to him the joy of prayer. It is the harp which hangs over David's bed at night as the east wind blows in from his open window in Jerusalem, and the strings begin to move and the melody is heard and David awakens and begins to adore God and compose his songs to Him (Berakhot 3b).

Who is David? David is the yearning Jew reaching upward and outward to God. Wherever one turns in the Psalms one finds the reflection of every possible facet of human life, of human anguish and joy, despair and triumph.

Who is David? David is the poet and warrior, the young shepherd who defeats Goliath and the Philistines. He is among the most complex of Biblical personalities, and the most human also. And David's love of God is symbolized most accurately by his harp. Who is David? David is represented by the kabbalistic concept of *mattah-maalah*, man below reaching up to God above.

Nothing was wasted from that ram. From its tendons were formed the strings of David's harp. That is, the sacrifice had in it an element of man reaching up, and this element continued to live, and surfaced again through the person of David. Not only does it surface in David, but his power originates in that sacrifice and in that ram.

But the sacrifice has another element in it: *not only man reaching up to God, but God reaching down to man.* And the concept of God reaching down into the affairs of man is also expressed by this Midrash: "the skin became the leather coverlet round the loins of Elijah."

Who was Elijah, and what does he represent? Elijah is the prophet of God, the zealot of I Kings 19:10, the protector of Israel. Elijah is the one for whom we open the door on Passover night, for he is the forerunner of the ultimate redemption. Elijah is the fiery prophet of God who confronts four hundred priests of the idol Baal on Mount Carmel, and Elijah assembles all the House of Israel below the mountain and hurls a challenge to them about religious fence-straddling: Get off the fence, he says; make your choice; decide today to whom you are willing to give your allegiance, to the God of Israel or the idol Baal.

Who is Elijah? He is the prophet of the covenant, the prophet of the *berit;* he is the one who attends every circumcision and protects every child when the child makes his own blood sacrifice. He is the fighter for God on earth, God's fearless messenger—the prototypical prophet, protector of Israel, fearless zealot of God.

Elijah's leather coverlet represents action, "girding one's loins" for God's battles. Elijah rides into battle with every Jewish soldier, so goes the tradition. Elijah is the prototype of *maalah mattah*— bringing godliness down to man. The original Akedah sacrifice had in it the element of God reaching down towards man. And this element continues and surfaces in Elijah. Furthermore, Elijah's power originates in the Akedah sacrifice.

David and Elijah: David brings man up towards God; Elijah brings God down towards man.This is the divine partnership of prophet and king. Just as Abraham and Isaac are in a divine partnership in the original sacrifice: Abraham finds God through his intelligence and rational faculties, and brings man up to God as he converts others to God; while Isaac, in his childlike and otherworldly inno-cence, knows God and senses Him and brings God down to man. David and Elijah, king and prophet; Abraham and Isaac, father and son.

David and Elijah may seem to be an unlikely pair, a strange union of contrasts: the humble shepherd and the brave warrior, the musi-cal poet, the scholar king, the psalmist—paired with the rough-hewn prophet who wears a leather-skin coat held together by a leather girdle, who is mocked by children, who speaks bluntly, directly, and simply the searing word of God which is branded into his soul.

But there is a common element which these two contrasting personalities share. He who brings man up to God and he who brings godliness down to man, he who is the author of carefully wrought lyrics to the Creator and he who is the author of the sharp, blunt outbursts ("if God is God, worship Him; if Baal is Baal, worship him") share together one common idea. We hear every Shabbat and every Yom Tov, in the blessings following the prophetic reading: *samhenu be-Eliyahu ha-navi avdekha*, "make us joyous in Elijah thy prophet." And in whom else do we ask God to make us joyous? *U-ve-malkhut beit David*, "and in the kingdom of the house of David, Thy anointed one" referring to the times of the Messiah. What David and Elijah share in common, then, is the Messiah.

For the Messiah will derive from the House of David, who is referred to in the tradition as *mashiah zidkekha*, "Thy righteous anointed," while Elijah is the herald of redemption, for it is he among all the prophets who will be the forerunner of David and will bear the tidings: it is Elijah who will lead the Messiah to us (Mal. 3:23).

For in the times of the Messiah, that which Abraham and Isaac brought into the world will have reached fulfillment and maturity: "the hearts of the fathers will be turned to the children, and the hearts of the children will be turned to their fathers" (Mal. 3:24) also refers to Abraham bringing man to God, and Isaac bringing God to man. The sacrifice par excellence which they together offer up results in a David and his Psalms, in an Elijah and his heavenly fire, and ultimately in the Messiah, who combines the two.

And what of the two horns of the ram? One, says the Midrash, was sounded at Sinai, and the second will be sounded at the final Messianic redemption.

The shofar at Sinai: God giving the Torah to man. The shofar at Messiah: all the world finally seeing that God is One and His name is One (Zech. 14:9). Thus it is that when we sound the shofar on Rosh Hashanah we have in mind two major events: one that has taken place in the past—the Torah at Sinai; and one that will take place in the future—the redemption of Israel and the recognition by mankind of one God. Two shofarot combined in one: the shofar of God reaching down to man, the shofar of Isaac and Elijah; and the shofar of man reaching up to God, the shofar of Abraham and David.

How amazing: the ram and its influence reaches from the beginning of time to the end of time, from Creation to the final redemption of man.

Abraham and Isaac: father and son.

Elijah and David: prophet and king.

Sinai and Messiah: the particularism of Israel and the universality of God; man reaching up to God, God reaching down to man.

A simple Midrash, but how perfectly balanced it is, how symmetrical. From this Midrash we glean a major and fundamental idea: just as the prototypical sacrifice, the quintessence of *korban*, echoes and resounds through human history—so does every single sacrifice, large or small, resonate beyond its immediate confines.

Abraham and Isaac branded upon the soul of Israel the ability to sacrifice, the ability to surrender to God our most precious possessions. But that is not all. All subsequent sacrifices, personal and national, contain elements of Abraham's and Isaac's sacrifice.

This is the point: somehow, somewhere, and in some way, nothing is wasted. Something vital remains as a residue from every sacrifice that a Jew makes. The simplest holy act, because it is godly, is eternal, a mirror of the eternal God who commands the holy act. Just as in the physical universe there is a law of conservation of energy, and mass never ceases to exist, so also in the realm of the spiritual: a holy act never ceases to exist. In God's world, nothing holy ever comes to an end.

God created that famous ram on the eve of the Shabbat of Creation. It is no wonder, then, that it remains significant until the end of time.

Two Immersions: Joseph, Exile, Redemption

THERE ARE TWO familiar immersions of food during the Passover Seder: *karpas* in salt water, and the bitter *maror* into the *haroset* mixture. There are a host of interpretations as to why these take place: some say that the salt water represents tears of oppression; others, that the dipping of food was a royal habit at banquets; still others, that *maror* in *haroset* represents the bitterness of the oppression, and that the *haroset* is a substance which resembles mortar.

But in addition to this symbolism, there is something here that does not readily meet the eye. According to one authority, these two immersions represent two incidents in antiquity which involve the dipping of a certain substance into blood; and each of these two incidents has had a profound effect upon the ultimate history and destiny of the people Israel.

The first occurs when the brothers of Joseph tear his cloak from upon him, dip it into the blood of a goat, and send it to their aged father Jacob as evidence that Joseph has been killed.

The second occurs at the redemption from Egypt: "Ye shall take a bunch of hyssop, dip it into the blood that is in the basin, and place it on the lintel and the two side-posts with the blood that is in the basin" (Exod. 12:22).

In the Biblical scheme of things, a terrible act cannot stand forever suspended in the air, unredeemed, uncorrected. Certain acts which affect the core of the Jewish soul must ultimately be rectified. For example, when the *kohen* on Yom Kippur sends out the goat, the *sa'ir*, into the desert for the atonement of the sins of Israel, this is certainly resonant of the slaughtered *sa'ir* into whose blood Joseph's cloak was immersed. When, in the daily Temple sacrifice,

27

there is a *sa'ir le-ḥatat,* a "goat for a sin offering," this too bears echoes of that original *sa'ir.* And when the *kohen* wears a special cloak, the *ketonet,* this is reminiscent of the *ketonet* which Joseph—who had been appointed by Jacob to be high priest over his brothers—had been given by his father.

But even prior to all this, we sense the prefigurings of atonement and redemption for the brothers of Joseph. For after that first immersion in blood, Joseph goes down into Egypt, followed by his brothers, followed by Jacob, followed by the enslavement in Egypt, followed by Moshe and the first stirrings of freedom. There is the demand to Pharaoh to let Israel go, and then finally the climactic moment comes when God gives to Israel its first commandment as a people: they must take the lamb (the domesticated counterpart of the Biblical wild goat) which the Egyptians worship; they must hold it, slaughter it, dip into the blood with hyssop, and smear it on their doorposts.

And here we have it: this second dipping into the blood comes to redeem and correct and atone for the first. This was failure of trust in their father Jacob. They knew better than Jacob; they would dispose of Joseph in their own way. And since they were convinced that their father was being fooled by Joseph, they would also fool their father by telling him that Joseph had been killed. But now the children of Israel, by defying Egypt, display their trust and faith in their Father in heaven. They hold the lamb for four days, in great danger to their own lives. And this risk to their own lives atones for the risk to the life of Joseph. There, Joseph's endangered life was accompanied by the slaughter of an animal; here, their own endangered lives are accompanied by the slaughter of an animal.

And in a number of other ways, this second dipping into blood repairs and redeems the errors of that first dipping. In the first, there is *pirud,* "separation." The brothers quarrel not only with Joseph but among themselves. Now, however, there is *yiḥud,* "union": in Hebrew "bunch of hyssop" is *agudat eizov; agudah* means "a union, a coming together, a oneness."

In the first immersion there is arrogance: I am right and no one else. Now there is humility, and the hyssop itself represents humility, as in I Kings 5:13 (cf. Rashi on Lev. 14:4).

In the first, the blood is the instrument of deception, dishonesty, and the impurity which defiles them. Judah, their leader, suffers an immediate spiritual descent: "And Judah went down" (Gen. 38:1). Now, however, the blood is the instrument of truth, Torah, and sanctity; it is the symbol of their becoming a kingdom of priests.

The two immersions of the Pesach Seder go even beyond this. In their themes of error followed by correction, and suspicion followed by trust, they bear within them the great, overarching framework of Judaism: *galut* and *ge'ulah*, exile and redemption. In fact, the Seder itself begins with *galut*: "We were slaves in Egypt": *avadim hayinu*. It ends with *ge'ulah*, redemption, with the *Nishmat* prayer of praise. All of Jewish history is a combination of these two strands of *galut* and *ge'ulah*, the ebb and flow of Jewish destiny. Even now, in the twentieth century, we can hear the same echoes in the destruction of European Jewry and the establishment of a Jewish State in Erez Yisrael and the homecoming of the Jewish people to their ancestral land.

The immersions at the Pesach Seder are hardly trivial; they are acts which contain the seeds of Jewish history and destiny.

Rachel the Silent

WHY IS RACHEL buried in Bethlehem? Because Bethlehem is the road which the Israelites will take when they go into exile, and God wants Rachel to pray for her children. So says Jeremiah: *kol be-ramah nishma . . . Raḥel mevakah al baneha*, "A voice is heard in Ramah, Rachel weeping for her children" (Jer. 31:15). Apparently there is something about Rachel which makes her prayers more powerful and penetrating. What is this special quality of Rachel?

The major character trait of Rachel, according to the Talmud, is that she is a *ẓanuah:* "quiet, humble, modest, private." Whatever she does is done in a non-public manner.

The primary example of this, of course, is the familiar incident in which her sister Leah is given in marriage to Rachel's beloved Jacob. Rachel makes no public outcry, no open protest, and no one knows of her goodness. In fact, to avoid humiliation for Leah should she be discovered, Rachel even provides Leah with the secret signs which Rachel and Jacob had prearranged between them.[1] She knows that she is destined to be Jacob's wife, and she will allow the process to run full course: the petals of the flower will unfold at their own pace.

Later on, her son Joseph will have the same characteristic: the true, inner Joseph will be unknown to all except to his father. And Joseph, too, without protest, allows the process of his life to arrive at its own fruition, in its own time.

And so it is with the other offspring of Rachel. Several hundred years later the Jews are in Canaan, and Israel awaits its first king. His name will be Saul, and he will be from the tribe of Benjamin, son of Rachel (I Sam. 9:1). And the Talmudic sages use the same word to describe Saul: *ẓanua* (See I Sam. 9:10–21, 10:16, 21–22, 27). Saul is the true descendant of Rachel.

---

1. See *Ba'alei Tosafot* on Gen. 29:25.

30

Generations go by: a thousand years. The Jews are now in Persia, threatened with extinction. A figure emerges who will save Israel. Her name is Esther, a direct descendant of Saul and Rachel. The Talmud uses one term to describe Esther: she is ẓanuah, "the hidden one." The name Esther itself is from *seter*, "hidden." *Ein Esther magedet . . .* "Esther does not tell her origin." Esther is quiet, asking nothing, speaking little, waiting for the redemption of Israel to unfold (see Midrash Rabbah, Gen. 71:8).

Rachel's power of ẓeniut extends long after her death. In fact, it is a great and curious irony: the quiet Rachel is responsible for quiet descendants like Joseph, Saul, and Esther; and yet each of them, though non-public by nature, becomes a viceroy, or a king, or a queen, with major impact upon the destiny and history of the Jews. Thus, Rachel's great saintliness, her inwardness and humility, ultimately creates a profound public impact upon Judaism.

When we hear the word ẓeniut, "modesty," we normally think of dress and clothing. But the ẓeniut concept extends beyond that. The most famous is in Micah 6:8: *haẓne'a lekhet*, "to walk humbly with thy God." The Talmud, commenting on that verse, states that Micah's term *mishpat*, "justice," refers to the laws of justice; *ḥesed*, "kindness," refers to deeds of lovingkindness; and *haẓne'a lekhet*, "walk humbly," refers to the following: taking the dead to burial, and taking a bride to her wedding; that is, to see to it that proper arrangements are made for funerals and weddings.

Interesting: the *haẓne'a* examples in the Talmud are all public acts. Neither funeral nor wedding arrangements, by definition, can be made in private. The Talmud continues: the performance of all mitzvot must be done humbly and quietly, and even when these mitzvot are by nature public, such as funerals and weddings, they still have to be done with a sense of modesty; your part in the arrangements must be as non-public as possible (Sukkah 49b).

The Targum Yonatan on Micah 6:8 is significant: he translates it as "worship God in a *modest* way." That is, not to wear piety on one's sleeve. It means: when serving God, do not make a display of it, do not make certain everyone notices; do it quietly. The essence of the religious life is that it is essentially a private matter. And the traditional synagogue attempts to maintain the polarity between these two apparent opposites: a private relationship between man and God, accomplished in a public place. (This is one of the reasons underlying the separation of the sexes within a synagogue. The separation is symbolic of aloneness and privacy, and yet at the same time it is an aloneness which takes place in a public context.) The truly religious personality is not even aware that he is religious.

Obviously, it is crucial to perform the mitzvot: tefillin, kashruth, Shabbat, mikveh, prayer, tzedakah, compassion, visiting the sick, comforting the bereaved. But it is not what you do, but *how* you do what you do, that truly marks the religious personality. And this is what the Talmud says about Micah 6:8.

And all this we derive from mother Rachel, whose life was marked by *ẓeniut* in dress, word, and deed, so that her children and children's children were affected for all time to come.

Little wonder, then, that above all others, God hearkens especially to her prayers. For prayer is essentially a private act, even when it takes place in public, an act in which the one, lonely, singular Jew reaches out to the one, lonely, singular God. Prayer is thus the quintessential gesture of the *ẓanuah* personality, the characteristic gesture of Rachel.

Joseph and the Biblical Echo

THE BIBLICAL JOSEPH: cloaks of many colors, dreams, jealousy among brothers, the pit, a cloak dipped in blood, the temptation of Potiphar's wife, the dungeon, interpretations of dreams, the elevation from lowly, anonymous prisoner to viceroy of Egypt, the journey of the brothers to Egypt in search for bread, the revelation of Joseph, the reunion with the old father, Jacob. Of all the drama in the Bible, is there any that is more poignant, more subtle, than this complex, serpentine tale which winds its way through fourteen chapters of Genesis?

Surprising: on the face of it, there is nothing intrinsically "religious" about the story. In the Binding of Isaac, God plays a clear and unmistakable role: He stays Abraham's hand at the last moment. In the dreams of Jacob, God stands at the head of the ladder. Throughout Genesis, God moves in and out of the narrative as if He were the central character—which He is in fact. But in the Joseph story God has apparently removed Himself from the scene.

But it is a mistake to think thus. In its deeper structure, the Joseph story is very much a religious one. It contains, in almost perfect symmetry, the single basic religious message of the Torah: everything man does creates a resonance, a reverberation, an echo which will be heard at some future point in history as inevitably as a sound made in an empty canyon. Echoes: this is the Joseph story.

Firstly, the *ketonet passim*, the cloak of many colors. Let us move beyond the typical Sunday School lesson and look anew at that multi-striped, many hued, many-splendored garment. Was this the reason the brothers hated Joseph—that the father favored him, that he received a cloak and they did not? Is this no more than a classical case of sibling jealousy?

"And Israel loved Joseph more than all his children, for he was a child of his old age, and he made him a many-striped cloak" (Gen.

37:3). Apparently he loves him because in him Israel/Jacob sees the future of the people Israel. He sees that Joseph and not the older brothers holds in his hands the destiny of the Jewish people. It is curious that it is "Israel" and not "Jacob" who loves Joseph. Surely Jacob loves all his children equally, but the Israel in Jacob loves Joseph in a way that he cannot love his other children. For Rachel is the mother of Joseph, and Jacob loved Rachel also, not merely because she was fair to behold, but because in Rachel, more than in Leah, Jacob saw the unfolding destiny of Israel. And the Israel in Jacob knows that it is the way of Joseph, his approach to God and to history, his view of the past and the present, which, more than that of the brothers, holds in it the seed of the future. And so Israel/Jacob gives Joseph the *ketonet passim*, symbol of dominance: with the cloak, Joseph is appointed high priest over his brothers. Many years later, when Israel has a Holy Temple, Torah law will require the high priest to wear a special garment, a cloak, which the Torah also calls *ketonet.*

The brothers, of course, are fearful of Joseph. They know that in their family there have been other sons who have fooled and deceived their fathers. There was Ishmael, who, were it not for Sarah, would have twisted Jewish destiny and would have dominated Isaac. There was their own uncle, Esau, brother of their father Jacob, who, were it not for their grandmother Rebecca, would have distorted Jewish destiny and would have sold it for a mess of pottage, bartered it for any immediate pleasure. And now they are sure that another Ishmael, another Esau, is in their midst. Once again a son was deceiving a father; once again a father was about to abort Jewish history because he was blinded to reality. But father Jacob, who has known Esau and Laban, is not fooled: Joseph is not Esau, not Ishmael. And to underscore Joseph's significance, he is given the symbolic *ketonet passim.*

Time passes. Joseph dreams his dreams, the brothers are further enraged. They find an opportunity to rid themselves of Joseph when he approaches them in Dotan, where he searches for them at the behest of Jacob. They see him approaching from afar, and they begin to conspire against him. What is the very first thing they do to him, even before they cast him into the pit? Verse 23: "And when Joseph came unto his brothers, they stripped Joseph of his cloak, the cloak of many colors that was upon him." Twice is the word *ketonet* written in the verse. No ordinary garment, this. It is to be removed even before Joseph is cast into the pit, and it will be dipped

into the blood of a slaughtered goat, and, according to Midrash
Rabbah 84, Judah, the leader of the brothers, will bring the bloody
garment to Jacob and will say to him, *haker na*, "Recognize, I pray
you, if this is your son's cloak" (37:32). Not "our brother's cloak":
"your son's." And if it is your son's cloak, noble father, what, then,
has happened to his dominion, his destiny, his spiritual leadership
which you tried to foist upon us? Is it possible that you, Israel/
Jacob, are like your father and grandfather before you, and that you,
like them, chose a son who was unworthy? And Jacob sees the cloak
and recognizes it and cries out, *tarof toraf Yosef*, "slain, surely slain
is Joseph," surely slain is my dream of him.

And so Jacob/Israel is deceived by a cloak. But cloaks, like everything else, have their own echoes. Is this the echo of an act which
Jacob himself performed? Did he not also fool his father, his blind
father Isaac? And how had he fooled his own father? By wrapping
himself in a garment not his own, in the skin of young goats, 27:16:
". . . and the skins of the young kids did she put upon his hands and
upon his neck," and when Jacob went in to receive the blessing of
Isaac he was disguised as Esau in the skin of a young goat, *gedi
izzim*. And—see how the echo persists—in which blood is Joseph's
cloak now soaked? Verse 37:31: in the blood of a young goat.

Of course, Jacob's early act of deception was necessary. Israel's
very destiny depended upon it: a catastrophe would have ensued
had Esau received the blessing, and desperate measures were called
for. Rebecca was quite right in doing what she did in forcing Jacob
to deceive his father, her husband. All true. But the fact, inescap-
able, is that Jacob was the instrument of deception and it is now
necessary that he be deceived himself—through the same devices,
through the cloak and through the goats.

But echoes create their own echoes. Who was the brother who
brought the bloody garment to the father Jacob and asked him to
recognize it? It was Judah, the leader among the brothers. And it is
odd that after the brothers sell Joseph into Egypt, the story suddenly digresses to the incident of Judah and Tamar. Tamar is the
daughter-in-law of Judah, married to his son Er. When Er dies,
Tamar is left without a husband. She desires seed from the house of
Judah, the house of kingship. The incident seems to be an intrusion upon the Joseph narrative:

And it was told to Tamar, Behold thy father-in-law goeth up to
Timnah to shear his sheep. And she put her widow's garments
off from her, and covered herself with a veil, and wrapped

herself, and sat in an open place, on the way to Timnah, for she saw that Shelah was grown and she was not given unto him as a wife. When Judah saw her, he thought her to be a harlot, because she had covered her face. And he turned unto her by the way and said, "Go to, I pray thee, let me come in unto thee," for he knew not that she was his daughter-in-law. And she said, "What wilt thou give me, that thou mayest come in unto me?" And he said, "I will send thee a kid from the flock." And she said "Wilt thou give me a pledge till thou send it?" And he said, "What pledge shall I give thee?" And she said, "Thy signet, and thy cord, and thy staff that is in thine hand." And he gave it to her, and came in unto her, and she conceived by him. And she arose, and went away and laid by her veil from her, and put on the garment of widowhood (Gen. 38:13–20).

Later, Tamar is about to be put to death, accused of having become a prostitute, but in 38:24 Tamar confronts Judah with the materials he has left with her, and the words she uses are: *haker na*, "recognize." And she proves that Judah is the father, and he, in a moment of luminescent truth, acknowledges it readily: *ẓadkah mimeni*, "she is righteous: it is from me." Surely Judah has heard the echo of his own words to his own father many years ago: *haker na* . . . The narrative's sudden intrusion is now understood.

Further echoes: the Torah says that when Joseph approaches his brothers, "he took him and cast Joseph into the pit" (37:24). Who is this anonymous "he"? Says Midrash Rabbah 84: it was Simeon. Twenty-two years go by. The brothers go down to Egypt in search for food. Joseph, now viceroy, detains one brother while the others go back to Canaan to fetch the youngest brother, Benjamin. And whom does Joseph detain? It is Simeon (Gen. 42:24). As if the Torah were saying: You, Simeon, are the one who cast Joseph into the pit; you represented your brothers in that act. Now you yourself will be cast into the pit by Joseph, and once again you will represent your brothers. Truly the echo that resounded down through twenty-two years was not lost on anyone, certainly not on Simeon. And more: twenty-two years earlier the brothers had willingly sold their brother Joseph down into Egypt: now they must forcibly bring their younger brother Benjamin down into Egypt.

Reuben, too, hears echoes. The Torah says of him, "And he saved him from their hands" (37:21). The Midrash says about Reuben: You were the first one to try to save Joseph, therefore when God allots the city of refuge, the first city of refuge will be in your territory (Deut. 4:43).

Joseph also hears echoes of all kinds. As a lad of seventeen, he accuses his brothers of violations of the family code. He tells Jacob, according to the Midrash, that the brothers denigrate the children of the handmaidens; that they are immoral with the women of the land; that they eat food without proper slaughter. These are inaccurate accusations, based on activities which Joseph misinterprets. Soon enough, Joseph himself is brought into temptation with the wife of Potiphar. It is as if Joseph is now challenged: let us see how you yourself resist temptation. The result is that though he resists, he ends up once again in the pit. And is it not strange that that which he leaves in Madam Potiphar's hands is the instrument of his newest incarceration: his garment?

Many echoes: when he sees Joseph's bloody cloak, Jacob tears his garments in grief. And in 44:12, when Joseph accuses his brothers of stealing the silver—which he has planted in their bags—the text declares, "and they tore their garments." And what of the silver itself? Does not this awaken the twenty-two-year-old memory of their selling him into slavery for twenty pieces of silver? And the twenty-two-year period during which Joseph has no contact with his father is in itself an echo, according to the Talmud (Megillah 16), of the twenty-two-year period during which Jacob had no contact with his own father, Isaac.

The symmetry of the narrative is immaculate: they had accused him of bearing tales against them to their father, of harming them with his words; Joseph now accuses them of being spies, of carrying information about Egypt back into Canaan, to the enemy.

None of this is petty revenge. Joseph understands the dark and mysterious ways of God, and Joseph knows that every act creates its own resonance. And just as what they did to Joseph did not result in harm but in ultimate good, so now with his brothers: this will only be a momentary fear, a temporary apprehension, and what he now does to them will not result in harm but in ultimate good. He suppresses his natural instincts for compassion—in verse 24 he silently weeps—but, in fulfillment of his prophetic dream, he acts instead as an instrument of the inexorable divine will which must bring the sweeping tale full circle, for unless it comes full circle there can be neither repentance nor redemption for the brothers, and thus no completion for their lives.

Nor are the brothers blind to signs. In verse 28 they tremble; in verse 36 they fear; in 43:16 and 33, and in 44:13 there is more fear and trembling. How can such powerful and brave men fear? Because to the religious heart, nothing is accidental: if something untoward occurs, the reaction is not *Why me, I've been good*, but *Why—to what act is this an echo, a response?* For every act of good ultimately brings good in its wake, and every act of evil will at some time and in some way create a resonance and bring something evil in its wake.

One further echo: when Rachel is barren she declares that she might as well be dead. Jacob replies, in some anger, *Ha-taḥat Elohim anokhi*, "Do I stand in the place of God?" It was, according to the Midrash, an unkind remark. And the stinging words are left hanging in the air.

Years later, long after Rachel dies, Joseph reaches up, as it were, and pulls down the hurtful words and redeems them, turning them inside out into words of generosity, kindness, concern for the other. It occurs after Joseph finally reveals himself to his brothers. Jacob has now died, and the brothers are fearful that Joseph will wreak his vengeance upon them. In verse 50:15, they come to him pleading for their lives. And Joseph forgives them, saying, *Ha-taḥat Elohim anokhi*, "Do I stand in the place of God?" The same words—but here Joseph, son of the wounded Rachel, has transformed the words into healing, and has redeemed the hurtful gesture.

The story is symmetrical not only in the literary sense, but in the religious sense. Actions and words bring in their wake other actions and other words. Nothing—no word, no gesture, no act—is without its unique resonance.

Just as stones cast into a pond will create ripples, so do the acts of life create their own echoes, inevitably, inexorably.

On Completing Genesis: More Echoes

THE POWERFUL NARRATIVES of the Book of Genesis form the soul of the people Israel. The events of Cain and Abel, Isaac and Ishmael, Jacob and Esau, Joseph and his brothers, are a true prologue to the story of the Jewish people. They are the ground upon which we are built.

Most striking are the overarching themes and patterns that recur and repeat themselves, the threads that weave in and out of the tapestry, a kind of rhythm and cadence that is heard over and over again—in a different form but always the same, in a different garb but never changing: certain ideas, concepts, truths, which are to become part of the eternal character of this people.

How curious it is that two themes seem to dominate this first book of the Torah: food and clothing.

The very first commandment to Adam and Eve deals with food: from this tree you may eat, from this tree you may not eat. They violate this food commandment with very serious consequences. Later on, food appears again, in the story of Jacob and Esau. Esau is the firstborn, the bearer of the destiny of Israel. He is undeserving of it, for his essence is material not spiritual. One day, Esau comes in exhausted from a hunting expedition in the field. Jacob is eating lentils (according to the Midrash, Jacob is eating the mourning meal because of the death of Abraham on that day). Says Esau: "Stuff me with this food, for I die of hunger" (Gen. 25:29). Jacob gives him the food in exchange for the rights of the firstborn. The text itself, in verse 34, testifies, almost in derision, that Esau sold these rights of primogeniture in exchange for food.

But we are not done with food, nor with Esau and Jacob. Time passes, Isaac grows old and wishes to give his blessing to his sons.

He is unaware of Esau's nature, and in 27:1, he orders Esau to bring him venison "that I may eat and bless thee." That is, perform the sacred mitzvah of honoring parents, and thus earn the blessing. Rebecca hears and orders Jacob, "Go to the flock and get two goats." Here also the role of food is a vital element in the narrative. And the two goats themselves are forerunners of the two goats to be offered up on Yom Kippur in the Temple, symbols of sin and repentance, of Esau and Jacob (Yalkut Shimoni). Here also the role of food is a vital element in the narrative.

But not only here: later again, with Joseph and his brothers, the Midrash tells us that when the brothers sold Joseph into slavery they were in the middle of a meal: *le-ekhol lehem*. And this fact is significant in later Jewish history. A thousand years later, the people Israel will be sold, bartered over a meal and a feast in the story of Haman and Ahasuerus. Haman offers money to Ahasuerus. Who redeems the Jewish people? It is Mordecai. From what tribe is Mordecai? Benjamin. Who is the mother of Benjamin? The same mother as of Joseph: Rachel.

Food: the staff of life, the stuff of life. More: food, which is representative of the physical, is not simply an object with which we assuage our hunger. Food the physical can be a means of serving the spiritual, of serving God. It can be a catalyst for rebellion or for submission, for good or for evil, a gesture of love or a gesture of defiance. No wonder kashruth is such a major ingredient of Jewish life. For the people Israel, food is more than food.

Clothing: that which protects us, hides our nakedness, shelters us, disguises us. Clothing is very significant in Genesis.

Who wears the first clothing? Again, Adam and Eve. *Katnot or,* "garments of skin," are made by God for them after their sin: clothing to hide their sudden awareness of their bodies, clothing to symbolize modesty, to deemphasize and downplay the physical and at the same time to emphasize their desire to return to a spiritual state. Later, a garment covers up Noah's drunken nakedness. A piece of clothing is also significant in the story of Esau and Jacob: Jacob is commanded by his mother to dress in disguise, in false clothing—clothing which will be hairy, and which will deceive the blind Isaac into thinking that this is in truth Esau. So Jacob dons goatskin around his neck and on his hands. But he also wears something else: "Rebecca took the garments, the *hamudot* ["precious ones"], for her son Jacob" (27:15). A Midrash: "God made a cloak for Adam and Eve, and this was handed down to Seth, to

Enoch, to Methuselah, to Noah. Ham stole it, gave it to Cush, to Nimrod. Esau stole it from Nimrod, and Rebecca took it from Esau and gave it to Jacob." And it is this same cloak, multicolored and precious, which Jacob ultimately gives to Joseph as a sign of his dominion over his brothers (cf. Midrash ha-Gadol 195:5, Kuk ed. p. 472; and Pirkei de-Rabbi Eliezer 24).

Clothing in the Torah is more than a mere covering of the body. It is a statement: of modesty, humility, disguise, dominion, accusation. In the Torah, clothing is not trivial, or casual, or frivolous.

Echoes, patterns, scenes: see how they recur. The matriarchs are all barren at first: Sarah, Rebecca, Rachel. Yet each of them ultimately gives birth to an Isaac, a Jacob, a Joseph. (And later on also: Hannah is barren and then gives birth to Samuel; Manoah's wife, Zelelponit, is barren and gives birth to Samson.)

There are other themes: older and younger brothers: Cain and Abel: Cain is older, but Abel is more acceptable in God's eyes. Ishmael and Isaac: Ishmael is older, but Isaac is to have dominion. Esau and Jacob: Esau is older, but it is Jacob who inherits the mantle of leadership. The brothers and Joseph: they are older, but it is Joseph to whom they must ultimately pay allegiance. And, of course, Moses is younger than Aaron. Much later, Saul, the first king, refuses the kingship. I Samuel 9:21: "From the youngest tribe, from the youngest family in the tribe." And still later, further themes of younger and older brothers: I Samuel 16:1: "Among the sons of Jesse, a king." Jesse parades his seven sons before Samuel, but none of them is chosen. Are there no more? Jesse answers, in verse 11: "There is one more, he is feeding the flock." He turns out to be the youngest son, the future king, David.

But the most striking of all the themes in Genesis is the theme which we have already explored: the echoes which reverberate from generation to generation. Echoes of reward and retribution which, if one reads the Bible with heart as well as mind, one feels and senses.

One act, one event, engenders another. Nothing goes unanswered. Furthermore, past and present are all one, and precisely because the brothers are exquisitely and painfully aware of echoes do they think Joseph himself is an echo of Esau deceiving his father Isaac, and an echo of Ishmael deceiving his father Abraham.

There is much more: note the repetitions of dreams; the similarities in the lives of Jacob and Joseph; note especially the sending out on journeys, and the role of messengers: the messengers of God to Abraham; Eliezer is sent by Abraham; Joseph is sent to find his brothers; Jacob sends messengers to Esau; Saul is sent to find the lost animals and becomes king.

Note also the subtle repetition of words when Abraham takes Isaac to the Akedah. Isaac says: *avi*, "my father." Abraham replies, *hineni*, "I am here." Years later Jacob is about to deceive his father, the same Isaac who had called his father *avi*. And Jacob says the same word, *avi*. And Isaac, who had once heard his father say *hineni*, now says to his son, *hineni*. Of what did Isaac think at that moment when he heard his son address him by the word *avi*? Did it conjure up memories of the long ago when he accompanied his father to Moriah to be sacrificed? Isaac did not know then what was about to befall him, and now once again Isaac does not know what is about to befall him. When Isaac hears *avi* does he realize that something shattering is about to happen to his life once more?

In truth, the Akedah story permeates the entire book. Abraham takes Isaac to another place, offers him up on the altar, and at the last moment Isaac is saved. Jacob, the son of him who was bound on the altar, apparently repeats this same act with his son Joseph. Jacob knows that the brothers hate Joseph, yet Jacob sends Joseph out to another place to find his brothers, a place where Joseph will be alone with them. And here, too, Joseph responds to his father's request with the fateful word, *hineni*. And when Joseph is cast into the pit, is this an adumbration of Isaac being bound on the altar? Joseph is saved finally by Reuben and Judah. Are they echoes of the earlier voice of God which stays Abraham's hand and saves Isaac? And when the brothers slaughter the goat and send its blood to Jacob, informing him that this is the blood of his beloved Joseph, is this act resonant of the ram which is slaughtered at the Akedah in Isaac's stead, and whose ashes represent a sacrificed Isaac? And, finally, does not the Jacob-Esau story reverberate with the sounds of Cain and Abel? The envy between brothers; the older brother hating the younger one; Cain killing Abel, and Esau vowing to kill Jacob.

Genesis is an echo chamber: food, clothing, older and younger brothers, childless women, measure for measure, retribution. The future is a continuation of the past. More: the future and the past are one, and each individual affects his or her future by his past and by his present. Past, present, and future all merge together and become one.

The Royal Conflict: King David and Michal

ONE OF THE classic domestic disputes in the Bible takes place in the story of King David and his wife Michal (II Sam. 6:12–23).

David, king of Israel, has finally established Jerusalem as the Holy City, the capital of the land. Many years earlier the Philistines had captured the Holy Ark, the *aron kodesh.* King David has now brought the Ark back to Jerusalem, and he leads a great celebration in honor of the event. He is ecstatic, and as verse 14 tells us, he dances in the streets "with all his might," leaping and shouting to the sounds of the shofar trumpet.

But not everyone is happy. Michal, the queen, watches from the palace window, and as he hops and springs before the populace she despises him in her heart.

Finally, the Ark is placed in its special tent, David offers up sacrifices to God, distributes cakes and bread to the people, and returns to his own household to give them blessings.

In verse 20, Michal greets her husband the king with bitter, taunting words: "How did the king of Israel get himself honored today, who uncovereth himself today in the eyes of the handmaidens of his servants, as one of the empty fellows shamelessly uncovereth himself." It is unseemly, unbecoming, unworthy, undignified to behave in such a manner.

King David replies: "I will rejoice before the Lord, who chose me king over thy father Saul, and I will be even more contemptible than this and will abase myself even more; and by the handmaidens of whom you have spoken, by them I shall be held in honor" (v. 21).

That is, one's own self and one's dignity count for naught when one serves the Lord; only God is noble and has greatness and dignity; man exalts God by humbling himself. And on this note the story ends, with the laconic statement that Michal bore no children.

It is tempting to dismiss Michal out of hand: shrewish, concerned with status, position, appearances. But Michal is no ordinary person. She is, after all, the daughter of the anointed one, King Saul. She has been raised in his palace, and knows something about giving proper honor to the Creator. Surely there is more to this story than its surface reveals, more than a queen angry at her royal husband for dancing in the streets. Perhaps we can hear in this powerful narrative a distant reverberation and echo of something we have experienced long before the times of King David.

For the source of this echo we must look at the genealogy of the protagonists: David is a direct descendent of Judah, whose mother is Leah. Michal is the daughter of Saul, who descends from Benjamin, whose mother is Rachel. As we see in the Joseph stories, the children of Rachel and Leah represent two prototypes of the Jew, two diverse though equally legitimate approaches to God. And in the words which ring out between David and Michal there is somehow an echo of the ancient differences between the children of Rachel and the children of Leah.

The first manifestation of these differences takes place in the conflict between Joseph and his brothers: Joseph, son of Rachel, against the leader of the brothers, Judah, son of Leah. Their dispute concerns the proper way to serve God—not merely the symbolic dispute concerning the cloak of many colors. Is the primary service of God to be open, outward, public—or is He to be served inwardly, quietly, in a hidden way?

Elsewhere we have suggested that Joseph represents the mind, the intellect.[1] He is otherworldly, remote, distant, removed from the mundane things which for him detract from the service of God. Joseph represents the worship of God by solitude, withdrawal, reserve, reflection. By contrast, Judah and the brothers represent the qualities of heart and emotion. God is to be served from within the world, by community, by a coming together, by utilizing and elevating the world.

For Joseph it is enough to love God, to serve him in quiet ways, concealed behind a veil. It is not necessary to demonstrate to others this love for Him; but for Judah, the love of God is so overwhelming that is must be shared and demonstrated to all, so that others may join in reaching for Him and loving Him. How can love of God, so

---

1. See below, "Mind and Heart: Joseph and His Brothers."

powerful, be kept to one's own self? As we have already seen, this philosophical conflict has never been resolved throughout Jewish history. It appears here once again, a distant echo of that ancient struggle, in the personalities of Michal and David.

David is the *ne'im z'mirot*, the "sweet singer" of Israel. He will serve God in all ways: by composing and singing his Psalms, by studying God's word, by prayer. And, if the occasion demands it, he will serve God by dancing, springing, jumping, hopping. He cannot contain his exuberant joy: his inner fire and his enthusiasm know no bounds. And if this king dances together with the commoners, with the servants, with the rabble, what of it? Before God we are all rabble, we are all servants. David's love of God is so overwhelming that it must be shared with others: it cannot remain private, hidden in a quiet corner.

Saul, on the other hand, is contemplative, brooding. Even after Saul is appointed king by Samuel, Saul is *neḥba el ha-kelim*, "hidden among the vessels" (I Sam. 10:22). (Is this why Saul initially finds David so intriguing and refreshing?) And Michal, the daughter of Saul, tracing her lineage to Joseph and Rachel, approaches God with reserve, thought, inwardness, quiet: God is served in a whisper, just as Rachel whispered her secrets to her sister Leah on the wedding day. And when Michal sees her husband the king dancing wildly in public, the ancient dispute erupts once again, and we hear David's angry retort. (There is an interesting echo of the Joseph story here as well: according to the tradition, one of the charges that Joseph leveled against Judah and the brothers was that they treated the children of the servant wives as inferiors. But now King David [Judah] is accused of behaving before the servants as if they were equals. Is this a correction of Judah's mistakes? Or is it an indication that Joseph's original accusation was wrong?)

It is an issue which will remain unresolved until the end of days, when the way of Leah and the way of Rachel, the way of Joseph and the way of Judah, the way of Michal and the way of David—heart and emotion, mind and intellect—all will be seen to be part of the way of God, whom we serve in private and in public, with heart and with mind, in concealment and in openness.

Biblical Personalities

. . . of Abraham and Jacob, and Ishmael and Judah and Elijah. But mostly, somehow, of the mysterious, silent, middle patriarch, Isaac; and of Isaac's equally mysterious, silent grandson, Joseph, and Joseph's silent mother, Rachel. Perhaps it is the silent ones who speak most eloquently.

Making Sense: Isaac and Ishmael

TWO SONS ARE born to Abraham: Ishmael, then Isaac. Abraham is content with Ishmael as the bearer of the destiny of the Jewish people. He has a very good upbringing; his mother Hagar is a righteous woman, a princess who voluntarily joins this household so that she might live under the beneficent religious influence of Abraham and Sarah.

Lu Yishmael yiḥyeh le-fanekha, says Abraham. "Would that Ishmael live before thee" (Gen. 17:18). Clearly, Abraham is content that Ishmael should be the inheritor of Jewish destiny. But God demurs. Ishmael cannot be the progenitor of a future Israel: he simply will not suffice. And although Ishmael is not evil, it is Isaac who will be the next patriarch: *u-le-Yishmael shematikha . . . v'et beriti akim et Yiẓhak,* "And as for Ishmael, I have heard thee, I have blessed him . . . but My covenant I will establish with Isaac" (Gen. 17:20–21).

What is the fundamental difference between Ishmael and Isaac? Each is brought up in the same home and with the same devotion to God. The difference is that Ishmael's life is symbolic of things that are rational, that appeal to the mind, to one's understanding. For example, he is born of a mother of childbearing age: this is perfectly normal. When he is thirteen, his father learns about the requirements of *berit milah* (circumcision), and then, according to the tradition, explains the significance of this mitzvah to his son. The young Ishmael understands it, appreciates its importance, and is circumcised at the age of thirteen. For at this age, a child is a man and possesses understanding.

Thus Ishmael represents service of God which emanates from

logic, from thought, from understanding why it is important and good to be an adherent of God and His mitzvot.

In stark contrast is Isaac. He represents something outside the natural order of events, something not easily understood. He is symbolic of things that do not easily appeal to the mind. Isaac's mother is beyond childbearing age: "After I am old shall I have delight, my husband being old also?" (Gen. 18:12). Nevertheless, she has a child, an extraordinary act which transcends nature. And the mitzvah of *berit milah* is performed upon Isaac when he is eight days old. No one can explain the significance of circumcision to Isaac; the father cannot appeal to his logic and to his understanding; it is beyond comprehension. This is a precursor of Isaac's life: everything will be beyond understanding, beyond mere reason.

Which kind of individual does God choose as the progenitor of the people Israel? Is it he who represents the order of nature, who serves God only when he understands why? Or does God prefer him who lives in a realm beyond the natural, who serves God not because he understands but because he trusts and believes, and who knows that not everything can be comprehended by mortal man?

God wants to have a suitable father for His people Israel, because His people is going to defy all understanding. His people's journey through history will not be on a natural path. Nations, empires, mighty military machines would destroy Israel, but Israel will not go under. The entire civilized world will delight in its suffering and persecution, and will stand idly by while it seems to go under. But Israel rises up. The world's major religions will declare war on its people and burn them at the stake or try to seduce them with a kiss. But Israel will remain true to its God.

This is a people which will puzzle historians. It will defy all the rules of historic logic; it will exist without a land for two thousand years, a stubborn, stiff-necked, proud, unbending people which will refuse to follow the siren call of the outside world and will remain true to its own calling.

To be the father of such a people God chooses a man whose life does not represent rationality. Instead, God selects an individual who is a true servant, who will serve even though he does not always comprehend.

To be the father of such a people, God does not choose Ishmael, who performs the mitzvah after he understands it. God chooses an Isaac, who performs the mitzvah even before he understands it.

With Ishmael, Abraham could not have gone to the Akedah. Only with Isaac could he have performed this astounding act of faith.

Ishmael would not have understood; he would have fought back. For to agree to be circumcised is one thing: He can understand the need for a physical sign of the covenant, a sign that would be a distinguishing mark of honor upon his flesh and the flesh of his seed forever. And he can comprehend also that inherent in the covenant are certain benefits to himself to which God is obligated. But to surrender one's life, for no particular purpose and for no evident benefit, makes no sense, and is so far removed beyond the realm of nature that Ishmael would have had to reject it out of hand.

Isaac, however, understands that one cannot always understand; therefore, Isaac is taken to the Akedah, and therefore Isaac is chosen to be the bearer of Israel's destiny.

He Who Laughs: Isaac and Ishmael

ONE OF THE most fascinating personalities in the entire Torah is certainly Isaac, the silent one, the mysterious one, the hidden one, he who was bound on Moriah.

Who is Isaac? He is the child of Sarah and Abraham. Sarah is a prophetess, and her divine spirit knows that it is Isaac, this son for whom she prayed and hoped, who will be the bearer of the destiny of the Jewish people. Therefore she watches his upbringing with care and attention.

Isaac has a brother, Ishmael. Somehow, the mother knows that Ishmael is a detrimental influence on Isaac. How does she know this? She sees him *mezaḥek.* She sees Ishmael doing something which immediately causes her to demand that he be banished from the home: "for he shall not inherit together with my son," he shall not share in the destiny of the people Israel (Gen. 21:1–9).

What is it that she saw? *Mezaḥek* is difficult to translate. The ancient sages say that it refers to three heinous transgressions: idolatry, murder, immorality. Others say that it means "to mock" or "to ridicule." We are not quite certain what it is. Obviously, Ishmael did something so terrible that it causes the gentle Sarah to go immediately to Abraham and demand his removal from the house.

One fact is clear: *mezaḥek* is from the word *zeḥok:* "laughter." It evidently is a special kind of laughter, a kind of derisive, scornful laughter. She sees that her older son is mocking and ridiculing something quite significant.

This is very strange, because the name of her own son, the actual bearer of the destiny, the child for whom she prayed and whom she is now protecting, also stems from the word "laughter": the name Yizḥak/Isaac means literally, "he will laugh." Why, then, in Sarah's

52

eyes is one kind of laughter unacceptable and another laughter important enough to be the name of her son?

Perhaps Sarah understood that much depends on what one laughs at, on what is scorned, on what is ridiculed. Yes, *zehok* means "laughter," but what matters is what causes the laughter, the ridicule, the mocking. And here is the key to the puzzle: *mezahek* is in the present tense; Yizhak/Isaac is in the future tense. *Mezahek* refers to the here and now, the immediate, the current, the instantaneous. Yizhak/Isaac refers to the future, to that which is beyond time, the ultimate vision, the eternal.

Now we begin to see what Sarah saw so clearly. Each one laughs, yes. But one son represents and emphasizes the immediate and the now, and scorns the future, while the other son represents and emphasizes the future, the promise, the vision—and scorns the immediate, the now.

Each one is *zehok*. Each one has the ability and the power to laugh and mock and scorn, but it makes all the difference what you laugh at, and what you honor.

One son ridicules God and His promise, the vision of a great people, all in favor of the now. The other son laughs at the now in favor of the ultimate future and the vision and the promise.

One son says that God and His law and righteousness are trivial. The other son says that physicality and materialism are trivial.

Each son laughs, each one is *zehok*. But one is a *mezahek*, present tense, and one is a Yizhak/Isaac, future tense. And it was this that Sarah saw with her prophetic insight. She saw precisely this talent which sets Israel aside from the nations of the world: to forgo the now. And therefore Ishmael, the *mezahek* of the present, must be sent away, lest he defile the destiny which is Isaac's.

Present versus future, the immediate versus the eternal, animal versus human, ape versus angel: this is a struggle that resounds from the dawn of history until the end of time.

The beginning of time: God creates Adam and Eve, places them in the Garden that they may enjoy the delights of everything in the Garden. There is only one restriction: from one tree they may not eat. (Even in Paradise there must be discipline.)

Enter the serpent. He is the symbol of the now, of instant gratification. What is this silly law about your not being able to eat fruit? he says. Take it now, why wait. You want to get old so you can't enjoy it? Enjoy it now!

But, says Eve, it is God's law. We will die.

Scoffs the serpent: Don't worry about later, the future, the morrow. Let us think about today. Look how luscious it appears: "The woman saw that the tree was good for food, that it was a delight to the eyes, that the tree was to be desired" (Gen. 3:6).

The issue is clearly drawn: immediate gratification versus self-discipline; rejection of God versus adherence to God; the now versus a higher good. At first our progenitors resist, but finally they succumb, and they are banished from Eden.

Move down through history, back to Isaac. He has grown up, he has twin sons, Jacob and Esau. Here we have a repetition of his own youth: he does not see the evil of his older son, Esau; and just like Sarah before her, so now Rebecca knows that Esau is not worthy of carrying on the destiny of this eternal people.

How does she know that he is not worthy? Recall the famous scene in Genesis 25: Esau is the hunter, Jacob the dweller in tents. Esau comes in from the field, ravenously hungry. Jacob is eating *nezid*, which the rabbis say was lentils, part of the mourning meal for his grandfather Abraham, who has just died. But Esau cares nothing about these mourning rites: he is out hunting. When he finally returns, he says, *haliteni na*, loosely translated as "stuff me with that food; gorge me with it." It is an expression which is vulgar, coarse, crude, uncouth—to be expected from one who goes hunting on the day of the funeral of his own grandfather Abraham. Shall this first-born be the heir apparent to Jewish destiny? Jacob seizes the opportunity: "Sell me this day your birthright," transfer to me the rights and privileges of the first-born.

Here is the test for Esau. Does the future mean anything at all to him? Esau does not hesitate: how can Jewish eternity and Jewish destiny and Jewish future and Jewish hope and Jewish aspiration compete with his stomach? How can the promise of a holy people compete with his appetite?

And so Esau says: *anokhi holekh la-mut, ve-lamah zeh li be-khorah;* "I am about to die this instant, who needs the birthright?" Get me food, fill my stomach, this is all that matters. And so he transfers his birthright and all of its duties and privileges to Jacob. And the Torah adds, "and Esau humiliated the birthright" (Gen. 25:34).

Learning of this incident, the mother Rebecca sees in her older son Esau what Sarah had seen in her older son Ishmael: an emphasis on immediate gratification as against the timeless and the eternal. Such a son shall not inherit the destiny of Israel; only Jacob knows how to forgo the present moment, and therefore only he can inherit the future.

Again and again this theme appears. Centuries later, in the wilderness, there are those to whom there is only the now. They long for the fleshpots of Egypt, for immediate gratification, for the "leeks and melons" of their erstwhile oppressors. Not for them a promise of Land and Torah. Later, they will create a golden calf, because they want a god now, immediately, one which they can see and touch. Not for them this invisible God of vision and promise.

The struggle has no letup. In every generation it reappears. We even find it reflected in the Jewish concept of God.

Moshe confronts God in one of the classic scenes in the Torah. "Who are you, what is your essence, teach me your ways. When I go down to Egypt and tell Pharaoh to let my people go, and when I speak to the children of Israel to tell them to follow me, they will ask me, who is this God, and what is His name and His essence?"

God replies to Moshe in one of the most profound and mystery-laden utterances in the entire Torah: "I will be that which I will be." Tell them "that 'I will be' sent me" (Exod. 3:13, 15).

"I will be." Not "I am that I am." That is present tense. "I will be": future tense. I am vision, I am promise, I am eternity, I am future, I am the end of days.

I am here but invisible. I am ever-present, but my essence is not of the now, but of the tomorrow. It is the pagan gods who are limited and present now, who are tangible and visible and knowable immediately. But the pure concept of the God of Israel is not limited by time. His ineffable name begins with a *yod*, the letter of the future. It is above time, beyond space, of the world and beyond the world.

And therefore we are called the people of God, the people which will be, which is of the future, and which is above time.

Throughout history the world scoffed at Jewish dreams and ridiculed the Jewish obsession with tomorrow and called on Jews to follow in its ways, to give up our historic calling and turn our back on the essence of the name of God.

But Jews are the children of Yiẓḥak and transcend the now—children of the *meẓaḥek* who is rooted in the now.

And because Jews are not rooted in the now, we prayed for Zion three times a day for two thousand years, and our grandparents hung in their houses faded drawings of the Wailing Wall, in total defiance of present reality.

In medieval Spain, wealth, comfort, rank, nobility were offered to us if we would but renounce our faith—and if we refused, the alternative was torture and burning at the stake. All reality called for rejection of our faith. But Jews maintained the faith in total defiance of the present moment. While Cossacks spilled Jewish blood in the streets of Russia, our grandparents prayed for the redemption and the restoration of the Holy Land in total defiance of the present moment. And while millions were herded like cattle into the ovens in our own time, we transcended the now and cried out *ani ma'amin*, "I believe," in total defiance of the present moment.

And when the hordes of Arab armies threatened again and again to overrun the fledgling Israel, tens of thousands threw themselves bodily into the fires of the enemy in order to preserve the future of the people—again in total defiance of the present moment.

For throughout our history we have been trained to withhold, to wait, to think, to wait, to anticipate. Our history has taught us; the name of our God has taught us.

And even our mitzvot have taught us to overcome the infantile needs of feeding on demand. Food in the hand cannot be immediately eaten: there must be a *berakhah*, there must be sanctification of the moment, because we are not beasts but human, and the *berakhah* reminds us that something is beyond us, that there is a Creator and we are His subjects, and somehow, before we swallow the food that will fill our stomachs, we have an intimation of immortality, a feeling that we have transcended the immediate moment for a glimpse of eternity.

Kashruth too is not just cleanliness but a transcending of the now. You say that you want what you want when you want it? But you are not a beast: you must wait, examine, think, pause, listen for the echoes of eternity. You can transcend the now, the momentary pleasures of fleeting delight. You are not controlled by immediacy. You can laugh at it.

And thus there is *taharat ha-mishpaḥah*, the sacred laws governing marital relations: again the present can be transcended, and even the most physical of drives, while not denied, can be sublimated, heightened, and infused with eternity and immortality.

Let the nations of the world scoff at the future and immerse themselves in the present moment. We march to the words of a different Commander.

Shabbat is not of the now but of the future, an attempt to bring into the world some eternity, a hint of the eternal Shabbat. The present, workaday world is shunted aside not because God wants us to live in a straitjacket, but because He wants us to experience the delight of a moment in time that is beyond time, beyond the immediate—an allusion and a foreshadowing of eternity and sanctity.

A people raised for thousands of years on such a regimen will be able to overcome the Pharaohs, Hamans, Torquemadas, Stalins, Hitlers, and Arab potentates who wish to destroy us, for they are of the now—*meẓaḥek*—and we are of the tomorrow—Yiẓhak/Isaac. This is our mission and our destiny: to remain true to the people of Yiẓhak/Isaac, the people of godliness, in a world too willing to sell its birthright.

What a pity if in this generation, after all these years, we, the heirs of Isaac, were to sell our birthright back to Esau for the paltry return of a mess of pottage. What a pity, after all that we have undergone and withstood.

We have faith that despite intermarriage, ignorance, defection, we are still a people which transcends time, and that there will yet come a day when, in the words of the psalmist, *az yimale seḥok pinu,* "our mouths will be filled with joy" and our tongues with song, and we will return to the Garden of Eden which we left, and the future promise and vision will become a present reality.

Laughter and Laughter: More on Isaac and Ishmael

ISAAC, THE STRANGE, mysterious, quiet figure, the great and fearsome bridge between Abraham and Jacob, is the most fascinating and intriguing of the patriarchs.

Perhaps the most intriguing aspect about him lies in his name, a strange and peculiar name. Isaac/Yizhak means literally "he will laugh." How does he receive such a strange name?

When the barren Sarah is told that at her age she will give birth to a child, she laughs in disbelief. And when Abraham is informed, he falls on his face, va-yizhak, "and he laughed" (Gen. 17:17). Two verses later God says to him, "you will have a son and you will call him Yizhak." In 18:13, "Sarah laughs to herself." She is asked, in verse 14, "Why does Sarah laugh?" and she replies, "I did not laugh," and is told, "No, you did laugh."

There is a great to-do here about laughing: laughing about the wrong things, and laughing at the wrong time. Clearly, laughter is not a laughing matter, not trivial or frivolous. God Himself comes along and tells them that the name "laughter" will be the name of their newborn son (Gen. 17:19).

Let us follow the narrative: Yizhak is born, and on the day that he is weaned, Abraham has a great celebration. Though he is apparently content, Sarah is not content. She is worried about the future: who will be the spiritual heir of Abraham? Who will carry forth the destiny of the Jewish people? Will it be Ishmael, the older son, or Yizhak, the younger?

Sarah knows the answer: it will not be Ishmael. Her reason is given succinctly in 21:9 and 10: she sees Ishmael in the act of mezahek, and she declares that he will not be the heir with her son Yizhak. Abraham is grieved by this, but God intercedes and tells him that he should heed the opinion of Sarah because the seed of Abraham's destiny will be carried on through Yizhak and not through Ishmael.

What was Sarah's reason for refusing to have Ishmael as the heir apparent? The word *mezahek* which she saw in him must have had quite terrifying connotations. According to the tradition, she saw him committing three heinous transgressions: murder, sexual immorality, idol worship.

What is curious about this is the fact that the Torah uses the single, suggestive word *mezahek* to describe the evil of Ishmael. And the question is: why is the grammatical root *zehok* acceptable when it is used for the name of Yizhak, and unacceptable when Ishmael engages in it?

This is a profound and elusive semantic problem—but it is more than a matter of semantics.

What does *zehok* really mean? It means "laughter"—but it means more than that. It connotes everything that laughter expresses: joy, pleasure, satisfaction, contentment. In a broader sense, it suggests the fulfillment of the heart's desire, the fulfillment of dreams, happiness, everything that one has always wanted.

The only questions are: (a) what is true *zehok?* (b) how does one obtain it?

The answer is not easy: entire civilizations have risen and fallen in an effort to arrive at an answer.

Isaac offers one answer, while Ishmael offers another answer, and that difference in approach is hidden in the grammatical form of *zehok.*

Yizhak/Isaac is from the root *zehok,* with the Hebrew prefix *yod.* The *yod* prefix has the power to take the present tense and transform it into the future tense.

But the *zehok* root in relationship to Ishmael is *mezahek.* Here, the prefix is not *yod,* but the Hebrew letter *mem.* And the *mem* in Hebrew denotes the present tense, something going on now, immediately, at this very moment.

Yizhak/Isaac means "he will laugh"; *mezahek* means "now laughing." Thus, the difference between Yizhak and Ishmael is the difference between something happening in the future and something happening now, in the present.

To the question, What is *zehok* and how is it obtained?—how do I achieve joy, pleasure, satisfaction?—Ishmael answers: You achieve it by emphasizing the now. Whatever is available at this moment, whatever will satisfy you quickly, take it, grab it, use it. There is no tomorrow, there is no *yod*, there is no future tense. There is no laughter other than now. If you like something, then take it, get it, work out some way to obtain it, because if you want it, you should have it—now.

Do you want to feel good, to feel high? Ingest, inject, eat, drink, sniff, smoke—whatever will give you pleasure now, do it without delay. Do not worry about the future, about addiction, about your health, about those around you, about your own life: the key to pleasure, joy, satisfaction, and *zehok* is that it not be postponed no matter what the cost: do it now.

This is the classic conflict between Yizhak and Ishmael: a conflict dealing with laughter.

Ishmael says that there is no laughter in the world other than now; if pleasure is not taken immediately, it might be lost forever.

Yizhak says that there is much laughter in the world, much joy, tranquility, serenity, love, pleasure, delight. But if your only standards of judgment are your nerve-endings, you will end up an animal and not a human. If you insist on the now, your future might be lost forever.

This is their conflict, and this is what Sarah sees.

In point of fact, this is a choice that everyone must make. Yes, there is laughter in the world. There is the present laughter of Ishmael, which turns hollow tomorrow; and there is the future laughter of Yizhak, and the future is forever.

There is the laughter of joy, and the laughter of derision.

There is the laughter of trust and faith, and the laughter of mockery and ridicule.

There is the laughter of fulfillment, and the laughter of bitterness.

There is the laughter that heals and caresses in times of trouble, and there is the laughter that wounds and causes pain.

There is the laughter of love, and the laughter of hate, the laughter of Yizhak, and the laughter of Ishmael.

There is laughter in the world: the laughter of Shabbat, a family shutting out the cares of the world, greeting one another and greeting God, winding down the burdens of the week, releasing themselves from the slavery of machines, understanding and experiencing the serenity of the world-to-come.

And there is the laughter of dominion and conquest, of never-ceasing pursuit of things, goods, and possessions—the laughter which at the end of days becomes heartache and shame at the realization of a wasted life.

There is laughter in the world: the laughter and jubilation of a family on Yom Tov, tasting not only the true *simḥah* of observing God's holy days together, but the exhilaration of celebrating God's holy days in God's ways.

And there is the raucous, empty laughter of stolen pleasures, of living lies, of cheating in business, of cheating on one's mate, of dishonesty in personal and professional life—the hollow laughter of self-loathing and disgust, aware that you are not what you might have been.

There is laughter in the world: the genuine joy of watching children grow into God-fearing, learning Jews, who are aware of themselves, their heritage, who care about Torah and synagogue, who know and are secure about who they are and where they come from.

And there is the empty laughter of parents raising their children without Torah, without Jewish consciousness, watching them grow up and learning nothing other than how to make money and how to get along in a non-Jewish society.

There is the present laughter which tomorrow turns into a moan and a cry as Torah is abandoned, Jewish tradition thrown overboard, and children, now grown, wonder aloud why their parents are now distressed about the disappearance of their own seed through intermarriage, when after all this is what the parents really trained the children to become.

There is laughter in the world: the gladness of knowing who you are, aware of your responsibilities to your faith and to your people, living according to sacred ideals, delighting in surrendering for a higher purpose, living a tranquil, serene life.

And there is the laughter of anguish which one feels in the dead of night, after the party is over and the guests have disappeared, and the dirty, empty glasses of life stand on the banquet table, and the cracked, broken shards of a tragic, wasted life lie unswept on the floor: mocking, derisive laughter.

There is laughter in the world: kindness, understanding, compassion; and there is the empty, bitter laughter of selfishness and greed.

There is the laughter of the open hand of giving, helping; and the forlorn laughter of the clenched fist which gives nothing and knows only to strike at the other.

There is laughter in the world: in the excitement of knowing that God lives, of seeing Him in the sunrise over the ocean, in the still calm of moonlight on the trees, in the sight of a vast desert, a jagged mountain, the power of a thunderstorm, the revelation of lightning, the fragrance of the first spring flower, the recurring, bitter-sweet beauty of autumn leaves, and of trees standing bare in the sunlight.

And there is the present laughter, the initial pleasure of seeing only the "me," catering only to the "me," blinded to the other, unaware of anything beyond the body of the "me," open to nothing new, to nothing holy; inspired by nothing, uplifted by nothing, caring about nothing, seeing nothing: the present laughter which tomorrow turns into melancholy, tedium, boredom, ennui, and regret.

There is laughter in the world: the pageantry of Sukkot and God's protection; the warmth of Pesaḥ and God's freedom; the purity of Shavuot, the triumph of Ḥanukkah and Purim, the solidarity with Jewish history of Tisha be-Av.

And there is empty laughter, the grieving, lonely, forlorn laughter of the poor Jewish soul which knows only that it is hungry and yearns, but knows not for what.

There is the *ẓeḥok* of Isaac with a *yod:* future, permanent, eternal, triumphant, joyous laughter; and there is the *ẓeḥok* of Ishmael with a *mem*, present laughter, temporary laughter that dissipates and evaporates like the morning mist, with promises unfulfilled, possibilities untouched, laughter soon drowned out by tears.

How wise was Sarah when she saw Ishmael *meẓaḥek*. The tradition tells us that *meẓaḥek* refers to him in the role of murderer, spiller of blood. Are you angry, do you resent, have you been wronged? Then take immediate action, immediate revenge, strike out at your opponent, express your rage and fury: hurt, maim, humiliate.

Sarah saw him also as an idolater. The idolater worships god as he himself wants to worship. He wants a tangible god here and now: god as a figurine which he can carry in his pocket and call on when needed. If god does not meet his needs, god can be discarded and another god can be obtained. (That is why there are thousands of idols but only one God.) The idol is shaped and molded according to one's needs; there is no higher good, no higher god. The idol is used to meet physical gratification, to glorify and exalt the body.

Sarah saw Ishmael also in his mode of sexual immorality. Here, too, immediate gratification of human desires is the key. There is no "thou shalt not" where my appetites are concerned: I take what I want, eat what I want, have what I want when I want it—now, immediately.

How wise was Sarah: a world which accepts the Ishmael/*mezahek* way is a world which will destroy itself.

Look at our world: who are the heroes of our day, our models and those of our children? Look at the list of heroes who are specialists in present laughter and soon enough destroy themselves in premature death. The heroes of our society, the Elvis Presleys, the Janet Joplins, the Judy Garlands, the Marilyn Monroes—the idolized and lionized pantheon of our culture—laugh themselves to death literally, destroy themselves, because they are slaves to an ethic which preaches: Fly now pay later, laugh now cry later.

This is what Sarah saw. Ishmael says, "This is what I require; give it to me now"; Yizhak says, "This is what God requires of me, I will give it to Him."

The mystery of *zehok* in this world all depends on a little prefix—a *yod* or a *mem*, the future or the now; laughter which is permanent and deep, or laughter which is ephemeral and gradually turns into a scream of terror.

In the final analysis, Yizhak laughs at Ishmael, for Ishmael destroys himself; and Yizhak lives.

Isaac, the Silent Patriarch

ISAAC IS THE silent figure among the patriarchs. He darts like a shadow across the pages of the Bible, saying little, doing little, essentially a passive figure. Even when he is mentioned in the Torah—and he is given less space than either Abraham or Jacob—the events that occur to him revolve around others. He does not do things; things are done to him. It is as if he has no role to play in the ordinary world, and all that takes place about him is not at his initiative.

Three great events occur in Isaac's life. The first is the great act of sacrifice, the Akedah. But when the Torah discusses the Akedah, it emphasizes Abraham. What of Isaac? He is, for the most part, completely silent. He merely asks, "Where is the sheep for the sacrifice?" (Gen. 22:7). He lets himself be bound, he lies on the altar, he watches as his father begins the ritual slaughter. He does not act; he is acted upon.

What went through Isaac's mind at that moment? The Torah does not say, but a Midrashic source informs us that God regards him as if he had died (Midrash ha-Gadol, Gen. 22:19). They also indicate that Isaac entered Paradise (Yalkut 109), that at the moment of the sacrifice the angels wept, that the tears fell down from heaven into the eyes of Isaac and blinded him, that Isaac saw the *Shekhinah*, the heavenly presence of God, and that it was from the sight of the *Shekhinah* that he subsequently became blinded.

Blinded to what? Perhaps he was blinded to the mundane, the materialistic, the physical. Perhaps he became, because of the experience, a thoroughly spiritual creature, almost as if he had no body—all spirituality, all holiness. As a matter of fact, when the Torah speaks of the period immediately following the Akedah, there is no mention at all of Isaac. It is as if he has become transformed. He is still in this world, but what he has now experienced makes him

64

of another world, no longer really involved in the ordinary affairs of men. And perhaps this is what his blindness means: he no longer can see evil, he no longer is able to recognize evil.

The second great event in his life occurs when he takes a wife. Here, too, all is done for him. His father Abraham sends a servant to find a wife for him, and the servant finds Rebecca. Rebecca leaves her home, and it is she who comes to Isaac. The Torah gives us much detail about Rebecca's decision, but it tells us nothing about Isaac at this point. The choice of the wife who will bear him the sons to carry on the destiny of the people Israel—this is being taken care of. The destiny is unfolding: Isaac knows he is an instrument in that destiny, and he observes it as it unfolds. He is not completely of this world.

When Rebecca approaches, towards evening (Gen. 24:63), she finds Isaac in the field, conversing with God, in eternal dialogue with his Creator (see Rashi ad loc.). And when Rebecca first sees him from a distance, she covers her face with a veil. Why? Because he is like an apparition, really more godly than human. And the sight of him in the field causes a fear and trembling to well up within her. She cannot gaze at him directly. She can only look at him as one looks at the brilliant, powerful sunlight—through a veil. For he has seen the *Shekhinah* at the Akedah, and the glow and the fire still emanate from his countenance, and Rebecca senses it immediately, and she dons the veil. And for the rest of her life with Isaac she will have to deal with him as through a veil, not directly (as pointed out in *Ha'amek Davar,* the commentary of R. Naphtali Zevi Yehuda Berlin, on Gen. 24:65).

Note, for example, how different is Rebecca's relationship to Isaac from that of Sarah to Abraham, and of Rachel to Jacob. When Sarah has something to say to Abraham, she speaks her mind clearly, forthrightly. When she feels that Ishmael is an evil influence on the family, she relates her misgivings clearly to her husband Abraham. Similarly with Rachel. In Genesis 30:1, she complains about her inability to have a child: "If I don't have a child I will die." These great women speak their minds to their husbands. But Rebecca, for some reason, does not. She sees that her wicked son, Esau, is about to obtain the coveted blessing which may affect the future of Israel and the destiny of mankind, and she goes to extreme efforts to make certain that Jacob receives the blessing instead. Why does she not simply go to her husband and tell him of her misgivings? Why does she not follow the example of her mother-in-law and have Esau evicted from the house? Perhaps it is because Isaac is of another world: he does not recognize evil, and Rebecca's relationship to him is constantly hidden, unspoken, as if through a veil.

And so the third great event in Isaac's life, the blessing for his children, is not given in the way he intended, and is in fact taken away from him. Once again he is passive, once again the drama is played out by others—by Rebecca, by Jacob, by Esau—while Isaac sits in the shadows. For he was the sacrificial lamb at the Akedah, and he was blinded by the tears, and he was blinded by the sight of the *shekhinah*. Not for him are the intrigues of this world.

Nor for him are the words of this world. Note how little he speaks in the chapters devoted to him. Abraham has much to say: to Sarah, to the angels, to God, to Lot. For Jacob, too, speech is an integral part of life: he speaks to Esau, to Rebecca, to Laban, to Leah, to Rachel, to Joseph, to his sons, to Pharaoh.

To whom does Isaac speak? To his father at the Akedah he says six words. To Jacob his son he utters just over one hundred words, including the famous blessing. To Esau his son, less than ninety words, including the blessing. To Abimelech and his general, Phicol, eight words. The phrase *va-yomer Yizhak*, "and Isaac said," is rarely seen. The total number of words which Isaac speaks in the entire Bible amounts to less than two hundred and fifty, perhaps one quarter of the words allotted to Abraham or Jacob.

(There are moments in life when mortal words do not suffice, when in fact they interfere with one's sense of the Infinite. Aaron the high priest knows such a moment when his two sons are struck dead at the hand of God during the dedication of the Tabernacle: *va-yidom Aharon*, "and Aaron was silent" [Lev. 10:3]. Hannah, not yet the mother of Samuel, knows such a moment when she enters Eli's Temple and empties her heart before God in prayer for a child: "her lips moved, but her voice could not be heard" [I Sam. 1:13]. The godly wordsmith, the singer and poet of Israel, whose Psalms form the main body of Jewish prayer, knows such a momemt when he realizes that words interfere with his apprehension of the divine Presence: "To Thee, silence is praise" [Ps. 65:2].)

Isaac the sacred one lives always in such a realm. In the face of the Infinite, in the presence of the divine *Shekhinah* whom he first encountered at Moriah, words are an intrusion. In the presence of God, only stillness will suffice. For example, when the shepherds of Gerar quarrel with the shepherds of Isaac over the two wells, Isaac does not react as his father did, by referring to it as *gezel*, "theft," and complaining to the highest councils of the land. Instead, he simply gives each well a name, esek and sitnah, "strife," and "contention," and then turns and digs another well in another place (Gen. 26:20).

Why give the wells a name? Perhaps because this is how Isaac protests: he will not argue with them, will not discuss thefts and rights and legal niceties with them. He inhabits a different world with different concerns. Not for him discussions and words over real estate and over wells. He simply calls it by its name—"strife"—and then leaves.

The revolutionary father, Abraham, and the dramatic angel-wrestling, ladder-dreaming son, Jacob: how remarkable is the contrast with Isaac. His father is born outside the confines of the Land and dies in the Land; his son is born in the Land and dies outside the Land. Isaac alone is born, lives, and dies in the Land, and never steps outside the Land. When it is time to go down to Egypt because of the famine, God approaches Isaac and says to him, *al tered mizra'imah*, "do not go down to Egypt." Egypt and all it represents is not for you. His life is complete sanctity, even in its geography. Note also that it is God and not his parents who gives Isaac his name (Gen. 17:19). This is not the case with Abraham nor with Jacob. Again the same concept: Isaac is a sacred, silent, godly creature, above understanding, fascinating and awesome in his complexity.

The Ladder and the Wrestling: Jacob's Two Visions

TWO MAJOR EVENTS occur to Jacob in the form of dreams or visions. The first is the dream of the ladder; the second is the wrestling with the strange *ish* ("man".)

What is the meaning of these two profound events, which are among the most mysterious in the entire Torah?

The ladder *(sulam)* incident is, on the surface, understandable. It takes place when Jacob flees Esau, at the urging of his mother, and is on his way to another land, to the house of his uncle, Laban. He is *levado,* "alone," and he lies down and dreams the famous dream of the ladder, standing on earth, reaching up to heaven, and of angels of God who are ascending and descending.

On the face of it, the dream is optimistic, hopeful, clear, crisp, precise. God promises him that the land in which he lies—the tradition is that he was lying on Mount Moriah in Jerusalem—will belong to him and his children's children forever.

The second major event takes place twenty years later. Jacob now has wives, children, servants, cattle. He has worked for Laban during this entire time. He is on his way back to his own land. He is about to meet Esau again, who is still lying in wait for him to destroy him. And once again he finds himself *levado,* "alone," and a strange man—called *ish*—wrestles with him the entire night through.

This event is a mixture, a fusion of reality and dreams. The reality is that Jacob emerges from this event with a limp. The dreamlike quality is that this *ish* is apparently an angel of God, who insists upon leaving at the break of dawn so that he can, according to the tradition, "sing hymns" to his Creator. The event hovers in that marginal zone between dream and reality.

Obviously, this incident does not have the calm and soothing effect of the *sulam*. It is frightening; there is danger of physical harm; the stranger wants to destroy Jacob; Jacob fights back and conquers the *ish*; the *ish* begs, "Let me go"; they raise *avak*, "dust," the entire night through. And the dust is also upon our comprehension.

Let us try to comprehend it. Firstly, these things are happening to Jacob, who is the son of Isaac, the grandson of Abraham, the conscious bearer of the destiny of Israel. He is partly Isaac and partly Abraham.

But having said this, we have almost stated a contradiction. Abraham and Isaac are very different creatures. Abraham is active, dynamic, a mover, he makes things occur. He converts people to monotheism. He is not a dreamer, not passive, not a silent figure. He is constantly moving: from Ur Kasdim to Canaan, to Egypt, back to Canaan again. Abraham is a man of this world. He is born to Terah, and has seen idolatry. He is a decisive individual, he does not vacillate, he does not turn away from crisis. When necessary, he fights battles, as he does in order to save his nephew Lot. He even argues against God Himself, as he does at Sodom. He rejects his father's ways and goes on to new ways. He is a revolutionary; he confronts. He is able throughout his life to make the decisive and painful decision: he is able to cut himself off from his birthplace, from his son Ishmael, from his wife Hagar, from his nephew Lot. He performs his own *berit*; he faithfully heard God at the Akedah. He knows that man is captain of his fate and master of his soul. He believes that he can change destiny, mold and shape the affairs of life. He reaches out from earth to heaven.

This is the grandfather of Jacob; this is one of the sources of Jacob's being.

But Jacob's father, Isaac, is something entirely different. Things happen around him, to him. And he observes, he watches, he knows that things take their time to unfold. Is it time for him to have a wife? His father sends Eliezer to find a wife for Isaac. But Isaac stays put. The cataclysmic watershed event of his life, the Akedah, is done to him, not by him. Isaac is the silent one: he says very little. Isaac is the blind one: he sees very little. For what is there to say about this world, and what is there to see in this world? Once you have seen the real world, the world above, the world of Paradise; once you have been bound and willingly bared your neck to slaughter and have in your mind already given up your life to God as an offering—things of this world are of no great import. You submit passively to that which takes place. Later, God tells Isaac, "You shall not go down to Egypt."

Not for you is this foreign land. Your father Abraham may go there, your son Jacob may sojourn there, but not you.

And Isaac is deceived by those around him. Esau deceives him. Even his beloved Rebecca and Jacob deceive him in order to wrest a blessing from him. For he is of another realm, this Isaac. This world is as nothing: Isaac waits for the real world. Isaac's is the world of heaven and beyond.

From this genealogy emerges Jacob, who is now entering the hostile world alone. His brother Esau has sworn to destroy him; he now faces the unknown. He needs a plan, a way, an approach for his life. Shall it be the way of his grandfather, shaping and molding this world, or the way of his father, living in another realm beyond this world?

All this sets the stage for the *sulam*. His dream is a ladder connecting this world to the heavenly world. His grandfather is that part of the ladder which is *erez*, "earth." But his father is that part of the ladder which is *shamayim*, "heaven." The dream is a comforting one, yes, but only on the surface. In a more profound sense, it is a reflection of his inner turmoil: shall the way of Abraham be dominant in me, or shall the way of Isaac? Shall I be an active participant in this world, and shall I and my children attempt to alter, perfect, shape, mold the world? Or shall I and my seed essentially withdraw from this world, turn our sights away from it, passively accept that which occurs? Shall I be that part of the ladder which is *muzav arzah*, "standing on earth," like Abraham; or shall I be *maggiia ha-shamaimah*, "reaching heaven," like Isaac? The *sulam* dream states the question and the dilemma, but provides no answer. God blesses him, but as to what way he shall finally choose—on this there is only silence.

Jacob goes on to the house of Laban. Twenty years pass by. Now that he is about to return to the land of his father and grandfather, that haunting decision can no longer be delayed. Once again he finds himself alone on the other side of the river Jabbok. And the *ish* wrestles with him until the morning.

We normally view this wrestling as a separate, discrete event. But what occurs here is an integral part of the *sulam* dream, the resolution of the conflict first expressed in the *sulam:* will Jacob be primarily heaven or earth, passive or active, confronting or submitting? Now there can be no delay, no postponing.

Question: who is the mysterious stranger with whom Jacob wrestles? Is he an angel of God? Is he the spirit of Esau? According to our commentators, he is one or the other. But we are permitted to add many suggestions to this incident.[1]

Perhaps another reading of this event is in order. The mysterious *ish* with whom Jacob wrestles and strives through the long dark night until the dawn is none other than Jacob himself: Jacob struggling with Jacob, the Jacob who is Isaac and the Jacob who is Abraham. Each half is struggling for dominion over the other, striving to break the other's hold and power over the future of Jewish destiny.

Who wins the struggle? The text is deliberately ambiguous: in Genesis 32:26, we find "he could not prevail," apparently referring to the *ish*. And so he touches the hollow of Jacob's thigh and dislocates it. That is, the heavenly force, the force of Isaac, is the apparent victor.

But suddenly the *ish* cries out, in verse 27: "Let me go, for the day breaks." Here the other aspect of Jacob, the earth, the Abraham, has the upper hand, and Jacob says: "I will not let you go unless you bless me." That is, unless you acknowledge that my way is primary. The heavenly force submits and gives his blessing. (Is there an echo here of Jacob wresting the blessing from Isaac?)

Who, then, wins, and who loses? The Jacob of Abraham wins because he wrests a blessing from the Jacob of Isaac. But the Jacob of Abraham loses, because after the struggle he emerges with a limp.

The Jacob of Isaac wins, because he has inflicted injury on the Jacob of Abraham. In this reading, the injury on the thigh represents a lessening of the value that is placed on this world, the thigh being a symbol of the material. In that sense, the heavenly Jacob is the victor.

The Jacob of Isaac loses, in that he is forced to acknowledge and concede that his antagonist's approach has merit.

And how is this concession made? The *ish* says: "Not Jacob shall be your name but Israel, because you have striven with God and with man, and you have prevailed." That is, you have fought the battle which is the result of your two-pronged heritage of Abraham and Isaac, *va-tukhal*—"you are able (from *yakhol*), you are capable, you can." That is, you are capable of being both Abraham and Isaac—for in you there is a merging of the two. They are not mutually exclusive, not either-or.

---

1. See the commentary of *Keli Yakar* (R. Ephraim Luntschitz) on this incident, who says that the "interpretations are endless."

And, in truth, we see in Jacob's younger years a merging of the two. He has to be told by Rebecca what to do to obtain the blessing, and yet he himself takes the initiative when he deems it necessary to obtain the firstborn rights from his brother Esau. He has to be told by Rebecca to leave his house because Esau will destroy him, but when he comes to Laban he does not permit Laban to take advantage of him.

This is what the children of Israel are as a people. We too have bared our necks, undergone *akedot* like Isaac; in our national soul we, too, are not overly moved by the things of this world; we know how to submit and how to surrender to God and renounce the pleasures of an earthly existence. We know what it is to be silent, to be blind to the temptations of the world. We are a patient, long-suffering people, allowing history to take its own time to unfold. We have seen God many times and, having seen Him, we have been less anxious about worldly events.

But we are also Abraham: stiff-necked, revolutionaries, visionaries. We want to change the world, to teach the world godliness, decency, compassion; we want to rid it of its brutality, bestiality, animality. We fight, strive, yearn, like Abraham, for the way of God in this world.

What aspect of our national psyche shall be dominant and primary: the perspective of him who lives in a higher realm, or of him who lives within this world and wishes to bring God into this world?

Isaac and Abraham, Joseph and the brothers, Saul and David, heaven and earth: these are the two golden threads which run side by side through all of Jewish history and will be fused together at the end of days. It is the glory and wonder and mystery of Jacob that he bears within him these two magnificent, golden threads.

The Ladder Between Heaven and Earth

JACOB HAS HIS first prophetic vision precisely when he is alone. Not when he is in his father's house, not with his mother, but in the dark of night in a lonely field with wild beasts around him and the hard earth beneath him and a rock for a pillow under his head, under the open skies.

In this setting he sees a *sulam*, "ladder," which stands on the earth but whose top reaches the heaven.

Jacob is Israel: Israel, too, is alone, apart, separate. And because we are apart we also see a unique vision. We behold a special prophecy which other people do not perceive.

The essence of this vision is its view of the relationship between earth and heaven. The *sulam* is the theme of the Jew. In fact, the *sulam is* the Jew, created from the earth, out of the dust, who aspires to go heavenward—but whose climb towards heaven is not direct and uninterrupted. Rather, he moves upward and then retreats. He is angelic, Godlike—but the dust resists. The angels are *olim ve-yordim*, "ascending and descending," in a symbol of the magnificent and heroic struggle of mankind.

But the Torah does not despair of man, despite the fact that he is *yesodo me-afar*, "rooted in the earth." Judaism does not look upon man as evil, damned, hopelessly sinful. On the contrary, man's material nature, his fleshly origin, his physicality, are indispensable elements in his sanctity.

The Torah was given to man, not to angels—because man is mortal, weak, and subject to temptation: he is *muẓav arẓah*, "planted on earth," like the ladder.

For us, holiness exists not in the monk or in the hermit or in the monastery, but in man—born of woman, created from the dust.

Because only man is able to triumph over his self, as rung by rung, mitzvah by mitzvah, he creates a miracle and transforms the earth of his being into godliness, the ape of his essence into an angel.

This is the essential teaching of Judaism: that man can triumph over his baser nature, that man can become better, become even more perfect.

In fact, it is because man is from earth and not all spirit that the Torah was given to man, as indicated in the famous Midrashic discussion on Mount Sinai between Moshe and the angels. And man has been given the power by God to sanctify and hallow and invest meaningless objects with meaning.

For example, take a parchment scroll and a drop of ink: by themselves, they are nothing. Add a Jew, add thought, intent, *kavvanah*—and the parchment and ink are transformed—by physical, mortal, earth-bound man, and only by him—into sacred objects: a Torah scroll, tefillin, a mezuzah.

Take a woolen string: by itself it is nothing; add to the string a Jew; add thought, add *kavvanah*—and the woolen sting is transformed—by physical, mortal, earth-bound man, and only by him—into *ẓiẓit*, into a *tallit*.

Take food: by itself it has no religious significance. Add a Jew, add thought, add *kavvanah*—and the food is transformed—by physical, mortal, earth-bound man, and only by him—into an act of worship. And the table is transformed into an altar; and the flour becomes holy showbread—*leḥem mishneh* and *leḥem ha-panim*. Similarly, matzah, which emanates from wheat and flour, becomes a mitzvah only because of man.

Take time: of itself it is an abstraction, a number, a date. Add a Jew, add thought, add *kavvanah*, and time is transformed by physical, mortal, earth-bound man—and only by him—into a Shabbat, a Yom Tov, a Rosh Ḥodesh, a Yom Kippur, a Rosh Hashanah, a Pesaḥ.

Far from being profane, only man has the power to create sanctity. The ladder reaches heaven, but it is clearly standing on earth.

The great teaching of Torah is that in order to be spiritual one must be mortal, physical, material. The earth needs heaven, yes; but heaven needs earth as well. Undisciplined idealism is as dangerous as undisciplined materialism. True idealism involves rules and regulations: charity (tzedakah) has its own halakhah; loving God has its physical expression; loving fellowman has strict rules of conduct. The idealist may not act according to his whim or mood of the moment, but must find expression of his idealism through physical mitzvot and halakhah.

The world by now should have learned this, after two thousand years of a spirituality unrooted in physicality, of idealism without strong discipline, of love of God without mitzvot—which led inevitably and logically to Auschwitz. The tragedy is that not only does the world not know this fact, but Jews do not know it yet either. For generations, young people have been taught that you can be a Jew without change in your life: that nothing is required, or demanded, that nothing needs to be surrendered. No wonder the Jewish youth has rejected this form of "Judaism."

The rungs of the *sulam* connect earth and heaven, and through them, man the brute can become man the angel.

Two Types of Holiness: Joseph and His Brothers

THERE ARE TWO types of holy days in Judaism: Shabbat and Yom Tov. By understanding the essential difference between Shabbat and Yom Tov, we gain a new insight into the differences between Joseph and Judah. Though Shabbat and Yom Tov are each holy days, each is of a different order of sanctity. Shabbat is characterized by the single key word *kadosh*, "holy." In the Friday night prayers we say, *Attah kidashta et yom ha-shevi'i . . .kidashto mi-kal ha-zemanim*, "You have sanctified the seventh day, hallowed it above all other times." In the Friday night *Kiddush* we also say, *va-yekadesh*, "and He sanctified it," and in the Prayer After Meals we refer to Shabbat as *yom zeh gadol ve-kadosh*, "this great and holy day."

Kadosh does not refer only to that which is holy and sacred; it also means that which is separate, apart, unique. What is the ultimate *kadosh* in the universe, the zenith of sanctity? It is God Himself: "For I am holy" (Lev. 19:2).

Kadosh is removed from the ordinary, and *kadosh* is alone, singular, solitary. God is one and His name is one: *attah ehad ve-shimkha ehad*, "Thou art One and Thy name is One" (Shabbat *Minhah* service). *Kadosh* and one have similar qualities of aloneness.

What is the essence of Shabbat? The Jew leaves the ordinary world and is alone with God. "It is a sign between Me and the children of Israel forever." This is the ultimate purpose of Shabbat: to establish a relationship with God, "For in six days God created . . ." Shabbat attests to a Creator, and on Shabbat the Jew withdraws from the mundane world and endeavors to know, in a more intimate way, his Creator.

76

Kadosh is conceptually related to *oneg*. Isaiah, referring to Shabbat, says: *ve-karata la-Shabbat oneg*, "you shall call the Shabbat *oneg*" (Isa. 58:13). And although *oneg* on Shabbat does involve some physical pleasure as well, this by itself is insufficient. For Isaiah in the next verse describes the quintessential *oneg: az titanag al ha-Shem*, "you shall have *oneg* unto the Lord." The connotation is one of inner delight. This inner *oneg* is derived primarily from an intellectual and deeply spiritual meditation and contemplation. Pure *oneg* requires aloneness; it cannot be attained in a crowd, in community, among friends. This may explain why Shabbat is described as *me'ein olam ha-ba*, "similar to the world-to-come" (Berakhot 57b).

For Shabbat, like the *oneg* which is its hallmark, is essentially a disengagement from this world, an adumbration of another realm of being. Thus, in its deepest sense, *kadosh* and *oneg* are bound together by their shared elements of solitude, apartness, withdrawal, singularity. Shabbat is nurtured and sustained by two deeply imbedded and complementary roots, *oneg* and *kadosh*.

The Kabbalistic tradition considers Joseph to be the embodiment of the Shabbat: a disengagement from the mundane, a withdrawal from the ordinary. This, says Joseph, is the way to God: to become a personification of Shabbat. (Note, incidentally, that this is another manifestation of the *sur me-ra ve-aseh tov*, "withdraw from evil and perform good," concept which we first saw in the Jacob-Esau narratives. To Joseph, withdrawal from the dailiness of the world is an essential first step in reaching for the good.)

Festival/Yom Tov is also holy, but its essence differs from Shabbat's *oneg* and *kedushah*. Yom Tov is characterized by the concept of joy, *simhah: ve-samahta be-hagekha*, "thou shalt have *simhah* on thy festivals" (Deut. 16:14). For example, one of the considerations by which we are permitted to utilize fire for cooking *(okhel nefesh)* on Yom Tov—while fire is prohibited on Shabbat—is the factor of *simhah*. To refrain from the use of fire may deprive one of the joy of properly cooked food on Yom Tov. *Simhah* requires the physical experience, and the experience of community. According to the Talmud, *simhah* is made manifest by the use of meat and wine (Pesahim 109).[1] And one cannot withdraw and disengage from

---

1. See Bezah 15b concerning the dispute between R. Akiva and R. Eliezer. According to R. Eliezer, the celebration of a festival with food and drink is only a suggestion, not an obligation. For R. Akiva, however, it is an obligation. R. Joshua adds: "Divide the festival: half to God and half to yourselves." Cf. also Pesahim 68b.

others and still have *simḥah:* "a person is obligated to have *simḥah* with his children and his family on Yom Tov" (Beẓah 15a, Pesaḥim 109a, and see Rosh Hashanah 16b).

So powerful is this *simḥah* that it abolishes even the laws of mourning. On both Shabbat and Yom Tov there is no public display of mourning. However, a mourner continues his mourning rites immediately after the Shabbat ends, and the Shabbat day itself is numbered as one of the seven days of mourning. Not so Yom Tov, which totally cancels formal halakhic mourning and eliminates it completely, so that after Yom Tov the formal rites of the first week of mourning cease to exist. The *simḥah* of Yom Tov is so intense and so powerful that it completely overcomes the requirement to mourn.[2] This-worldly mourning is completely vanquished by *simḥah*, which is also of this world. But the *oneg* of Shabbat is otherworldly and has no sway over the this-world of mourning. Although the public manifestation of mourning is forbidden on Shabbat, this is merely out of respect to the day; Shabbat intrinsically is no contradiction to mourning. It requires only *oneg.*

Oneg is alone, withdrawal, like *kadosh; simḥah* involves others, a coming together.

Oneg is essentially private; *simḥah* is essentially public.

Shabbat is the world-to-come; Yom Tov is at least partly of this world.

On Shabbat, the Jew does not so much praise God as observe Him, contemplate Him, and bask in His presence, while on Yom Tov, the Jew engages in exuberant, fulsome praise of God through the recitation of the *Hallel* prayer.

Shabbat is God's day: it falls every seventh day, regardless of whether or not the earthly court acts. But Yom Tov can only take place when the human, earthly court, after hearing the testimony of those who have sighted the moon, officially pronounces the advent of the New Moon.

Thus it is that the Kabbalists tell us that Joseph is Shabbat, while the brothers, in the person of Judah, are Yom Tov. More: the brothers are twelve, which represents this world: the twelve months of the year. But Joseph's name in Hebrew means "additional, beyond, more, added to," that which is not satisfied with things as

---

2. See Tosafot to Mo'ed Katan 23b, "Mourning on Shabbat." For further discussion of the issue of *simḥah* on Shabbat and the views of the Jerusalem Talmud, see Menachem Genack, "Mitzvat Simḥah Be-Shabbat," *Or ha-mizraḥ* 34, nos. 3–4 (Spring 1985): 229–234.

they are but with things as they might become. Therefore he dreams and he understands the dreams of others. It is the dream of one who lives in the realm of "beyond." When Joseph dreams that the sun, the moon, and the stars will bow down to him, he is dreaming that all of physical nature will admit to his view, which is above nature, above time, above the understanding of man.

Judah represents this world, the harnessing of the forces of nature into the service of God. Precisely by confronting the physical, by living the mundane, ordinary life in a holy way does one achieve sanctity. Not only the synagogue, but the kitchen, the bedroom, the workplace can be transformed into holiness.

Joseph and Judah, Shabbat and Yom Tov: two facets of man's eternal quest for the way that leads to heaven.

Mind and Heart: Joseph and His Brothers

THE CONFLICT BETWEEN Joseph on the one side, and Judah, the leader of the brothers, on the other, often falls victim to banality about rivalry for a father's affection or jealousy about a multi-striped cloak. In fact this is a conflict about how to serve God and man, and how best to preserve the destiny of the people Israel.

According to the Jewish mystical tradition, Joseph represents the intellect: thought, logic, analysis; Judah represents the heart: emotions, affect, feeling. Joseph is contemplative, looking inward; Judah is active, reaching towards the other. In addition, Joseph is seen as man reaching upward to heaven, and Judah is man bringing heaven to earth.

Joseph is both in this world and yet not of this world. His essence is concealed, withdrawn, hidden: he is silent, alone, private, closed. Like his grandfather, Isaac, he lives behind a veil. His father characterizes him twice as *nezir ehav*, "separate among his brothers" (Gen. 49:26, Deut. 33:16): he is more than "separate"; he is, as the word *nezir* implies, like a Nazirite, living a life apart. Judah is fully in this world. His father characterizes him as *attah yodukha ahekha*, "your brothers will acknowledge you" (Gen. 49:8): he is open, revealed, active, part of the community of men—as befits one who is the forerunner of kings.

Each is a source for a major motif in the Jewish soul. Joseph, ever contemplative, holds that we worship God primarily through thought and mind. The physical universe must take second place if one is to achieve holiness. Judah, recognized leader of the brothers, agrees that the world is impure, unholy, defiled, but—always reaching to the other—he holds that defilement and profanity can be sanctified and transformed into holiness. This is adumbrated in

80

Judah's name, which has in its Hebrew root the word for gratitude and acknowledgment: *odeh et ha-Shem.* "I will acknowledge the Lord," says Leah when she names him (Gen. 29:35). Judah will acknowledge God in all ways and in all aspects of life, for the entire universe is a legitimate field for godliness. Judah will confront every facet of the world which opposes sanctity; he will subdue it, dominate it, and turn it towards holiness, for holiness is found not only in the ethereal heights of withdrawal, contemplation, and loneliness, it is found in the mundane hubbub and cacophony of everyday life. And in his personal life, Judah ultimately will demonstrate that it is possible to stand up before evil and physicality—to recognize the things of this world—and to transform them into the service of God. Furthermore, says Judah, holiness will be achieved through the community of men, not through individuals alone. But Joseph, who represents the quality of aloneness and hiddenness, maintains that even a single righteous person, a lonely *tzaddik*, can, through his very presence, pull all Israel towards God and thus sanctify the entire community.

The Judah/Joseph conflict is put into clearer focus by a major Kabbalistic concept. There are two types of wisdom: the *hokhmah tatta'ah*, the "wisdom of the lower spheres"; and the *hokhmah ila'ah*, the "wisdom of the upper spheres." Judah's is the *hokhmah tatta'ah*. He knows how to deal with earth, with appetites and desires and hungers. He will transform the physical into a vehicle for the sacred. Because his way is within nature, his way to God is also within nature and does not strive to transcend it, as does Joseph's. He will lift the entire community by his acts, for his acts will be within the world and will be open and public—as they are in the case of Tamar, when, in an act of utter selflessness, he publicly admits his guilt; as with his descendant Nachshon, who, in a supreme act of faith, publicly inspires the children of Israel to walk into the sea (Sotah 37a).

Joseph is the bearer of the *hokhmah ila'ah*; he sees and understands the nature of heaven, and withdraws from this world. The text describes Joseph as *ben zekunim*, which is normally translated as Jacob's "child of old age," but which the Targum translates as *bar hakkim*, "wise child" (Gen. 37:3). Pharaoh says to him, "There is no one as wise as you" (Gen. 41:39), and refers to him as *zafnat pane'ah*, "revealer of secrets" (Gen. 41:45). For Joseph, the way to God is godly: as God is One and private and alone, so Joseph is one and private and alone. (It is characteristic that Judah represents the group, while Joseph is alone.)

Since the approach of Joseph to God and to man is private and hidden, and since the essence of Joseph is concealment, the brothers can hardly know the true Joseph, the righteous one, the saintly one. Only Jacob the father can know this. What the brothers. see is merely external, a youth grasping for power and dominion. They consider him a threat to the future destiny of Israel; they perceive him as another Ishmael, another Esau. Especially an Esau. And, in truth, Esau and Joseph are similar in one regard: in their ability to mask their individual essence. Esau masks his evil and reveals everything but evil; Joseph masks his goodness and reveals everything but good.

What does Joseph see that is so evil in his brothers that he brings *dibatam ra'ah*, "reports of their evil," to father Jacob (Gen. 37:2)? It is this: their very openness, their very conviviality, their active participation in the life about them, their willingness to enter the mundane universe. Joseph misunderstands the purpose of their behavior and speaks to his father about them: the precursors of a holy people must behave in a holy way. Holiness for Joseph is not in this world; it transcends this world.

They are two separate entities. Joseph, child of Rachel, withholds speech, just as Rachel withholds speech. What words of protest does Rachel utter when her older sister Leah and not she is given in marriage to her beloved Jacob? No words at all: she is silent (Midrash Rabbah, Gen. 71:5, 73:4). On the contrary, according to the tradition she passes along to her sister the secret signs which will save Leah from humiliation on the wedding night (see *Ba'ale; Tosafot* on Gen. 29:25).

And Joseph, too, is silent. What words of protest does Joseph utter during the long ordeal when he is accosted by his brothers, cast into the pit, and sold to the passing traders? Where are Joseph's cries of hurt and pain? There are none. He allows events to develop at their own pace, and for the next twenty-one years he takes no active role in his own destiny. God's plan will unfold: man must be passive in this regard, and thus he makes no contact with his father during the long years of their separation. But Judah says that although God's plan will certainly unfold, man will help it unfold, for man must be actively involved in his own destiny. Judah's is not the passive voice, but the active voice. It is he who says to his brothers, "Let us not kill Joseph, let us sell him" (Gen. 37:26–27).

In what is surely one of the most intensely dramatic scenes in the entire Bible, these two forces confront one another in the court of Pharaoh (Gen. 44). Joseph is now viceroy of Egypt, the monarch who plays nasty little games with the brothers. But on another level, this is the climactic encounter between the intellect and the heart, between Joseph, who seeks truth and holiness through pure thought and intellect and contemplation unsullied by things of this world, and Judah, who seeks truth and holiness through the heart, through the public uplifting and sanctification of this world. The concealed meets the revealed.

Judah—future king and bearer of royalty, destined to be the forerunner of the monarchy of Israel, which will include David, Solomon, Hezekiah, and ultimately the Messiah—Judah pleads for Benjamin, who is in prison, offering himself as a slave in the place of his younger brother.

And Joseph is hidden now as always, this time concealed behind an inscrutable Egyptian mask of royalty. Earlier, it was behind a mask of youthful frivolity and preoccupation with his physical self. Even as the brothers did not recognize the true essence of Joseph twenty-two years earlier, so is it now: when they first appear before Joseph in Egypt we are told that "Joseph recognized his brothers, but they did not recognize him" (Gen. 42:8). They never perceived who he truly was, although Joseph now does recognize their essence. Earlier, they had felt that he was the family usurper, that he was falsely parading his qualities before their aged father, even as Esau had done to his own aged father in a previous generation. And now the brothers once again are misled by the concealed Joseph. They see only a diabolical, scheming monarch bent on destroying them through mischievous demands.

Judah and Joseph: for twenty-two years they have been separated from one another, each walking his separate path. For Judah it has been a path rising and falling and rising again. First, he is the leader of his brothers, but after Joseph is sold into slavery the Torah tells us, *va-yered Yehudah,* "and Judah went down" (Gen. 38:1). He went down not only geographically to another place; he went down spiritually as well. He is accosted by a woman disguised as a harlot, who is in reality his widowed daughter-in-law, Tamar. He tries to resist her temptation, but as if in a daze he succumbs to her. Later, as she is about to be put to death for harlotry, Tamar confronts him with the evidence that he is the father of her unborn child. Judah publicly acknowledges his guilt, this time resisting a different kind of temptation—the temptation to lie, to deny, to save his name and reputation as leader of the sons of Jacob.

Joseph, too, has lived through a crucible of pain. He is sold to Ishmaelites, who sell him to Midianites, who sell him as a slave to the house of Potiphar. Gradually, he becomes a leader there, in charge of Potiphar's domain. The wife of Potiphar is attracted to Joseph's physical and spiritual beauty, sensing that in him there is the seed of great destiny. And though Joseph is attracted to her as well, he resists her, attempts to flee, is falsely accused, is placed in a dungeon, becomes leader of the prisoners, and ultimately the leader of Egypt.

It is noteworthy that in the life of Joseph and in the life of Judah the matter of sexual attraction is the crucible which transforms each individual into his true self.

By resisting the blandishments of Potiphar's wife, Joseph's essential nature will come to the fore: the ability to turn his back on the merely worldly. And when he turns his back to her and flees from her chamber, this is the great watershed in his life, the supreme test of his essence. Here he becomes what he has been preaching: theory becomes actuality. The physical temptation is to be given no quarter, and by resisting his own strong desire for her, he will become the true Joseph. He becomes what he is destined to be, and because of this the tradition refers to him as *Yosef ha-zaddik*, Joseph the Righteous.

Judah is attracted to Tamar as well, and though, according to the Midrash, he tries to resist, he is overwhelmed by a supernatural desire—because his test in life is to learn to deal with the temptation of the physical. And later when he publicly humiliates and disgraces himself as she is about to be put to death, and declares to the populace that *zadkah mimeni*, "she is right, it is from me" (Gen. 38:26)—this act of luminous honesty and pristine integrity on behalf of the helpless girl sanctifies God's name in public. Through this act—his repentance and his self-inflicted public humiliation— Judah is transformed and reaches his essence as a man. From the broken shards of his own self-destruction after the selling of Joseph and the incident of Tamar he rebuilds a greater Judah. He has in fact navigated the treacherous reefs of the earthly and has reached greatness: evil has been transformed into good, material into holiness, physical into spiritual. He has wrestled with the earth, has dominated it, elevated it, has become whole again; and thus he will be the forerunner of kings and of the Messiah.

It is no coincidence that the crucial event in each man's life takes place as a manifestation of each man's essence: Joseph's resistance to Potiphar's wife takes place in private; no one knows about this act of resistance except Joseph and the wife of Potiphar—and God. Judah's great moment, the public admission of his own guilt, takes

place in public. Thus the Talmud declares that while Joseph sanctifies God's name in private, Judah sanctifies Him in public (Sotah
10).

It is through the sexual temptation that each man is transformed,
because the sexual drive, as the most powerful and most uncontrol-
lable of human desires, contains both physical and spiritual elements. It can be a source of debasement and animality; and it can be
a vehicle of love, the source and continuation of life. Joseph rejects
this-worldliness, and becomes *Yosef ha-zaddik*, Joseph the Righteous One.[1] And Judah, by his subsequent correction of his earlier
inability to resist temptation, becomes Judah, the leader of this-
worldly matters.

And so they stand, in the forty-fourth chapter of Genesis, Judah
and Joseph, brothers united in their concern for that unique Jewish destiny which will spring from their loins; united in their desire
to sanctify God and to reach closer to God. But brothers divided in
their approach to God, to themselves, and to mankind.

This great, wrenching final confrontation is to be read on two
levels. On one level, Judah is going to plead for Benjamin and offer
himself in his stead. On a deeper level, Judah and Joseph are going
to step closer to one another, to reach over into one another's realm,
to adopt some of the other's qualities, to begin their ideological
reconciliation.

The reconciliation begins with the words *va-yiggash Yehudah*,
"and Judah approached" (Gen. 44:18). It is fitting: Judah, the
outreaching one, makes the initial approach. He comes nearer to
Joseph; that is, he admits that there is significance in Joseph's way
to God. Note also that Judah is not speaking in public: according to
the Midrash, he is speaking softly into the ear of Joseph: a private
act.

And after the speech, Joseph—who has been able to keep himself
under control, as befits the private, silent Joseph—now makes a
declaration of fealty and love to his brothers. And he declares it in
public, and he weeps—again publicly. Though he makes a characteristic attempt to have the Egyptians leave his presence, all Egypt
becomes aware of it: "and Egypt heard" (Gen. 45:2).

Thus the entire history of the Jewish people now comes to a point.
The reconciliation is in fact a precursor of the future people Israel,

---

1. The term *zaddik*, or "saint," is applied primarily to him who demonstrates
control over his sexual passions. Cf. *Zohar* 159b, *Nizozei Or*, ad loc. 5 and 6; and
Sotah 36b.

when these two elemental forces in man's service of God, the concealed way of Judah and the revealed way of Joseph, are merged into one, in fulfullment of Ezekiel's prophecy in 37:16–18. This chapter of Ezekiel, not by coincidence, is the Haftarah reading accompanying the Joseph-Judah confrontation section. In it, the prophet is commanded to write the name of Judah on one tree, and the name of Joseph on another tree, and "they shall become one tree."

In point of fact, normative Judaism has always contained byways and extensions of the two paths first established by Joseph and Judah.

There is the concept of *gillui shekhinah*, God openly revealing Himself; and there is *hastarat panim*, God hiding His face.

There is God's *middat ha-raḥamim*, which brings the community—sinners and righteous alike—into the holy embrace, overlooks errors, forgives weaknesses, understands that man's origin is dust; and there is His *middat ha-din*, which pushes aside the evil, shuns the sinner, refuses to overlook the fissures in our being, for it knows that our origin is from God.

There is the sacred fire on the altar, the fire which glows before God's throne (Deut. 33:2), isolated, alone, reaching ever higher, untouchable, silently devouring all in its path as it yearns for higher spheres; and there is the sacred water which flows beneath the altar, water which reaches down lower and lower until it touches those who themselves have reached the depths and says to them with the prophet, *u-sh'avtem mayim be-sason*, "you shall draw water with joy."

There is service of God through man's rational faculties, and there is service of God through his intuitive faculties.

There is service of God through the mind, and the service of God through the body.

There is the Shabbat, man reaching up to God; and there is the Biblical festival/Yom Tov, God reaching down to man.

There are the tefillin of the head, the intellect; and the tefillin of the arm, adjacent to the heart.

There are prayers which must be recited aloud, and there are prayers which must be recited silently.

There is public prayer, which can be recited only in the company of others; and there is private prayer, uttered only in the privacy and loneliness of one's heart.

There is the Written Torah, its essence concealed, hidden behind a veil, not fully understood on its own; and there is the Oral Torah, open, expanding, revealing, clarifying.

There is Michal, wife of David, child of Saul, and offspring of Joseph's mother Rachel, who considers David's public demeanor to be unseemly, unfitting, unregal (II Sam. 6:20); and there is King David, offspring of Judah's mother Leah, who dances and shouts in front of the populace in his unbridled joy before the Ark.

The two paths may diverge, but Ezekiel envisions the Messianic time when opposing spiritual forces are reconciled and merged into one: when mind and heart, the concealed and the revealed, the way of loneliness and the way of community, are no longer mutually exclusive but miraculously blend into one whole, when the way of fire/*esh* and the way of water/*mayim* join together into the supernatural fusion of the Biblical *shamayim*/heaven; and the way of Joseph and the way of Judah finally merge into one path which leads towards sanctity.

The Great Silence: Joseph, Jacob, and the Brothers

THREE SEEMINGLY DISPARATE but related questions about Joseph and Jacob:

1. In his final blessings to his sons, Jacob berates Simeon and Levi for what they did to the inhabitants of Shechem. How is it that Jacob makes no mention at all of what the brothers did to Joseph, how they cast him into a pit and sold him into slavery?

2. Jacob ultimately learns that Joseph is alive, and goes down to Egypt to see him. What does Jacob think about the action of the brothers, what does he say to them, what does he do about it? The Torah is silent about this.

3. During the twenty-two-year period that Joseph is away from his father, why is it that he who was always so close to his father does not contact him at all during that long span of time?

To this last question, one of the most intriguing in the Bible, a number of answers have been suggested: (a) Joseph knows that his dreams are prophetic, and that all aspects of the dreams will ultimately come true. He knows, therefore, that the brothers must ultimately acknowledge him as the leader, and were Joseph to reveal the truth to his father, it might abort the fruition of the prophecy. (b) Joseph wants to make it possible for the brothers to correct and atone for their sins against him, so he engineers the events towards that direction: he holds Simeon hostage, demands to see his younger brother Benjamin, plays "tricks" on the brothers—all with the defined purpose of raising their consciousness about what they have done, and about the need to atone for these deeds. And the brothers must atone on their own, without remonstrations from their father.

There is, however, a possible third reason that Joseph does not contact his father, and this will answer the first two questions.

Joseph *does not want* his father to know what his brothers did to him. For Joseph fears that should his father find out, the brothers will be cut off totally from the destiny of the people Israel. That which befell Ishmael, that which befell Esau, would now befall the brothers. Just as Abraham banished Ishmael from the family because Ishmael's behavior violated the standards of the covenant community, just as Isaac and Rebecca banished Esau for the same reason, so now Jacob would have no choice but to banish the brothers, to drive them from the fold for behavior unbecoming precursors of a holy people. And once this takes place, the covenant between God and Israel comes to an end, because the covenant requires both Joseph and his brothers; it requires unity between the two great thrusts of Jewish life: the approach of Joseph and the approach of the brothers. And if the brothers are banished and cursed by Jacob, this will mark the end for the people Israel and the end of God's promises for the future. The foundation of the Jewish people crumbles, and God's role in the world comes to a crashing end.

Therefore, Joseph does not contact his father. To do so would mean to inform him about what has happened. And so, rather than jeopardize the future of the people, Joseph—the beloved of his father, the student and disciple of Jacob's wisdom, the son of his old age, he whose visage reminds Jacob of his own lamented and beloved Rachel—Joseph keeps this terrible secret to himself lest his brothers be harmed: better for Jacob to be in the dark (once again in the dark, as he was when he thought he had married Rachel but instead found Leah; as he was when the brothers showed him Joseph's bloody cloak) than for all of Jewish history to enter an eternal night.

It is amazing: the Midrash tells us that after Joseph is sold into slavery, the brothers make a vow and take an oath never to reveal the secret to anyone. God, though disapproving of the selling of Joseph, nevertheless gives tacit approval to their vow and also promises never to reveal the secret (Midrash ha-Gadol, Gen. 37:27, 30). God Himself, apparently, does not want his own promises to Abraham and Isaac to come to an end. And so the brothers, and Joseph, and God Himself (and some say even Isaac, who was still alive) all conspire to keep the secret from Jacob.

Thus the answer to the third question is also the answer to the first two: Jacob never says anything to the brothers after he goes down to Egypt to see Joseph, because apparently Jacob goes to his grave never knowing the full truth.

In all this, Joseph does not spare himself. While Joseph awaits the full and complete repentance of his brothers, he himself is repenting, correcting, and repairing his own misdeeds. For he himself had misused the power of speech against his brothers. He had made assumptions about them, ascribed evil motives to their actions, and had spoken unfavorably about them to his father Jacob. Perhaps his twenty-two-year silence—which surely causes him anguish and suffering—is a *tikkun*—a repairing, repentance, and correction for his evil speech against his brothers.

Thus it is that Joseph emerges even nobler than before: protecting the reputation of his brothers who wronged him; sacrificing his overwhelming desire to reach his father—all in order to preserve the destiny of the people Israel.

Biblical Ideas

The Traditional Jew and Biblical Criticism

THERE WAS ONCE a time when the field of Biblical criticism was anathema to any believing Jew. The vestigial remains of this are still evident today. After all, the Torah is not a man-made book, subject to the caprice of literary critics, but rather a record of God's revelation to man. It is to be regarded as a manifestation of God's will for man, and is to be followed as an expression of man's love for God. What point is there, then, in a preoccupation with styles, with special usages of divine names, with literary influences?

The Biblical critic may have laughed at the traditional—and mythical—concern about the number of angels dancing on the head of a pin; the critic was not aware, however, that the traditionalist was laughing at him and his critical concern about the number of documents and strata which could be discovered in, say, one chapter of Genesis.

The two had absolutely no contact with each other. They inhabited two different worlds, and each looked upon the other with scorn.

This mutual antagonism is responsible for the fact that despite the radical changes which have shaken the world of Biblical scholarship in the last generation—changes which have moved it much closer to the traditional position—traditional Jews still view that world with suspicion. And while it is true that for one who is immersed in the study of God's word Biblical criticism has no relevance, it is also true that those who know and understand Torah have little to fear from Biblical criticism.

It may be helpful to one's faith to deny that it exists. But the paradox is that, as it is constituted today, it may be even more helpful to one's faith to grant Biblical scholarship at least a *de facto* recognition and to become acquainted with the new approaches and methods which have revolutionized its thinking.

Biblical research of a generation ago rested on two major premises, one literary and one philosophical. The literary premise stated that the Bible, primarily the Pentateuch and Joshua, was not one single book, as had been assumed for millennia, but a composite work of various authors who lived between the ninth and fifth centuries B.C.E. The philosophical premise was the evolutionary theory prevalent in the nineteenth century, which posited the thesis that all of history developed from lower to progressively higher stages. From this Hegelian hypothesis it was but logical to assume that, in similar fashion, the religion of Israel had developed gradually from a primitive idolatry to the advanced monotheism of the prophetic period.

It was with these two apparently solid underpinnings that Biblical criticism proceeded systematically to demolish the traditional view of the Bible as the unified work of an Author or, at least, author.

It did not occur to the scholars of the time that their presuppositions might themselves be demolished a generation later. They claimed that it was self-evident that there is no unity in the Bible. And their methods of textual analysis seemed to demonstrate that in the Pentateuch various authors and strata are visible. Already in the eighteenth century, Jean Astruc had pointed to different usages of divine names, to differences in style and language, to seeming inconsistencies and contradictions, to repetitions and redundancies. All of this could only mean that the material must have had several authors, and that later editors, or redactors, tried mechanically to fuse together all of these various documents into one whole.

This theory, attractive on its face, was expanded and refined by many scholars. It reached its classical formulation in the works of Julius Wellhausen (1844–1918). Under his influence, Biblical criticism became primarily a search for various sources within the text and a concurrent effort to separate strands and strata, to discover their historical and religious background, and to assign the various strands to their own redactors. Thus was born the Documentary Theory. There was a J document, based on the use of the Tetragrammaton; an E document, which used Elohim as the divine name; a D, or Deuteronomic, document; and a P document, written by priests and containing ritual and cultic legislation. Under Wellhausen's dominance of Biblical criticism, the Torah was no longer Mosaic in authorship; it was a mosaic in design.

Since the basic assumption was that the Bible was really quite unreliable in anything it had to say, changes and emendations were made as a matter of course. Even a wild speculation was considered more reliable than an untrustworthy text.

It was also an age in which the spirit of the day insisted on categorizing everything. Before long, the Documentary Theory became expanded, and scholars were referring with great assurance not only to J, E, D, and P, but to new sources, such as C, K, S, Pg, P1, P2. A cursory look at some of the older critical texts reads more like algebra than the Bible. The pigeonholing knew no bounds. Style and content were the major criteria, and since the question of what is style and what is content has no satisfactory answer, the number of the new Biblical documents and sources mushroomed. Accounts which remained stubbornly inconsistent were further distributed, then joined together and reconstructed. Soon an "adjective" phase set in: sources began to be described as popular, naive, erudite, reflective, theological, anthropomorphic, interested-in-chronology, supernatural, culturally superior, nationalistic, ad infinitum.

The times were Hegelian, and it was *de rigueur* for all disciplines to create theses and antitheses. And so Biblical scholars created their own Hegelian systems. Prophet was set up in distinction to priest, moral law was said to be different from cultic law, there was a preexilic and a postexilic Judaism, and Judaism itself was a synthesis of the preprophetic faith and the prophetic reaction. It was all very neat, precise, and orderly. It was, after all, a neat, precise, and orderly age.

Clearly, then, this entire critical view of the Bible was in reality a reflection of the temper of the times. Contemporary philosophy and science were dominated by the hypotheses of gradual development and growth in history—the concept of evolution. In history and philosophy Hegel dominated the horizon, just as Darwin was later to dominate the natural sciences. Hegel's philosophy of history was one of constant, never-ending change. He promulgated the theory of "becoming" instead of "being": nothing was static, all was dynamic, and the process of history was a proper waltz with its own predictable rhythm and beat. Progress and more progress was the key. Civilization had advanced from the primitive stage, and as it moved westward it advanced to a higher stage until it reached its pinnacle in Hegel's Germanic culture. Human history, he pointed out, had its infancy in Asia, reached its childhood in Greece, adolescence in Rome, and its full maturity—or synthesis—in western Europe. To Hegel, the more a culture is removed from Germany in time and geography, the more infantile it is. Thus, the Chinese language even sounds like baby-talk and is written with pictorial characters; the Hindu character is childish and dreamlike, without vigor. It follows, of course, that since Persia, Assyria, and Egypt are geographically closer to Europe, they are slightly more advanced.

Though this concept of gradual evolution sounds somewhat naive to modern ears, it was a major philosophical motif of the age, and Biblical criticism, as did other disciplines, found itself operating under its assumptions. Israel's Bible and her history were entirely reconstructed to fit into this mold. Everything was neatly rearranged in logical progression. The major thrust of Biblical criticism, under Wellhausen's leadership, became an attempt to show how Israel's history had developed from lower to higher forms. Development was now no longer a theory but a fact; the only issue remaining was to discover the nature of that development.

This had profound implications. For since evolution had now graduated from theory to law, it was, for example, inconceivable that the patriarchs could have lived in the sophisticated type of civilization ascribed to them in Genesis, with monotheistic belief, a settled way of life, and an advanced state of culture and economy. It follows, therefore, that Israel's history must have begun not with the patriarchs but with the Exodus from Egypt a millennium later. It had to be thus, since human development invariably proceeds from the lower to the higher. Therefore—and here the philosophical base of Biblical criticism forced the literary hand of its practitioners—the patriarchal narratives were untrustworthy, and were really nothing more than anachronistic "back-projections" reflecting the concepts and ideas of authors who lived in a much later age—between the ninth and fifth centuries B.C.E.—and were reflecting the conditions of their own times rather than those of which they purported to tell.

Still working within the evolutionary framework, Wellhausen and his school tried to show that the religion grew more complex as the Israelites adopted the cultic practices of their Canaanite neighbors. The prophets transformed the simple idolatrous and monolatrous religion of early Israel into the advanced concept of strict monotheism. They, and not their forebears—not even Moses—created monotheism.

The premises, if tendentious, were neat and crisp. The order was logical. The reconstruction of Israel's history was appealing. Freed of the restraints of the older traditional views, the new approach had scope and breadth. It brought Biblical criticism, long an outcast in the scholarly world, closer to the respectable scientific circles of contemporary times.

But the beautiful edifice, unknown to its designers, was deteriorating as it was being built. The first telltale sign came in 1887 when the Tel El Amarna letters were discovered. This was a rich collection of cuneiform tablets containing correspondence between diplomats in Egypt and those in Babylonia, Assyria, and Palestine. It revealed a well-developed culture in the ancient Near East which had hardly been expected as early as the fourteenth century B.C.E.

This had shattering implications for the theories then in vogue. It meant, for one thing, that real credence had to be given the patriarchal narratives, and that they could not be considered the product of a writer who lived much later. It portrayed a world quite advanced in intellect, commerce, trade, and diplomacy—one that could hardly be termed primitive. It suggested that ancient Israel was deeply involved in the history and culture of the ancient Orient. And it showed that Israel's history began long before the times of Moses.

All of this should have called for a new look at the methods of studying the history of Israel. A radical revision of Wellhausen was now in order. But Wellhausen himself failed to understand the significance of the new evidence, and ignored it completely. His conclusions remained unchanged. Nor were the other adherents of his school more receptive to the discoveries. Together with their master, they continued to build their theories as if nothing had happened, totally oblivious to the fact that the very foundations were crumbling beneath them.

But it was not an isolated discovery which signaled the fact that changes were coming. The times themselves were beginning to change. Science and philosophy were progressing away from the apparent certainties and assured results of an earlier day. They became much more tentative, and a slow reaction began to manifest itself against the concept of a neatly progressing development in human history. In a word, the temper of the times changed, and with it, Biblical criticism.

Over twenty years ago, Albright anticipated the reaction of our day against the older system.

> The evolution of historical patterns is highly complex and variable; it may move in any direction. . . . Wellhausen's Hegelian method was utterly unsuited to become the master-key with which scholars might enter the sanctuary of Israelite religion and acquire a satisfying understanding of it.[1]

---

1. W. F. Albright, *From the Stone Age to Christianity,* 2nd ed. (Garden City, N.Y.: Anchor, 1957), p. 84.

Albright then proceeded to annihilate the very methods of the older school, referring to the evolutionary interpretation of history as "a bed of Procrustes," for if a phenomenon seemed too advanced it was assigned later; if too primitive, it was pushed back earlier. And only those facts which fitted the preconceived hypothesis were used, while the others were ignored or discarded.

Albright continued the attack:

In dealing with historical evolution there are many seductive errors of method into which historians have been beguiled by insufficient facts or by inadequate perspective. For example, the sequence of evolution is sometimes reversed [or it] . . . may be telescoped into an impossibly brief period, as has been done by the Wellhausen school in reconstructing the development of the religion of Israel. Evolution is not always homogeneous in human history—in fact the reverse is probably more common, as in the development of Egyptian civilization.[2]

Under Albright's trumpeting charge, the last vestiges of Wellhausen's suppositions went up in smoke. While much of Wellhausen's account of Israel's history and religion survives today, it is a fossil preserved mostly among amateurs in Biblical scholarship. One modern scholar has pointed out quite astutely that it is particularly current among those who would claim the label of religious or secular "liberal," and that "it is at least a justified suspicion that a scholarly piety toward the past, rather than historical evidence, is the main foundation for their position."[3]

This reaction against Wellhausen was made complete by the evidence of the maturing science of archaeology, which now began to provide a new, non-literary basis for Biblical study, and to throw light on aspects of ancient culture heretofore unknown. Unlike textual analysis, archaeology's focus is not on theory, but on matters concrete and material: ancient tombs and temples, houses and pottery and utensils, clay tablets and seals, bits of papyrus, stone inscriptions, contracts, works of art. History need no longer be a scissors-and-paste hodgepodge, but a disciplined science based on objective and material facts.

The patriarchal period in Genesis was one of the first beneficiaries of the archaeologist's pick and shovel. Biblical historians had long

---

2. Ibid., pp. 118–119 ff.

3. G. Mendenhall, "Biblical History in Transition," in *The Bible and the Ancient Near East* ed. G. E. Wright (Garden City, N.Y.: Doubleday, 1961), p. 36.

doubted the historicity of these Genesis narratives. We have already noted that the characters were looked upon as eponymous ancestors of writers who actually lived much later, and the traditions reflected in the narratives were said to be the actual conditions of the tenth century. To assert that such an advanced state of civilization was possible in the times of Abraham was not only unscientific in its non-evolutionary presuppositions; it was patently absurd.

Enter archaeology. The discovery of the Amarna letters and their implications have already been mentioned. Such discoveries began to pick up momentum. Time and again the excavations revealed evidence which clearly authenticated the Genesis narratives. Discoveries at Nuzi and Mari, dating from the Northwest Mesopotamia of the second millennium—the geographical and chronological place of the patriarchs—again revealed that period as quite sophisticated, with a flourishing literature and science, with a stable government, enlightened agricultural techniques, and a prospering economy.

The Nuzi site has had an important effect on our understanding of the Bible. Excavated in 1925–31, it has unveiled thousands of cuneiform texts which give us new insights into the social mores of the age. For example, Rachel's taking of her father's teraphim in Genesis 31:19, 30, had long puzzled many scholars. But the texts supply interesting background. Property, we learn, could pass to a son-in-law in certain circumstances, but in order to give it the proper sanction the father had to give the household gods— teraphim—to his daughter's husband. Or in the troublesome passages where the wife of a patriarch is referred to as his sister (Gen. 12:10–20, 20:2–6, 26:1–11), Nuzi shows that marriage was considered most sacred when the wife had the legal status of sister, and that the words "wife" and "sister" were used interchangeably in certain circumstances. Hence, by referring to their wives as sisters, Abraham and Isaac were actually protecting and praising their wives.

The most common topic in the Nuzi material is adoption. Couples without children would adopt an heir with the understanding that he would relinquish his privileges should a natural child be born later. Thus in Genesis 15:13, the relationship of Eliezer to Abraham is clarified.

These tablets also shed light on the Jacob-Esau conflict concerning their father's blessing. According to the conditions reflected in these tablets, birthright could be established by the father's decision regardless of when the child was born. Moreover, the blessing of a father was most solemn when it was given on his deathbed.

The Mari site has given us an even deeper insight into this age.

Here again all the evidence of history, archaeology, anthropology, comparative religion, and linguistic scholarship substantiates the historicity of the Genesis narratives.

Albright has dated Mari at eighteen centuries B.C.E., approximately the time of the patriarchs. The tablets contain five thousand letters and give us a thorough picture of the society which Genesis describes. We note that Haran and Nahor were extremely important cities; we come across names like Ja'qob-el, Abamran, Banu-Yamina, Arriwuk. The texts also reveal that there were no real barriers in wandering from city to city, and that Abraham's sojournings would have been quite possible. André Parrot, the major excavator of Mari, has even shown what those ancient Mesopotamians might have looked like. The men wore square, curled beards; the women, earrings, veils, and necklaces. They dressed in woolen tunics of red, black, and white. And that Abraham the iconoclast is not merely a children's tale is suggested by the extensive finds of Mari gods and goddesses, revealing an elaborate and pervasive cult of idolatry.

Nuzi and Mari are but two of the numerous sites which indicate that the Genesis narratives were transmitted accurately from the times in which they occurred. Had they been invented by later authors, they would have reflected later Hebrew customs and laws.

Furthermore, these finds have given the final blow to the old concept of religious growth as a development from the lower to the higher. They show that Israel's ancestors lived in a highly sophisticated society with highly developed notions of law and morality. (The Bible itself recognizes the existence of a universal moral law from primitive times, to which all men are subject. Cain, the Generation of the Flood, Sodom, are all punished for violating this law.)

Archaeology, then, has been of invaluable assistance in understanding the Bible. It has filled in our knowledge of the background of many of the social, historical, and religious currents in Israel's life; it has given us the explanation for specific bothersome words and has thus rescued many terms from the fate of emendation; and, most significantly, it has pushed back the dating of the Biblical books much closer to the traditional claims than could heretofore have been imagined.

For providing us with such positive support of the Bible, archaeology is greatly to be praised. But there is one caveat: archaeology is not the handmaiden of the Bible, and it is not invariably a support to Torah. Its traditional adherents frequently forget that its purpose is not to confirm the Bible, but to illuminate it. For the believing

Jew, scholarly and scientific support for Torah is pleasant, but it is not indispensable to his faith. Similarly, apparent contradictions to Torah do not disturb him. He remembers only too well that just forty years ago Torah had been "scientifically" disproved, only to find the disprover itself become the disproved.

It is important not to be misled by the fanatics of archaeology, just as it was important not to be panicked by the Higher Criticism of a generation ago. The radicalism of a Wellhausen has now given way to the neo-traditionalism of an Albright; but uncritical approval of the new conservatism may in the final analysis be as harmful as unqualified fear of the radical.

For one thing, we must bear in mind that archaeology is not simply a factual science, and that its evidence is rarely plain or direct. Its findings are subject to analysis, reasoning, deduction, comparison, evaluation—in brief, to *interpretation* of facts. The discoveries of potsherds or clay tablets deep beneath the earth are not automatic and self-evident "facts" or "truths." As in any other scientific discipline, speculation and intuition play an important role. Certainly archaeology is on much more solid ground than was the criticism of a generation ago. Its practitioners are more cautious, its methods are firmly based on the canons of dispassionate analysis, and it thus is infinitely more reliable. But it is a human discipline, and as such it is subject to human error. Belief in the authenticity of the Torah and a Jew's personal commitment to it do not depend on the caprice of critics, whether they be conservative or radical, speculative or sober.

In any case, the critical certainty and self-assurance of a generation ago are with us no more. Nothing has yet fully replaced it, but there is now a new willingness to study the Bible from within, from its own *Sitz im Leben*, as the form-critics call it, rather than from preconceived standards.

For, in truth, one of the major weaknesses of Biblical criticism has been its tendency to judge the ancient world by modern frames of reference. No attempt was made to understand the temperament and character of the Biblical world. For example, since we have an enthusiasm for writing and we have poor memories, we readily ascribed these characteristics to the ancients. And since we have no reliable oral tradition, we could not conceive of one in the Biblical world. In point of fact, however, writing was to them always secondary, and they put great stress upon the spoken word and upon an oral tradition which was highly reliable.

Modern critics are also fond of overemphasizing canons of style and vocabulary, of neatly separating different strata and distributing them into definite historical dates and events, and of showing the influences which one civilization may have had upon another. But now it has been shown that styles and documents are not always evolutionary; they are occasionally parallel and are found at times to be decreasing in complexity.

The older critics had also maintained that the prophets stood in sharp contrast to the Law, that they wanted a more "spiritual" and "ethical" faith, and that they opposed the sacrificial cult. But today we find that the Psalms, which are so similar to the prophetic "spirituality," had their origin in the sacrificial cult. Modern scholars are now much more sophisticated about the prophets' apparent hostility to cult and sacrifice: the prophets were opposed only to foreign cults, as in Amos; or to sacrifice as an end in itself, as in Isaiah and Jeremiah; or to ritual without proper devotion, as in Hosea and Micah. And excavations at Ugarit and elsewhere show that ethics in religion is pre-prophetic. The spurious divisions of prophet vs. priest, and moral law vs. cultic law, are the results of applying irrelevant modern categories to the Bible. To the ancient Israelite, however, worship of God—and the rituals and cults it entailed—was deeply involved with ethics; and the ethical-moral life was deeply tinged by ritual and cult. For the divine will is not limited to ritual: it includes man's relations with his fellow man. There is a great deal of overlapping between the ethical and the ritual, and it is likely that it never occurred to the ancient Israelite that there is a difference between the two.

There are evident today the first stirrings of an attempt to deepen our understanding of the Bible by means other than textual analysis and archaeology. Gradually, we perceive a cross-fertilization with other scholarly disciplines. For example, a new awareness is now evident of the techniques of ancient poetry and music, their unique rhythms and metaphors, and their special cadences. These can give us a clear perspective of many puzzling aspects of the Bible. Many apparent contradictions and inconsistencies have already disappeared because of the growing sensitivity on the part of Biblical scholars to the work of other intellectual areas. Over and above these welcome signs of change is the increasing realization that textual problems are natural, simply because we do not understand the ancient Hebrew well enough.

A recurrent stumbling-block for Biblical scholars has been their own insistence on viewing the Bible as merely an example of ancient literature. Those few who, like Albright, have occasionally taken into account certain divine elements have been labeled as mystics. And yet each of the merely rational approaches has led into a new web of difficulties which has in time left it completely helpless to cope with the Bible as a whole. For obviously the Bible is not a systematic or organic work of literature. It is huge, it is diverse, it contains narratives, poems, songs, legal codes, sagas, and is written in an infinite variety of styles and nuances and subtleties. To attempt to synthesize it all under contemporary frames of reference is a hopeless task—and it is for this reason that the critics themselves are seeking new methods and principles with which to approach their subject.

It is precisely because of this that the believing Jew need have no fear of modern Biblical research. Indeed, he can make a contribution to it. For the history of such research is bringing it inexorably towards some rapprochement with the divine Bible, if for no other reason than that all other avenues have failed. The Jew who is thoroughly at home in his Torah and in the language of criticism can provide the key to many of the Bible's riddles which have baffled scholarship for many years. It would be naive, of course, to expect the critics, for so long committed to a natural view of the Bible, to accept fully a view which is suprarational. But in an age where the merely rational has been clearly inadequate, those with a suprarational point of view need not be afraid to speak. And certainly the traditional view of the authorship of the Bible, until now categorically rejected, offers some way out of the vast maze of problems in which Biblical scholarship finds itself. For once having accepted the reliability of the text, traditional Jewish exegetes are not afraid to probe, to ask, to find apparent contradictions, and to question every jot and tittle of the text. The only assumption—granted, a major one—is that the answers lie within the text. The believing Jew's faith will hardly be disturbed by an exposure to the still shaky science of contemporary Biblical scholarship. On the other hand, Biblical criticism may hopefully lose some of its faith in itself through an acquaintance with the world of Jewish tradition.

Biblical criticism has come a long way since the first stirrings of Jean Astruc, Spinoza, and others of the seventeenth and eighteenth centuries. Whatever its future direction, it is safe to assume that never again will it arrogate to itself the magisterial role of judge and jury. And, who knows, perhaps its newly found sobriety will allow it to adopt some of the techniques and premises of traditional Jewish scholarship. This can only result in a more profound appreciation of the origins and sources of our faith.

Crisis, Morality, Decision: A Jewish View

ONE OF THE great catchwords of our time is the word "crisis." There is a crisis for every need: a crisis of faith, religion, morality. *Time* magazine writes essays on crisis, *Life* runs pictorial reviews, *Reader's Digest* presents cures, more serious journals devote their pages to it, and scholarly quarterlies give it entire issues.

Morality is no exception. There is a crisis here as well, and, we are told, this moral crisis is reflected in qualities characteristic of modern man: frustration, despair, loneliness, indifference. His life is said to be meaningless and absurd. In the face of the world's impersonality, he is helpless and totally irrelevant.

And, to be sure, there is much truth in all of this. Who can gainsay the fact that there is a deep spiritual distress which afflicts our time? And if it is true that other men in other days suffered their own form of malaise, it is equally true that in our time we seem to have stumbled, among the scattered ruins of false idols, upon the shocking discovery that it was ever thus and will always be thus. Human existence has always meant and will always mean insecurity, danger, fear, conflict. Loneliness, frustration, and despair are synonymous with man in an alien world.

It is this realization of the existential crisis of man—a crisis which transcends any specific time in history—which is the beginning of the crisis philosophy of today. In a word, man is in the midst of a terrible restlessness, and he is thrashing about in deep waters in a desperate search for some ultimate meaning. The traditional answers have offered little, so new ones are presented. But they offer as much difficulty as the old. In place of "yes" we now hear "maybe"; instead of "no" we hear "unlikely"; in place of "ought" there is "perhaps"; to the demand "thou shalt" we hear the response "it all depends"; to the question "What doth the Lord require of thee?" we hear the answer "What do you mean by 'Lord,' and by 'require,' and by 'thee'?" Everything is relative, ethics are situational, and words like "imperative" and "absolute," or "ought" and "must," or "God" and "law" are taboo. And since it all depends on the circumstances, issues such as slavery in our day, or famine, or poverty, or thought control, or the persecution of thousands and the willful murder of millions are not necessarily right or wrong, good or evil. And if my mind and my heart tell me they are wrong and evil? Well, nothing is absolute, and my mind and heart are not always right, are they? But what is right?

If the conventional rhetoric is bankrupt, the new jargon tends to be anarchic, and man is left to fend for himself. And for himself he fends: euthanasia? abortion? civilization? genocide? premarital sex? dishonesty? crematoria? It all depends on the circumstances. Law is out; love is in.

Some of this is called the new morality, but perhaps its roots are in a Christianity which has always sought to sublimate the law, to elevate it, to make the spirit overcome the letter. In classical Christianity law was transcended by love, and love was the standard by which all human behavior and decision were to be determined. In this view, law is mechanical and cold and rigorous, and love is the true spirituality superseding all else. While this is the usual phrasing of the classical Christian deviation from Judaism—spirit versus letter—from the Jewish point of view the issue was always one of law versus no law at all.

Is the new morality, the ethics of situation, so far removed from the classical Christian antinomianism? Joseph Fletcher, for example, rejects "legalism" as an approach to decision-making, because "solutions are preset and you can look them up in a book—a Bible or confessor's manual."[1] (He displays, incidentally, a myopic view of Jewish law, referring to the methods of Jewish law in discredited clichés, such as the "tricky and tortuous . . . business of interpretation the rabbis called *pilpul* . . . a logic-chopping study of the letter of the law." It "chokes its weavers . . . who are in its coils."[2] Such a caricature of Halakhah—defined later in this essay—is most regrettable from a student of Fletcher's stature.) He rejects antinomianism because its decision-making process, in the form of a "Gnostic claim to special knowledge, just *knows* what is right," because "it is

---

1. Joseph Fletcher, *Situation Ethics* (Philadelphia, 1966), pp. 18 ff.
2. Ibid., p. 19.

literally unprincipled, purely *ad hoc*, and casual. . . . they are exactly anarchic—without a rule . . . sheer extemporizers, impromptu, intellectually irresponsible." Only situationism will do. The situationist is fully armed with the ethical maxims of his heritage, which he treats with respect. "Just the same he is prepared in any situation to compromise them or set them aside *in the situation* if love seems better served by doing so." Is this not itself anarchic? No. Love "is a principle . . . the *only* principle that always obliges us in conscience. It is always good and right in every situation." Love "is an attitude, a disposition, a leaning, a preference, a purpose."

A committed Jew, attuned to the voice of his Torah and his prophets, is deeply troubled by these words, for he stands inside a tradition that is less concerned with attitude than with action. This kind of Jew, himself so often the victim of the frameless ideal of love, is even more convinced today, after Auschwitz, that unless love is pervaded and guided by law it can easily become satanic. A man therefore is required to do what he must do regardless of his inner disposition or leanings. Man is obligated to meet the other, the non-self, in a relationship of caring involvement, and Judaism is not content to leave this critical involvement to chance or to love.

It is precisely here that the special experience which is Jewish has something to say about the crisis of our day. What it offers is not necessarily found at the level of its theology or ethics or morality, much of which have long been evident in the larger framework of Western culture and Christian religion. On this level Judaic teaching is quite familiar and has become part of the daily life of civilized men. That which is unique about Judaism and which has a strange ring to modern ears can be described in two Hebrew concepts, *halakhah*, and *kedushah*. The Halakhah, literally "the path," or "the way," is the term for the all-embracing Jewish law which regulates every aspect of daily human behavior. *Kedushah* is sanctification, holiness. The purpose of Halakhah is *kedushah:* the integration of the secular and the holy, a counterforce against triviality and profanity, a suffusing of all human activity with a pervasive sense of religious meaning and direction. By governing every area of life—intellectual, physical, social, economic—the Halakhah helps the individual along the way, the path, towards the sanctification of self and environment—time, place, and person. The committed Jew has always asked, What does the Lord demand of me? His response to this divine challenge, according to Halakhah, must be a total one.

For Judaism, the dignity of man is not enough. Rather, it is the sanctity of man which is the ideal. Man in his totality must be consecrated to God through the halakhic way to sanctity. Each of man's actions must testify to his awareness of his own relationship to God. It is the halakhic genius which transmutes an ideal into practice, so that the presence of God is to be perceived in every area of life, even the most private and personal.

The inner logic of the Halakhah is such that the ethical becomes an integral aspect of religion itself. But not only does it view man as a moral agent, or provide an ultimate rationale for moral action, and thus turn morality itself into a quest for the good. In this it is not unusual. Halakhic ethics goes beyond this. It posits specific ideals as well as methods and standards of fulfillment.

Although the obligation to Halakhah is felt by the committed Jew, he is far from being a subservient vassal. There is in Judaism a remarkable rebellious element: man openly revolts against God. He strives mightily to preserve a balance between God and man. From Abraham's striving with God (Gen. 18), through Jeremiah's (12:1–2), Habakkuk's (1:2–3), the psalmist's (44:24–27), and Job's (27:2–6), up through the Rebbe of Berditchev in modern Hasidism, Judaism has kept man's prerogative under the covenant: to see to it that each side fulfills its responsibilities.

Nor is man a subservient vassal in his decision-making. Despite the specific halakhic directions, Judaism allows considerable autonomy and range for man to use his own mind and will and experience. With the exception of certain basic areas, decision-making via Halakhah is therefore not simply a matter of "looking it up in the Book." The mind and will are engaged, at every point, to an extent that would make the situationists quite happy. There are, however, prerequisites for proper decision-making, one of which is complete familiarity with Halakhah and its processes. Not only is the *how* of decision-making important, but the *who* as well. Often decision-making is done by dialogue and consultation with a competent halakhic authority, known as a *posek*. Within this process, itself subject to certain bounds and limits, there is a staggering degree of latitude, and boundless possibilities.

For example, the general question of contraception is often a subject for decision. Although Halakhah forbids its use in general terms, there are specific circumstances under which a married couple may be permitted the use of contraceptive techniques. But—paradoxically, agreeing with the situationists—the *posek* must evaluate certain aspects of the particular situation, such as the motivations of husband and wife in using the contraception. ("We want to travel first" may not be sufficient reason; medical considerations may well be: the one has little to do with the sanctity of human life; the other has everything to do with it.) The *posek* will also be concerned, among other things, with psychological factors of husband and wife, and with the compliance with the commandment "to be fruitful." In his decision he will reflect the complex halakhic view of the marital act, which involves not only man and his wife but the people Israel and the God of Israel as well.

It would be difficult, in view of the above, to envisage halakhic sanction for the dispensation of contraceptive pills to unwed university students, for this leads not to *kedushah*, "sanctification," but to a general callousness in the attitude towards sex, which, instead of becoming sanctified, is made trivial and profane.

The Halakhah, then, calls from within the particular situation, and in making the choice and arriving at decision, man comes ultimately face-to-face with God. Thus the halakhic ethic is one of tension between the realm of the ideal "ought" and the realm of actual choices.

The goal, of course, is *kedushah*. This is the *imitatio Dei* of Halakhah: "and ye shall sanctify yourself and ye shall be holy, for I the Lord am holy." If *kedushah* cannot be achieved by an anarchist, neither can it be achieved by an automaton, for God is *Elohim Hayyim*, a Living God. In an electrifying wordplay, the rabbis interpret the phrase in Exodus 32:16, "engraved on the tablets," in the following characteristic way: "Read not *harut* [meaning 'engraved']; read *herut* [meaning 'freedom']" (B. Talmud, Eruvin 54a). Since *harut* and *herut* have the identical Hebrew spelling, the rabbis give expression to their own authentic Jewish feeling: the very law is itself identical with freedom. "All is foreseen," says R. Akiva, "but freedom of choice is given" (Avot 3:19).

Furthermore, man is not only an equal partner in the covenant and a free partner; he is a creator in his own right. For in the halakhic scheme of things nothing is sacred unless man makes it so. In the Temple, the sanctity or profanity of the sacrifice depends on man's inward intention. The sanctity or nonsanctity of a Torah scroll depends on the intentions of the scribe. It has been pointed out, for example, that Mount Sinai, which God sanctified, never had a special historical sanctity for Jews, and its precise location is not even specified in Jewish tradition. By contrast, Mount Moriah, which man sanctified (Abraham in his near-sacrifice of Isaac), is eternally sacred, and ultimately becomes the site of the Temple. Man creates *kedushah* by his thoughts and decisions and acts, because through his thoughts and acts the divine meets the human.

Certainly, decision-making frequently depends on the situation. The Halakhah itself, for example, grants situational leeway in the rigorous area of dietary laws. A rabbi who is called upon to decide on the ritual fitness of certain foods may be lenient in passing judgment in certain borderline cases and may pronounce the food permissible (a) if the family involved is poor and would be hard-pressed to replace the food; or (b) if it is close to the Sabbath or a festival, and the family will not be able to celebrate the holy day properly without the food. But this situationism is bounded on all sides by the Halakhah and is ultimately responsible to an absolute *imitatio Dei* holiness in all of life. Euthanasia? Abortion? Sterilization? Not easy problems, not easy decisions. The halakhic decision process will be painful, but will proceed in terms of its own experience, instinct, knowledge, judgment, laws—and holiness. Genocide, crematoria, premarital sex, dishonesty? The disciplined holiness of man and life, structured within the Halakhah, will help the individual decide, through the *posek*, what is right and what is not; how and in what way my decision and act will testify to my awareness of my striving for *kedushah* and to my relationship to God.

Physicality and Holiness: A Look at Kashruth

THE FIRST TEN chapters of the Book of Leviticus deal almost entirely with the sacrificial laws. In the Sidrah of *Shemini* we come to another subject, that of the food laws—the basis for the laws of kashruth.

If, as we believe, each word in the Torah has profound meaning, then the sequence of subjects also has meaning. From the fact that the sacrificial laws precede the food laws, it becomes apparent that before we satisfy ourselves, before we meet our own personal requirements, we must first offer up a sacrifice. The giving of the self precedes the taking for the self.

And another truth emerges: the food laws appear after the sacrificial laws to teach us that one must offer up his worship and his service of God, not from a "full stomach," not with a feeling of self-satisfaction and self-contentment, but with feelings of need and dependence upon God. He who is fully fed, he who is fully content with his achievements in life, can never serve God properly, because his being, filled only with his own self, has no room for a Supreme Being. In order to teach this, the Torah presents to us first the laws of sacrifice and then the laws of food: true service of God is an act of genuine reaching out for Him—and this kind of reaching out which the Torah requires of us cannot be done on a full stomach. Which is why prayer-time always precedes mealtime.

That there should be laws about food is not unique to Judaism. Every culture and society has customs and mores on this subject, and entire careers and fortunes have been built on the subject of how to handle a fork and knife. Judaism also teaches food manners. But although there is an entire tractate in the Talmud dealing specifically with this subject, Judaism is not concerned primarily

110

with how we eat, but with what we eat; it is not the form but the content which is important. And it is this content, which comprises the eleventh chapter of Leviticus, that we call the kashruth laws.

Obviously, kashruth is not simply a custom or a practice which the Jewish people adopted because of hygienic reasons. It is a Biblical law. And the only reason which the Torah gives is a reason of holiness: "Ye shall make yourselves holy, and ye shall be holy, for I the Lord am holy" (Lev. 11:44). Hidden within this regimen of holiness is a profound Jewish worldview.

It is not unusual for cultures, particularly those of the ancient world, to forbid certain animals. But it is important to emphasize that in those societies where animals were forbidden, they were often forbidden because the *animals* were considered to be holy. But Judaism forbids animals because Judaism considers *man* and not the animal to be holy.

Note also that the very first words which God speaks to man deal with the subject of food. In the second chapter of Genesis, God creates man, places him in Eden, and speaks to him concerning permitted and forbidden foods. Thus, even a Garden of Eden, even a Paradise, contains restrictions and commandments. Only in a fool's paradise is everything permissible; a true Paradise has its do's and don'ts. For God creates man in his image: God wants to make certain that man retains his godliness within him. Therefore He gives man directives and guidelines—the first of which deals with that which is most dear to man and of most concern to him: his food. If man is to become a godly creature, the process must begin with his most elemental needs—with his stomach.

Thousands of years later, after Adam and Cain and Noah and the patriarchs, God decides to create an entire people in His image. God wants to make certain that this people maintains the image of God, and He is concerned that they carry forth His teachings. He chooses this people to be a light and a beacon unto the nations, and He wants them to teach all men that God exists and that this world can become a Paradise and a Garden of Eden. And just as He spoke to the individual Adam, so does God now speak to the group, to the people Israel, and He tells them, once again, which foods are permissible and which are forbidden. Just as Adam differed from all creatures, and was therefore given special requirements to maintain his special relationship to God, so is Israel different from all peoples, and is given special requirements to maintain its relationship to God.

Food is the basic element of existence. But man is not the only creature who eats: the beast also eats. Is there to be no difference? The animal takes what he wants when he wants it. Should the human being, the Jew, the man chosen of God, the bearer of God's word, behave in the same way as the beast? And if the very purpose of Torah is to elevate, to sublimate, to sanctify, to raise up the animal which is within every man, can we really expect that an area such as food will be neglected in Torah law? It cannot be neglected, because the path to holiness which the Torah requires of us begins with ourselves and with our basic drives and appetites. The state of holiness, in other words, is not a never-never fairy-tale land, where people sit with halos on their heads singing hymns to the Almighty. The Torah's idea of holiness is to be holy within society and among people. God Himself says in the Bible that His sanctuary dwells "in the midst of their impurity"—betokh tumotam. (Lev. 16:16).

The businessman who sees dishonesty around him and yet maintains his integrity—he is on the way to holiness; the professional man who sees unethical practices around him and maintains his honesty—he is on the way to holiness; the student who sees immorality and selfishness all around him and yet maintains and upholds that which he knows is right—he is on the way to holiness.

Holiness is a this-worldly phenomenon. And in order to underscore the this-worldly nature of holiness, the Torah gives us food laws—as if to say to us, If you wish to become holy, it must begin with the very basic appetites within you. It is no wonder, therefore, that these food laws close with the only reason that Torah gives for them: "Ye shall be holy."

Cherchez la Femme: Judaism and Women

AS A SERIES of magazine articles on the general concerns of contemporary Jewish women, Blu Greenberg's pieces went relatively unnoticed and for the most part were critically unexamined. Placed together in the less hurried confines of a book, *On Women and Judaism: A View from Tradition*, her attempts to graft certain feminist values onto normative Jewish tradition invite much more careful scrutiny and examination. She writes with lucidity and often with sensitivity. But, as indicated in her subtitle, Mrs. Greenberg claims to base her ideas on Jewish law, on classical Jewish texts, and on the vast corpus of the halakhic traditon, and it is on these grounds that her material does not sustain a critical analysis. Regrettably, her articles now emerge as a recounting of feminist arguments of the most conforming sort, papered over with occasional halakhic rhetoric which barely conceals that which lies underneath: imprecise scholarship, slippery logic, and major conclusions often based on nothing more than personal feelings, emotions, and intuitions. Her operating principles are taken from the same tedious catalogue of complaints offered by Betty Friedan and company for years, and her suggestions for tampering with Jewish law echo the dreary litany long recited by various non-halakhic ideologies.

What gives this work a certain notoriety, and compounds one's discomfort, is that it comes from an individual who claims fealty to the classical halakhic process. The pages are liberally sprinkled with protestations of allegiance to Halakhah: Mrs. Greenberg "wants to

This essay was originally published under the title "Women and Judaism" in *Tradition* 21, no. 3 (Fall 1984). © 1984 Rabbinical Council of America.

113

live life as a halakhic Jew," and "does not want to reject the basics" (p. 172); "Biblical law is revelation" (p. 127); "this is not to say that Talmudic and post-Talmudic literature is not the law of Moses at Sinai" (p. 44). In fact, this is a work which at best displays a very tenuous commitment to the integrity of the halakhic process. One wonders if the author has thought through the implications of being committed to Halakhah and whether she is at all aware that many of the positions she takes in her work are incompatible with such a commitment.

Halakhic discipline involves more than the punctilious observance of Shabbat, kashruth; *taharat ha-mishpaḥah*, and the rest of the mitzvot of the Torah. As expressed by Maimonides, there are certain beliefs which comprise the underlying structure of a Jew's commitment to Halakhah (see his *Hilkhot Teshuvah* 3:8, and *Mamrim* 1:1). These beliefs are: (a) the written Torah together with its interpretation, the oral Torah *(Torah she-be-'al peh)*, were given to the Jewish people by divine revelation; (b) part of this revelation provided for a mechanism, known as the exegetical principles, for further interpretations and derivations of the written Torah to be made by later generations; these, when used properly and accepted by the majority of the sages, have the status of all other Torah laws; (c) the Torah gives authority to sages of all generations to make rabbinic enactments which will protect and advance the laws of the Torah. Such enactments do not have the same gravity as Torah law but are no less binding upon a Jew, and become part of the body of Jewish law.

The laws and practices which stem from these three categories are what comprise the Talmud, which is the sum total of *Torah she-be'al peh* and Halakhah. Because *Torah she-be'al peh* represents what man has determined to be the will of God as expressed in the Torah, there has never been any doubt for halakhic Jews that the Talmud is binding. Indeed, Mrs. Greenberg apparently realizes as much.

What she apparently does not realize is that the basic prerequisites of the halakhic process are that its decisors/*posekim* master the entire body of Jewish law, and that they accept the entire body of Jewish law totally as ultimately stemming from divine revelation. In addition, these decisors/*posekim* in Jewish law—who are skilled and carefully honed scholars of integrity and repute—operate within a rigorous system in which canons of interpretation, themselves a basic part of the divine Torah, are objectively applied. To ascribe prejudice of male chauvinism to such scholars, or to insist that

Halakhah meet the standards of a Gloria Steinem, or to suggest, as Greenberg does, that halakhic changes can be influenced by public pressure ("Who can know," she writes, "the impact of a thousand Jews calling on the Bet-Din of the Rabbinical Council of America to re-examine current injustices in halakhic divorce" [p. 141]) is to make a mockery of the halakhic process and to render sterile Greenberg's protestations that she does not wish to "diminish the divine authority of halakhah and tradition" (p. 178).

This is precisely why, given this classic understanding of Halakhah, it is not clear that Greenberg is truly committed to, or fully understands the subtleties of, the halakhic process. It is not only that there is in her work a persistent note of denigration of the Halakhah; more seriously, there is a persistent misunderstanding of the nature of *Torah she-be-al peh.* For example, the Biblical law of granting a bill of divorce to a wife is clearly delineated in the Oral Law's tractate *Gittin.* The method of transfer of the bill, from the hand of the husband to that of the wife, is an undisputed element of the law, as is the derivation which forbids divorcing an insane wife. To Greenberg, however, divorce laws were "developed" by "rabbis of the Talmud," and the method of transfer was devised by male-chauvinist rabbis to reinforce the absolute right of the husband "by selective weighing of scriptural phrases" (p. 127). On the other hand, "the rabbis of the Talmud were not insensitive to inequities in Biblical divorce law" (the divine Source of the Torah was apparently not sensitive enough to these inequities), and they constantly changed the laws to protect the wife. In the case of the insane wife, they forbade her divorce, but "covered their humane tracks with legal rationale" (p. 128, n. 4). In other words, Talmudic interpretations of Torah were written with the intent of either crushing women or protecting them. How and why the Talmudic sages were able to achieve these two contradictory results at once is not explained. Thus, what Jews call *Torah she-be-al peh* is nothing but a rabbinic invention to meet various social needs. In all this, we are asked to believe that this work proceeds from within, and not from without, the Halakhah.

Another major problem in Mrs. Greenberg's work lies in her unusual dependence on intuition instead of the rigorous canons of research. What, for example, is her scholarly evidence that the Talmudic laws dealing with women are for the most part connivings by prejudiced sages who wanted to preserve male supremacy? She has none. Rather, she arrives at her conclusion because she feels "intuitively" that the values of feminism are truth. Thus she writes:

Intuitively and with a new awareness of the ethics of male-female equality, I find it hard to accept any notion that assigns to God a plan for a hierarchy of the sexes . . . That could be only a time-bound interpretation of God's will from which women ought now to be exempt . . . does the *fact* that this long-standing sociological truth has been codified into Halakhah oblige us to make an eternal principle out of an accident of history? (pp. 45–46, emphasis added).

Here we have a vivid illustration of the kind of slippery logic upon which much of her thesis rests: intuition (which becomes "fact" two sentences later) has convinced her that the Oral Law is an "accident of history." And once the oral tradition is intuited into an accident of history, all the rest is commentary, and it matters little that certain laws have been accepted without dispute since Talmudic times. Greenberg can reject them out of hand whenever she cannot discern any reason for them. Thus: "If *kol ishah* has any redeeming value it escapes me" (p. 36).

One marvels at the liberties that can thus be taken with Jewish law. Without the scholarly constraints of reason and analysis, and with personal feelings as the guiding principle, a certain impromptu, ad hoc, anarchic quality animates her writing, and it is hardly surprising that Mrs. Greenberg gives strong credence to contemporary notions of feminism while at the same time cavalierly dismissing the rigorous halakhic tradition. For example, regarding the mitzvot from which women are exempted, she writes: "What emerges is an exemption by gender rather than by function, a standard *called into question by contemporary notions of sexual equality*" (p. 83, emphasis added). And: "If the new feminist categories are *perceived* to be of a higher order of definition of woman than those that limit her . . ." and then proceeds as if her perception is unquestionable truth (p. 41, emphasis added). And: "Admittedly, I have been propelled . . . by the contemporary Western humanist liberation philosophy of the secular women's movement" (p. 42).

If the original impulse derives from feminism, certain corollary impulses are inevitable. Thus, regarding the exclusion of women from joining a quorum of men for Grace/*Birkat ha-Mazon*, which the Talmud says is designed to prevent possible immorality resulting from the mixing of the sexes (Berakhot 45b), she writes that it "borders on obscenity" to exclude a woman after she "has organized, prepared, and served a meal to her family" (p. 177),—as if making up the quorum is meant to be some sort of cooking award.

Nor is it surprising that she would reject the laws of *harhakot niddah*, the system of halakhic reminders to the married couple that a state of *niddah* exists, whereby even innocuous physical contact is avoided. She posits the thesis that these laws are a mistaken outgrowth of the laws of defilement which are not applicable today. Her evidence for this thesis? None. Rather, she states that these laws "evoke defilement" and that "certain institutions undoubtedly grew out of defilement" (pp. 113–114). Unfortunately, she has disregarded the critical fact that while defilement is a Torah prohibition, the *harhakah* laws are clearly a rabbinical "fence" and are in no way related. But no matter: these practices are not pleasing to feminism and the facts of scholarship need not stand in the way.

Having established this baseless thesis, she presents a cornucopia of inaccuracies in her purported history of the *niddah* laws. These include a misreading of a Talmudic passage, in which she erroneously states that touching one's wife during the "white" period entails the punishment of *karet* (p. 114); an inaccurate declaration that a *niddah* is obligated in a sacrifice by Torah law (p. 123, n. 8); a mistranslation of Naḥmanides' commentary to Leviticus 12:4, in which by mistakenly reading a colon instead of a semicolon, she arrives at an erroneous conclusion.

To add to the confusion, she finally concludes that proscriptions against certain physical contact should be rejected.

> Very few couples strictly observe all the laws of *negi'ah*, the interdiction against all physical contact. . . . As one who respects the laws of *negi'ah*—but also as a student of history who understands that after the destruction of the Temple the emphasis quite naturally shifted from *tum'at niddah* (separations for reasons of ritual purity) to *issur niddah* (proscription of sexual relations)—I find the emphasis on *negi'ah* excessive and onerous (p. 121).

In other words: although there are no proofs for it, we should accept her thesis about the source of these laws because she is a student of history. And the laws should be changed because she finds them excessive and onerous. Besides, very few people keep them anyway.

These same criteria could of course be applied to the laws of *niddah* themselves. But she leaves them untouched—indeed, she writes an entire chapter supporting the practice of *mikveh*. "*Niddah*," she writes, "has come down to us through three thousand years of Jewish living" and "obviously serves a deep human need" (ibid.). For some reason, the fact that the *harhakot* have also come down to us through thousands of years is ignored. Some laws are more equal than others.

Although some of the practices of old have lost their glitter for her, she is not averse to proposing new observances: "An annual Pap-smear should be tied ritually to, say, the first *niddah* after Rosh Hashanah to add new meaning to the mitzvah"; and, "on the assumption that we still place a value on virginity before marriage"(!), the abstention period of brides should be altered (p. 121).

A particularly unfortunate misreading of source material is evident in her discussion of time-bound commandments. She is disturbed by the exemptions of women from these commandments, and declares that women should be ruled as obligated in all such mitzvot. That the Mishnah explicitly states otherwise is no problem for her, because the principle that women are exempt is an "arbitrary" one. She gives as the source of this discovery *Kiddushin* 34a, where R. Yoḥanan, commenting on the women's exemptions listed in the Mishnah, states, "*ein lemedin min hakelalot*"—"that list was not exhaustive," upon which Greenberg comments: "To paraphrase, the principle [women's exemptions from the commandments] is not necessarily consistent . . . R. Yoḥanan's statement opens the door to emendation" (p. 83).

This is in total error. The phrase used by R. Yoḥanan appears several times in the Talmud, and simply means that any Talmudic catalogue of laws is not necessarily exhaustive, and that items excluded from the list are not to be construed as having another ruling. It says nothing about the arbitrariness of anything. But it is upon just such shaky readings of Jewish law that Greenberg would have us restructure Jewish life.

The keystone of Greenberg's thesis lies in her call for a reinterpretation of the Written Law. In order to rectify the injustices perpetrated by the rabbis, these reinterpretations would change the divorce laws, obligate women in some mitzvot and free them from others, and finally permit abortion on demand. As a vital plank in this program, she calls for *posekot* (female decisors of the law) to replace the present authorities upon whom all of Jewry rely, because, she advises us, the present authorities are really nothing more than manipulators for male supremacy: "What these *gedolim*, the principle decision makers of contemporary Orthodoxy, are really saying is that they feel a need to preserve the original male prerogative" (p. 47). Female *posekot* will reinterpret the law in line with feminism. But if the interpretations of the present decisors / *pose-*

kim are rejected because they are ploys for maintenance of male supremacy, why should interpretations by female *posekot* designed for female equality be any more binding? She fails to see that *Halakhah* designed not to meet God's will but to meet man's needs, feelings, and intuitions is by definition not Halakhah. Her call for responsa and explanations which will adjust Halakhah to what feminism perceives as truth can only be termed frivolous, in that, willy-nilly, it totally vitiates and destroys the authority of the Oral Law.

Perhaps the most startling aspect of this book is its treatment of abortion. It is in this section that we find a painful manifestation of the pitfalls of reliance on feelings and emotions when approaching the halakhic system.

She readily admits that "the Halakhic outlook opposes abortion on demand" (p. 18). This should be enough for any halakhic Jew to reject abortion on demand. But Greenberg is undaunted: "As Jews, we must demonstrate that abortion need not eliminate reverence for life nor joy in creating life. . . . an orientation of this nature will allow new halakhic attitudes towards abortion" (p. 18).

Apologetically, she relates that "when abortion was permitted by halakhists, it was performed . . . where not to abort would constitute a grave threat to the life or health of the mother." But in the case of malformed fetuses, "this seems insensitive to the potential suffering of the child" (p. 149). Apparently, keeping the child alive is insensitive to his suffering; the child would apparently prefer to be murdered.

Turning to the stubborn refusal of halakhists to approve abortion on demand, she asks why abortion "based on personal economic or family planning considerations was never dealt with in the Responsa." (In her view, evidently, dealing with a subject in the Responsa is equivalent to finding a reason to permit it.) To her, this is not because there was no question involved, although it was always universally recognized that this is murder—even destruction of seed is prohibited in the Torah. There is another reason: in premodern times "life was precarious. You had to have eight children if you wanted four to survive." Also, until modern times abortion was not "common to the general culture" (p. 150). This, then, is why abortion was never permitted. Here, as elsewhere, she indulges in her penchant for taking a single-cell amoeba and, in an instantaneous evolutionary leap, producing an elephant.

In another giant leap, she suggests that we broaden the framework of therapeutic abortion (by which the mother's life is given precedence in life-threatening situations) to include "quality of life" of the mother. Thus, "the circumstances under which abortion is permissible may be widened [to include] the need to support one's self (or spouse) through school, the time required for a marriage to stabilize, overwhelming responsibilities to other children, and so forth" (pp. 150–151).

If quality of life is to be the criterion for abortion, one shudders to think what excesses Greenberg's harmless "and so forth" might lead to. She even goes so far as to declare that "in these cases abortion should be seen as a necessity rather than an evil." Despite the fact that there are myriads of laws forbidding abortion on demand, in circumstances such as these "abortion is the higher morality" and overrides those laws which "were developed to express those very priorities" (p. 150).

As for deformed fetuses, "it is true that some children with deformities are more loved and evoke deeper feelings or compassion than do perfect specimens." In other words, one should argue that they should not be put to death, since they serve the social function of evoking emotions or compassion. Nevertheless, "institutions are full of pathetic, rejected, and malformed, non-functioning children who eke out a miserable, inhuman life and whose parents have deep wells of guilt" (p. 152). In still other words, we should put fetuses to death because there are so many who do not evoke feelings of compassion.

There is a certain unreality about all this. Is not life in itself, without any social benefit, sacred and inviolable? What is the "higher morality" of abortions referred to against this morality? Why is the Torah's reason for prohibiting the murder of fetuses never mentioned in her consideration; namely, "for man is created in God's image" (Gen. 9:6, see *Sanhedrin* 57b, where this applies to fetuses). Yet this author who is an observant Jewess has "supported abortion reform with the full knowledge of the ambivalence of my position" (p. 147). She who presumably would not write on Shabbat to get through college would nevertheless permit someone to kill a fetus in order to get through college. All this is based on "intuitions of a higher morality."

To dispel any notion that her decision to support abortion is based on reason, she writes:

Each time I seemed to nail down an idea something happened to make it come apart. . . . Just when I thought I had the most sensible Jewish response to abortion where Tay-Sachs fetuses are concerned, I'd meet a woman who would tell me: "Even knowing what I know now, the agony we went through for four years, I still don't think I would want an abortion. There was so much love there" (p. 177).

She had her reponse "nailed down" by the vision of "the institutions full of pathetic children" (p. 152), but it "came apart" by a comment of a woman who loved her baby. This is candid and touching, but hardly a basis for momentous decisions involving life and death.

In a frank recognition of the inconsistencies of her work, Greenberg acknowledges that at this stage in the feminist revolution, "perhaps . . . the only legitimate response can be a series of tentative remarks . . . with a stammer, one step forward and half a step backward" (pp. 177–78). Her forward and backward steps are confusing but understandable. She is, after all, a child of her generation, her original impulse derives from the stirrings of a secular feminism (p. 42), and she remains influenced by the society around her. At the same time, she has strong roots and attachments to classical Judaism. Unable to decide in which camp to place her total allegiance, she has opted—impossibly—to try to be loyal to both. This ambivalence shows throughout. On the same page she can complain that "halakhah . . . continues to delimit women . . . halakhic parameters inhibit women's growth . . . as human beings"—and then immediately backtrack: "I do not speak here for all of Halakhah," which has "so highly developed a sensitivity to human beings" (pp. 40–41). She can stoutly defend the beauty of Jewish law while in the same breath take it to task for its "injustices"; she can declare that Jewish law "demeans" women (p. 41) and on the same page declare that "throughout Rabbinic history one observes a remarkably benign and caring attitude towards women." And she is aware of her ambivalence, describing herself as "calling for a love of halakhah and tradition yet subtly tearing away at parts of its intricate tapestry, perhaps weakening other threads in the process" (p. 177). While admiring her openness, one must sadly agree that this is an accurate assessment.

This book is an object lesson in how not to approach the halakhic system, a demonstration of the ways in which loose analogies, half-baked sociological theories and personal feelings ("I have had some very good feelings in the course of doing this work" [p. 178]) combine to create a web of confusion in which Halakhah—and, ultimately, women themselves—emerge the losers.

One final point. How can it be that a halakhic system which, by her own admission, has retained the "ability to preserve the essence of an ancient revelation as a fresh experience each day; power to generate an abiding sense of kinship, past and present; intimate relatedness to concerns both immediate and other-worldly; its psychological soundness, its ethical and moral integrity. . . . with so highly developed a sensitivity to human beings" (pp. 40–41)—how is it that such a system can at the same time "demean" women or "delimit" them or "inhibit their growth as human beings"? Perhaps the answer lies not in the cliché which she repeats: "Judaism simply reflected the male-female hierarchical status in all previous societies in human history"—with all the inevitable negative humanistic-sociological-Western-liberation baggage that comes along with that response. Perhaps the true answer to that question lies in a patient, consistent, careful, analytical, whole, reasoned examination of the halakhic tradition from within, in search of the unique Jewish truths about men and women which still lie unexcavated beneath the surface practices so lovingly set into place by the Halakhah. Such an investigation, undertaken without the prejudgments and preconceived opinions of outside cultures, might lead to conclusions radically different from those presently arrived at. And in the hands of as talented and as engaging a writer as Mrs. Greenberg, such a study—a true "view from tradition"—would be a real service in the cause of women and of Judaism. It is a pity that this kind of study, from within the parameters of the Halakhah, still remains to be written.

Somewhat Poetic . . .

. . . *the following three essays are not designed for accountants, lawyers, engineers, computer experts, or other "literati," unless they have been provided with the divine gift of rising beyond the literal—which we call imagination.*

In the Beginning:
Seeds and Questions

IN THE BEGINNING is the question *Me'eimatai korin . . .*—"from when may the *Shema* be recited in the evening?" (Mishnah Berakhot 1:1). Thus, with a question, begins the first of the Six Orders of the Mishnah. Thus begins the Oral Torah.

A question is a window to man's awe and astonishment at being part of God's universe, and to his yearning for kinship with the Lord of Creation.

The sun rises over man's fields and over his towns, traverses its course in the heavens, and in the evening bows down beneath the distant hills. And the moon rises, and the stars, and the silence of the long dark night. In the lonely rhythm of nature, the Jew perceives the oneness of the Creator who moves beyond it. He wants to draw near to his Creator, and he cries out with a question: From when?

When and how shall I acknowledge God in this universe of order and awe and mystery which He in His unmeasured wisdom has given me, creature of disorder and confusion?

And the response is heard in the very first Mishnah:

In the evening and in the morning, at dusk and at dawn, know Him and affirm Him. When the *kohen* enters the Sanctuary at dusk to eat his sacred food, from that moment on you are to cry out, *Shema Yisrael*—"Hear, O Israel, the Lord is our God, the Lord is one."

And you are to love Him with all your heart when you lie down, for you too live in a sanctuary.

And in the morning, when the dark night ends and you can distinguish between the blue of the sky and the green of the grass, proclaim that you perceive the difference between heaven and earth, and affirm and acknowledge Him. In the dim light of the dawn, when you are able to recognize your fellow at a distance of four ells, recognize Him who is your ultimate friend and shield, and love God with all your soul when you rise up.

> In the beginning there are heaven and earth.
> In the beginning there is a question.
> In the beginning there is an answer:
>   *Shema Yisrael . . . the Lord is One.*
> And in the beginning there are seeds, *zera'im.*
> *Zera'im* is the First Order of the Mishnah,
> Seeds are of the earth which God created in the beginning.
> Seeds bear the mystery of life of the King of life.
> Seeds are origins and beginnings and growth.
> Seeds are continuation, future.
> Seeds are tomorrow.

God gives man a seed, and man tills the soil, and from the seed and soil there grows a fruit which bears another seed, which bears another fruit and then another seed. God and man and earth and seed.

The First Order of the Mishnah is *Zera'im.* And the first word of the First Order is *me'eimatai,* "when?"

Seeds and questions.

In the field grows fruit, and grain and corn and barley ripen. And in the town the grapes are pressed, and olives and dates and figs. The Jew knows he must bless Him who created all this and granted this bounty.

Keizad mevarkhin . . .—"how shall one recite blessings over fruit?"

Keizad—"how?" When and how? And where, and which, and why?

Questions and seeds. The first Mishnah of the Order *Zera'im* begins with a question, and the Six Orders of the Mishnah unfold God's response to the questions of man.

> In the beginning there are seeds.
> In the beginning there are questions.
> In the beginning there are blessings.
> *Berakhot,* "Blessings": this is the first tractate of
>   the First Order.

When you eat the bread of the earth and sip the fruit of the vine, and when you savor the goodness of the olive and the corn and the date and the fig, bless Him, for without the blessing you are a thief from the storehouse of heaven, but with the blessing the fruit of the seed becomes yours and you can eat and be satisfied.

Berakhot, the first tractate of the Mishnah.
Berakhah is berekhah, a well, a spring of water.
Berakhah is berekh, a knee which is bent in awe before Him.
Berakhah is blessing.
Barukh Attah, Thou art the One before whom alone it is
    proper to bend the knee.
Barukh Attah, King of the Universe,
    Who brings forth bread from the earth;
    Who creates the fruit of the vine, and the earth, and the tree;
    Whose power and might fill the universe;
    Who daily renews the act of creation;
    Who performed miracles for our fathers and for us;
    Who is the True Judge;
    Who sustains us in life and helps us reach this moment.

It is good to worship God, to bless Him, to bend the knee before Him, for in bowing down before Him you will understand and know that it is He and not you who is the ultimate owner of the land upon which you walk, and ultimate master of the earth in which you plant. And as owner and master, He teaches the Jew that it is not enough to bend the knee before Him.

For it is only God who is One and who is alone. But man lives among other men, and among men there must be responsibility and obligation and reciprocity and taking and giving. And the produce of the earth may not be enjoyed and consumed by the human land-owner until he shares and until he gives.

Acknowledge God; affirm Him and bless Him: this is *Berakhot,* the first tractate of Order *Zera'im.*

Acknowledge also the man who lives beside you: this, too, is the teaching of *Zera'im.*

Has the Lord granted you a portion of His earth? Has He granted you land, a harvest, given you a share of His treasures? And have you acknowledged the God above you? Do not close your eyes to the man beside you. He too is a creature of God, and if he is beset by poverty and has less to eat than you, all your praises and blessings and prostrations before God are of no avail if you close your eyes to him.

Tractate *Pe'ah:* there is a man beside you. Share with him.

Pe'ah, "Edge." The landowner who tills his field and sows his seed and works his soil and now is ready to harvest his crops and gather his grain and store his produce and place his food on his table, must first open his eyes to his fellow men. Thus it is written in the Torah, and thus does the Mishnah expand upon it.

In the Torah, in the nineteenth chapter of Leviticus:

> *U-ve-kuẓrekhem* . . .when you cut
> the harvest of your land you shall
> not cut the edge of your fields,
> and the gleanings of your cuttings
> you may not gather, nor the
> unripe clusters of your grapes, nor
> the gleanings of your vineyards.
> For the poor and the stranger
> must you leave them, I am the Lord your God.

How large an edge of the field must be left unharvested so that the poor may have some share in your bounty? The Mishnah lists the mitzvot which have no fixed measure, and *pe'ah* is among them. The edge has no fixed measure. The minimum measure is set by the Mishnah, but the maximum measure is the goodness of man's heart.

The gleanings of your cornfields and your vineyards, and the unripe clusters of your grapes, and the sheaves which fall from your arms, and the sections of field which you have forgotten to gather in—these too have no fixed measure, and these too belong to the poor.

Acknowledge the man who stands beside you, for in this way you acknowledge Him who dwells above you who is the Lord your God.

And the Mishnah is not only theoretical. Who is eligible for the benefits of *pe'ah,* and who is ineligible? What is the definition of poverty? Are there regulations about the time of day when the poor may come, the amount they may gather, the type of cutting implements they may use, the kinds of fields and produce which fall under the obligation? No detail is beyond the sweep of the Mishnah.

You live in the sanctuary of God's world; your fellow man lives there as well: I am the Lord your God.

"The earth is the Lord's, and that which it contains" (Ps. 24:1), and what is sown into it, or arises from it, or works upon it, is subject to His will. Mishnah *Kilayim* ("Mixtures") limns the details of Leviticus 19 and Deuteronomy 22: you may not sow certain seeds one with the other. And even certain animals which work the land may not plough in one harness together: "Thou shalt not plough with an ox and an ass together." Nor may you breed different kinds of beasts together, nor wear in one garment a *sha'atnez* mixture of the wool of your sheep and the flax of your field.

God and His reasons are shrouded in the dark veils of shadow and mystery, but the Jew affirms God and serves Him even when he does not fully comprehend.

And again the Mishnah is not merely theory. How shall the various seeds be planted in accordance with the will of God? Which seeds are subject to the laws of *kilayim* and which absolved? Who is subject to these regulations, and who not? Where do these restrictions apply: in the Holy Land alone, or elsewhere as well?

How and which and where and who? The Mishnah responds to the questions of man.

The earth is the Lord's, and certain fruits may not be eaten during the first three years of their growth. They are not yet mature enough and not yet good enough to be presented on God's table in His Holy Temple, and thus cannot be placed on man's table in his own house. The young fruit is called *orlah* (lit., "unopened"), and this tractate presents the practical details of Leviticus 19:23.

Because the earth is the Lord's, it must celebrate its own Sabbath every seventh year, and the entire land lies fallow—unsown, unplanted, untended, unharvested. For the land was given in trust to man and is never fully his, and since the owner does not truly own, even the landless have certain rights to it.

The land has its own life: just as man works six days and rests on the seventh, so may the land work and yield its produce for six years, and in the seventh it too must rest. This is tractate *Shevi'it*, based on Exodus 23:

> Six years shall you sow your land
> and gather in its fruit. But the
> seventh year you shall let it rest and lie still,
> that the poor of your people may eat.

There is a seventh day, there is a seventh year: again a reminder that He, and not you, is the Master. And so that you shall know that no man may forever dominate his neighbor, all unpaid debts are canceled in this seventh year, for this, says Deuteronomy, is a year of release.

Zera'im is a sharing of bounty, and not only the poor who dwell with you must be remembered, but the *kohen* and the Levite as well, for they devote their lives to the service of the Master. Acknowledge God, plant properly, work your field in accordance with His will, share with the poor your *pe'ah* ("edge") and your *ma'aser* ("tithe"), give offerings to the *kohen* with *terumot* and *hallah*, and to the Levites with *ma'aserot* even when they are doubtful *demai*, bring your tithes in the second year to Jerusalem and learn awe before your Lord, and present your *bikkurim* ("first-fruits") to God's sanctuary where you become transformed from a farmer to a servant of the Lord in Jerusalem.

Affirm the existence of God and of His ownership of the land.

Affirm the existence of your fellow man and of his right to share the bounty of the land with you.

Affirm the existence of the servants of the Lord who devote their lives to Him, and share with them: this is the First Order of the Mishnah.

Seeds and beginnings, questions and responses, blessings and affirmations, a God above you, a man beside you, an earth which is the Lord's. *Seder Zera'im* comes to an end.

Ends and Beginnings

WHERE DOES THE Torah end? Some say that it ends at Deuteronomy 34:12, the last verse in the Torah. Where does the Torah begin? Some say that it begins at Genesis 1:1. And this is technically true.

But there is a problem. The Torah is God's eternal Book: that which is eternal can have no beginning and no end. And that is not technical. That is true.

Certainly we do "complete the reading of the Torah" at the end of Deuteronomy. But no sooner do we complete it then immediately we begin again with Genesis. For there is no real ending to the Torah and no real beginning.

Endings and beginnings exist only in our finite minds, which have no concept of the infinite, of things without end and without beginning. For if Torah is God's blueprint for the world; if, as the sages tell us, it is God's plaything and His favorite companion which he permits us to share with Him—how could it be anything but infinite and eternal? And if it is infinite and eternal, how can we say it has an end or a beginning?

Observe: the last three words of the Torah and the first three words of the Torah form one conceptual unit. Whenever you have heard *Bereshit*, "In the beginning," you have already heard the last three words preceding it. When is the first time in the year you hear *Bereshit*? Simḥat Torah. But you never hear *Bereshit* without the preceding last verse in Deuteronomy, *le-einei kal Yisrael*, "before all Israel," echoing in your ears. And this is proper. For why must beginnings always precede endings? Perhaps endings should precede beginnings, just to teach us not to be so certain, positive, and absolute in our linear, sequential, chronological habits. In finite matters one and one equals two. But in infinite affairs perhaps two precedes one. Perhaps they are the same.

131

For example, the last letter in the Torah is *lamed*. The first letter in the Torah is *bet*. Combine them, *lamed* and *bet*, and what emerges? The word for "heart": *lev*. The Torah ends and begins with heart. God demands the heart. What is prayer without heart? What is service without heart, *teshuvah* ("repentance") without heart? *Raḥmana libba bai*, "God desires the heart." First and foremost know in your heart that *bereshit bara*, in the beginning there is a Creator.

Another interesting word among the "last three words" is *le-einei*—"before the eyes of all Israel." Eyes: here again, is a key element in the human being, a major element in God's service. Read the last three words and the first three words as if they were one sentence: "before the eyes of all Israel God created the world." That is, the eyes of all Israel are directed to the fact that in the beginning God created the world, that it was not by chance or accident, that there is a creator, a designer, an author, a lawgiver. All of this is there for the seeing: *le-einei*.

And in this combination of ends and beginnings, where the last words of the Torah precede the first words, as they do on Simḥat Torah, we find an interesting word hidden in the very first word, *Bereshit: rosh*, "head, mind." Feel it in your heart, see it with your eyes, know it with your mind.

Your heart, your eyes, your mind: direct them to God and you will find a paradise in all that you do. Misdirect them, and you are banished from the Garden of Eden.

Look at poor Adam and Eve. They have it all: paradise, pleasure, security. But one thing they do not understand: that there can be no paradise without demands and restrictions. And so Adam and Eve are commanded to refrain from eating from one tree in the Garden— but they look (with their eyes) and they see that it is to be desired (with their heart) and that it makes them wise (mind). They subvert the three great gifts of God.

And we often do the same. The Torah ends and begins with heart, eyes, and head. *Lo taturu aharei levavkhem ve-aharei eineikhem . . . le-ma'an tizkeru*, "You shall not go astray after your hearts, and after your eyes . . . in order that you remember." Again, eyes and heart and mind.

The most astonishing facet of Simḥat Torah is the reading of the end and the beginning. For then we see with our eyes, and feel with our hearts, and know with our minds. See how the last passage weaves inexorably into the first, how God created the Torah because He wanted to give it to Israel.

Where does the Torah end, where does the Torah begin?

Where does the horizon end and dip into the sea, and where does the sea end and merge into the horizon and disappear?

Where does the sky begin?

Where does the rainbow end?

Where does God begin, where does God end?

When the Holy Temple was destroyed the Messiah was born, say the sages: ends and beginnings, simultaneously. When God gave the Torah to Moses, all the ḥiddushim, "novellae," that Jews to the end of time were to discover in it were given to Moses. Discover it, it is new. But it is also old. What was, already has been, says Ecclesiastes. God created a world ages ago. When did His creation end? *Meḥadesh be-tuvo*, "He creates anew every day."

The world of Torah is a world where life is a continuum; it is not a line from here to there, but a circle.

Yizkor for the departed is recited on the holiday in which we complete the reading of the Torah. An anomaly? Not really. When we think about death we think of the end. But is it really an end? As we have seen, we really do not know about endings and beginnings. Who can say that life ends at the grave? Here too there is a merging into beginnings: a beginning of a life in another realm, a return of the soul to God. The mystery of life is like the mystery of Torah, unfathomable, down to the depths. Life is godly, for God is the God of life, Torah is the Torah of life, and God and Torah and life are without end and without beginning, for they are eternal. Shemini Aẓeret and Simḥat Torah are the end of the holidays in Tishrei. The end? These holidays do not come to an end. They are just the beginning. Their influence on our lives is just beginning.

May our lives be marked by renewed contact with eternity, with prayer, with mitzvot, with tzedakah—which we can achieve with heart and with mind and with eyes searching upward for the endless, infinite, limitless eternity of God and His Torah.

God and Man in the Shofar Sound

ASHREI HA-AM YODEI TERUAH, "blessed is the people which knows [understands] the *teruah*" (Ps. 89:16). This means that it is not enough simply to hear the sound of the shofar's *teruah* with the external ear; it is necessary to listen with the heart. The sound of the shofar is not for external use only; rather, it is internal—and eternal.

What does the shofar attempt to convey? How and why do the notes and sounds differ? And just how does each sound convey a different message?

To comprehend the answer, we need not only a mind, but also a soul. It is not with the conscious self that the shofar speaks, but with the inner self, the soul. For the shofar speaks the mystical, hidden language which is understood only from within.

The first sound of the shofar is *tekiah*—a long, clear, steady, unbroken, piercing sound. What does it say, in its own language?

Tekiah represents the call from God: God calling to man in all the elemental, natural, primal power which is God's.

Tekiah: the call is frightening, piercing, penetrating, searing the soul. Imagine that you are asleep in the dark of night and suddenly this kind of awesome sound awakens you. With fear and trembling you try to hide, but the sound is heard again and again: *tekiah, tekiah. Ha-yitaka shofar ba-ir*—"can a shofar sound in the city and the people not tremble?" (Amos 3:6).

This is the first shofar sound of Rosh Hashanah, the call from God to those who have been spiritually asleep: awaken from your slumber, from smugness, complacency, contentment, self-satisfaction. Wake up and remember that I am God, that there is a Ruler who gave

134

you mitzvot with which to serve Him, and paths to walk upon with Him, and a Torah by which to follow Him.

This is *tekiah:* that shrill, penetrating note which seems to emanate from the bowels of the earth: there is a God, a Ruler, a Master, a King.

This is not as obvious as we think. If we know that there is a God who sees all that we do, then how can anyone lie, or cheat? If we know that there is a God who gives us our possessions, how can we not give more? If we know that there is a God who listens, how can we utter a falsehood? If we know that there is a God who observes our every act, how can we deal falsely, how humiliate another, how can we gossip? The truth is that we have put God into a separate compartment, locked Him in a special cabinet not to be used except in emergencies; boxed Him inside a synagogue, as if in a museum, to be visited only on special occasions, such as Bar Mitzvahs, weddings, funerals, festivals.

In such a context the call of *tekiah* is important: there is a God who sees and who commands. This is the opening call: the elemental, unadorned, unvarnished, unpretentious sound of the shofar calling to the authentic soul of the Jew.

But as we know, there is more to the sound of the shofar. There are two other sounds: *teruah* and *shevarim.* The *teruah* sound consists of a minimum of nine rapid, staccato blasts; *shevarim* is three short half-notes.

What do these sounds represent? The answer is that they are a *response* to the call of God, to the call of *tekiah.* And it is the Jewish soul which is responding.

And what is the sound of response? The sound of three sighs, called *shevarim,* followed by the sound of weeping: nine broken sobs, called *teruah.*

Shevarim, the three half-notes, represent the soul suddenly aroused from her slumber; half-asleep and half-awake now, she cries out, partly in fear, partly in joy. She faintly recognizes the call of God.

Teruah is the soul in full-throated sobbing, weeping, crying—because now she recognizes fully that her own Maker has returned and is calling for her.

Why does the soul weep in fear and in awe, in joy and in happiness? Because she has been separated from her Creator for so long that she thought she had been abandoned by the heavenly Father. And now, suddenly, she hears a familiar call, calling as of old, as He called at Sinai through the shofar, as He called at Jericho through the shofar, as He called at every critical juncture in Jewish history, at every battle and at every victory.

And so the soul weeps—hesitatingly at first—but as a kind of sighing in the *shevarim* and then as the full sobs of recognition in the *teruah*.

Why does the soul weep? The soul weeps because she hears God's voice and she recognizes the truth of His demand: that there is only one Master, one King, one Ruler, and she wants to cleave to Him. The soul weeps, just as any man may weep when he is deeply stirred by some great and profound truth.

Why does the soul weep? The soul—that which makes us human—weeps because she knows that because she is fettered to earth, her essential purity is encrusted, weighed down, tarnished, corroded, with the accumulation of man's neglect, and so she weeps and sighs and moans.

The soul, the essential Jew, wants to be what it once was meant to be: at one with God, cleaving to Him.

In the course of time, the Jewish soul has wandered off and forgotten her roots. She tried false gods, dead gods, and found no peace—because the Jew has only one identity, and no Jewish soul is truly at peace with herself until she comes to grips with her identity. Shunted aside, ignored, she constantly returns. Try to eradicate the soul, change names, change faces: it does not matter. At certain moments the soul reminds you who you are: you hear a word, a sound, see a headline, and in a fleeting instant you remember who you are.

No Jew today is more than a generation or two removed from a traditional Jewish forebear. This is the kind of proximity that is hard to hide. Ultimately, each Jewish child emanates from Abraham, Isaac, and Jacob. Ultimately, each Jew has as his forebears David and Solomon. Each Jew comes from the family of Isaac, Jeremiah, Hillel, Akiva, Rashi, Rambam. It is difficult to run away from this kind of *mishpaḥah*.

And on Rosh Hashanah, as the shofar sounds, it blasts away all the veneer and gloss and pretense that we have accumulated, all the poses and masks. The sound penetrates our hearts, and the soul begins to awaken.

God calls again and again. We listen to the note: the sounds vary, the patterns and combinations change. Every combination begins and ends with *tekiah*—God calls; and immediately there follows *teruah*—the soul's full, sobbing, weeping response: "I recognize you,

my Father, I remember. Yes, I have wandered, but I wish to return."
Again and again the dialogue is heard like a shepherd piping for his
lost sheep. God calls, man responds; God calls, man responds. Over
and over, flowing up from the subconscious, from the innate awareness of the Jew—one hundred sounds in all: God and man in
elemental, primordial, wordless dialogue, a symphony of God and
man.

After the repeated calls, after the urgent supplications and en-
treaties and urgings, the shofar concludes with *tekiah gedolah*—
the long, climactic, majestic sound of triumph and of victory. Man
has fully responded, has recognized the truth in its entirety: that
God is King and we are His subjects.

God is King and we are His subjects. This is the essence of
Judaism.

Somewhat Brief . . .

. . . in which are found some significant ideas, unelaborated and unadorned.

Two Kinds of Remembering: The Shema

THE QUESTION HAS often been asked, Why is the word "remember" mentioned twice in the last paragraph of the *Shema:* "it shall be unto you for a fringe, and you shall look upon it *and remember* all the commandments of the Lord and do them, that you not stray after your hearts and your eyes. . . . so that *you shall remember* and do all My commandments and be holy unto your God. I am the Lord your God that brought you out of the land of Egypt to be your God. I am the Lord your God."[1]

Why does this critical passage, recited by Jews twice each day, contain two commandments to remember? Why would not one suffice?

The Torah refers here to two stages of man's relationship to God, one preceding the other, one less advanced than the other. The *ẓiẓit* fringes are first designed to help us remember all the commandments of God—*u-zekhartem et kal miẓvot ha-Shem.* This is the first level: looking at the *ẓiẓit* reminds us of the mitzvot of God (who is here referred to as an abstract, nonrelated Being). In addition, this first stage will keep us from "straying after our heart and our eyes." The first stage of doing mitzvot, then, is to prevent us from wandering away from God.

The second stage is much higher: *le-ma'an tizkeru,* "in order that you may remember and do all My commandments." Here, the commandments are not simply those of an abstract third-person God, but they are "My commandments," the commandments of the God

---

1. Num. 15:39–41. On this passage, see the remarkable comment of R. Ephraim Luntschitz, known as the *Kli Yakar,* citing the Sifri on the underlying motif of the "cord of blue" on the *ẓiẓit.*

who is intimately related to man. If man learns first to refrain from wandering after his heart and his eyes, from falling to his own temptations and desires, then he will be ready for the second kind of remembrance, the higher remembrance, a remembrance which will place him in an intimate relationship with God. And then, "and you shall be holy unto your God." This second remembrance creates the highest level of relationship between man and God, that of holiness.

The very last sentence of the *Shema*—"I am the Lord your God, who brought you out of the land of Egypt to be your God; I am the Lord your God"—contains two references to "I am the Lord your God." Each of these parallels the two earlier stages. The first "I am the Lord your God" refers to the lower stage, where service of God is reflected simply by refraining from following the heart and the eyes. This is "I am the Lord your God, who brought you out of the land of Egypt to be your God"; that is, the lower level of relationship to God—one which serves Him only because He took us out of the land of Egypt and we therefore owe Him something, and therefore we do not stray from Him.

However, the highest level is to serve God without reason, to "remember and do all My commandments and be holy unto your God." This is symbolized by the second "I am the Lord your God," in which there is no reason. It is simply man's obligation to serve God without cause, without reason, without any benefit that may accrue to man from this service. This second statement parallels the second statement above: "and you shall be holy unto your God."

Did Moses Waste the Forty Days?

IN A VERY touching Midrash, R. Avahu says: "All the forty days that Moses was on Sinai, he studied Torah and forgot, studied and forgot. Finally he said, 'King of the Universe, I have studied for forty days and I don't know a thing.' What did God do? When Moses finished the forty days, God gave him the Torah as a gift, as it is written, *Va-yiten el Mosheh*, 'and He gave it to Moses' " (Midrash Rabbah 41).

Does this mean that the forty days that Moses spent on Sinai were wasted? Furthermore, why did God put him through it in the first place? And why is the Torah always referred to as having been taught to Moses during the forty days, when in fact God was unable to teach it to him, but was forced to present it to him as a gift?

Perhaps the answer lies in the idea that the effort put in by Moses, though he kept forgetting, made of him a vessel which was able to receive this gift of Torah. Had Moses not worked, he would not have been ready to accept this gift. Each day of work and study and effort of the forty days made it possible for Moses to receive God's gift, and not to forget the contents of the gift.

The same holds true about the six days of the week and Shabbat. During the mundane week, we try to serve God. We have good intentions, we even perform mitzvot. We try, we labor, we yearn to comprehend. But our effort often seems wasted, and we forget. All the effort seems to have no impact upon us. But on Shabbat, all the effort and attempt come together. For an impression, a mark, has been branded on our souls, and on Shabbat it all comes to the surface, and nothing is lost. From all of the effort a receptacle, a vessel is created, and we are therefore able to accept the gift of Shabbat, and appreciate it, and cherish it.

143

This is the lesson: let a person not be discouraged. Let his heart not fail if he finds himself trying and failing, trying and failing, for everything shapes and molds. Sincere effort, invested with heart and will and earnestness, though it may not yield immediate fruits, does yield ultimate fruits. For this is the difference between holy work and ordinary work: with holy work, we become vessels ready to receive.[1]

---

1. In this regard, see the comment of the Gaon of Vilna on sidrah *Ki Tissa:* he cites the Talmud about the person lost in the desert who forgets when it is Shabbat. When should he observe the Shabbat? The final halakhah is that he must count six days and then keep the seventh. This underscores the concept that Shabbat requires preparation in advance, and that part of the essence of Shabbat is the preparation that precedes it. Through the preparation, we become vessels ready to receive the grace and joy of Shabbat.

The Dual Element in the Mitzvah

THERE IS A well-known Midrash (Sifre on Deut. 33:2; Pesikta Rabbati 21) which says that God tried to "peddle" the Torah to the whole world, but that all the peoples of the world rejected the Torah and its precepts, insisting first on examining its legislation and on editing out certain rules of morality and behavior which did not appeal to them. Only Israel, says this source, accepted the Torah sight unseen, with the declaration recorded in the Torah, *na'aseh ve-nishma*, "we will do and we will hear" (Exod. 24:7).

There is an equally well-known text (Shabbat 88a) which states that Israel was reluctant to accept the Torah, and that it was only after God lifted Mount Sinai physically, held it over the heads of the people, and threatened to drop the mountain down upon them, saying, "If you accept My Torah all will be well; but if not, that will be your burial place"—only after this did Israel accept God's Torah.

Do not these two sources stand in stark contradiction to one another?

Perhaps not. There are two elements in the performance of every mitzvah. The first is the personal element, that which one brings to each commandment from within one's heart and soul and mind: a sense of love, obedience, or gratitude to the Creator; a desire to please God, or to honor Him. These inward feelings vary from person to person. The second element is the universal requirement to perform the commandment, whether or not one comprehends it, or feels like it, or is in the mood, or desires to do it.

In brief, the performance of each commandment contains a personal, subjective element, and this differs with every single individual, depending on what he or she personally brings from within the self to the performance of the commandment. In addition, the performance of each commandment contains an objective element, and this falls equally upon every Jew.

The first source, in which Israel willingly accepts the Torah, refers to the personal, subjective element in the commandment, that which one brings from within, and which differs with every individual. "We will do"—we will certainly perform Thy commandments, because they are commanded by Thee. But "we will hear"—each person "hears," understands, perceives differently, and therefore will bring to the commandment his or her unique soul. This is the voluntary aspect within the performance of each commandment.

On the other hand, the incident in which God holds Mount Sinai above Israel and "forces" them to accept the Torah may be symbolic of the objective element in every mitzvah: the requirement to perform it regardless of one's own personal feelings. This is the nonvoluntary aspect of the mitzvah: commandment as commandment and nothing else.

Thus, in each mitzvah that we perform, there is a fusion of the subjective and the objective, of the voluntary and the involuntary, of God's immutable will and man's loving response.

When Contradictions Make Sense

THE MIDRASH RABBAH mentions that there are four mitzvot which are apparently contradictory in their nature. There is the wife of one's brother, who is prohibited, according to the Torah; and yet, if the brother should die without children, the remaining brother was required, according to Torah law, to marry the widow. In the case of the *sa'ir ha-mishtaleach*—the scapegoat—it helps purify all of Israel; nevertheless, the one who sends it into the desert becomes impure himself. *Kilayim*, mixtures of wool and linen are prohibited; but in the case of *ẓiẓit*, the ritual fringes, it is permitted. Finally, in the case of the red heifer, its ashes purify an impure man, but they render impure the priest who prepares it.

In this Midrash, the rabbis give us a profound insight into the Torah. We like to know the reasons behind the laws; but the Midrash seems to say that ultimately the Torah goes beyond mere reason. We like to think that reason and logic and the mind are supreme; but the Midrash seems to say that there is a realm above reason and beyond logic. If the same object can be pure and impure, permitted and forbidden, there must be a realm of understanding, a different level of meaning, which we have not yet attained. And the Midrash seems to tell us that if we really want to understand Judaism, we must enter a new dimension of thinking and feeling. We must throw ourselves into a new world of mystery, of shadows, of paradox, where contradictions seem to exist and yet together they somehow create one totality, one whole.

And the truth is that all of life is contradictory. Man is part angel and part brute: he is a fusion of love and hate, pride and humility, humanity and bestiality. The very contradictory nature of man makes him human. And the rabbis tell us that one of the primary meanings of the word *eḥad*, "one," in the *Shema* is this: that in the end of days everything will be *one*: everything that seems now to be contradictory will be reconciled, and that which seems evil will be seen to be in actuality an aspect of good.

In other words, that which seems contradictory is only a reflection of the surface view. Beneath the surface these paradoxes, this duality, are seen to be essential and really complementary.

The nub of the matter is this: the Midrash tells us that we really do not know any reasons for any of the mitzvot. We think we know, but upon examination we find that we are as ignorant of those mitzvot for which we think we know the reasons as of those for which we know we do not know the reasons.

Take, for example, the mitzvah of tzedakah. Why should I share my possessions with someone who is poor? Objectively, what is mine is mine. My possessions belong to me because I worked for them, sacrificed for them, gave up much time and pleasure for them. What I have belongs to me, and therefore there is no earthly reason why I must share it with anyone else. Let him work and he too will have his own possessions. So goes the litany of selfishness. And, objectively speaking, there is no good, arguable, logical reason for tzedakah. It is only because it has become ingrained in us through the Torah, as part of our moral heritage, that we accept charity and tzedakah as a very sensible and rational law. But fundamentally we do not really understand it or grasp the rationale behind it.

Or take the law of loving one's neighbor. Why should I love my neighbor if I find him unlovable? How can the Torah expect me to be as concerned with someone outside me as I am concerned with myself? It is, in a literal sense, unreasonable: without reason. We do not really understand the essential reason for this law.

And if we do not understand the rationales for charity and love, certainly we cannot demand reasons for tefillin or kashruth or Shabbat, and others of the so-called ritual category, since we do not completely understand the "understandable" laws. We provide our own rationale: we speak of "Jewish survival" or "Jewish identity," but these are superficial explanations. Ultimately we do not know. Of course there are reasons for every law, but some of the reasons are so profound that they are beyond our understanding—and these are the *ḥukkim*. Some are even more profound and even seem to be contradictory, such as the laws of the red heifer and the others described by the Midrash.

The primary motive in practicing Judaism is that there are commands of God. This is not to say that we may not search for reasons.

Ours is an intellectual faith. We search, we ask, we inquire. But we must always remember that our inability to provide an answer is not sufficient reason not to practice the laws. And the reasons we may ascribe to mitzvot may change from generation to generation, just as our insight changes, but the mitzvot themselves do not change.

There is a science of *ta'amei ha-miẓvot*, rationales for mitzvot. Originally, *ta'am* meant "taste." As Rabbi Aaron Soloveitchik points out, when one observes God's commandments, the observances and the acceptance of the discipline are the meat, the substance, the essence. The reasons we may ascribe to them are the *ta'am* which adds taste and flavor. Just as it is important for meals to be tasty and flavored, so is it important to learn and discover *ta'amei ha-mitẓvot*. But we must always remember that it is possible to survive on a bland diet provided we have the proteins, the vitamins, the carbohydrates, the minerals. But you cannot be sustained by sugar and chocolate and flavoring alone. The essential foodstuff in our spiritual diet is obedience and submission to the will of God. The taste and flavor may make it more pleasant, but ultimately it is the substance and the essence of the meal that make the difference.

Holy Space, Holy Time: Shabbat and the Tabernacle

THROUGHOUT THE TORAH, when Moses speaks to the Israelites, he in fact speaks only to the elders and teachers, who in turn impart his words to the rest of the people. But in Exodus 35, Moses insists that all the children of Israel come together to hear him. Why is this particular occasion so special? Why is this so crucial that Moses must insist that the people hear it directly?

What we find in this chapter are laws dealing with the *mishkan* (sanctuary) and laws dealing with the Shabbat. These are in fact two types of sanctity, and they present interesting contrasts and parallels.

The *mishkan* is created by man for the indwelling of God. Shabbat is created by God for the indwelling of man.

The *mishkan* is tangible, physical and material: it is constructed from gold, silver, brass. The Shabbat is an abstraction: a moment in time.

The Jew must do, act, perform, engage in creative labor in the *mishkan*. The Shabbat is primarily an abstinence from creative labor.

Melakhah (creative labor) is that which was needed to build the *mishkan*. There are thirty-nine types of *melakhah*, and it is precisely these thirty-nine types which are prohibited on Shabbat.

The *mishkan* is the physical made holy. The Shabbat is an abstraction made holy.

The *mishkan* is holy space. The Shabbat is holy time.

The sanctuary is limited to Jerusalem. The shabbat is *be-khal moshvoteikhem*, "in all your dwelling-places."

The *mishkan* is the *Shekhinah*, the spiritual entering the world

150

of the physical. The Shabbat is the physical (man) entering the world of the spiritual.

The *mishkan* is temporal, destructible. The Shabbat is eternal, indestructible.

There is one common element to each, and that is man. He is commanded to enter both the *mishkan* and Shabbat.

In our day, we have no sanctuary, no *mishkan*; we have only the Shabbat. Normally we think of the purpose of Shabbat as rest, rejuvenation, spiritual withdrawal from the world, and an opportunity to be at one with one's own soul.

This is all true, but there is one additional aspect of Shabbat: its observance serves as *atonement* for the cardinal sin of idolatry.

Talmud Shabbat 118: "Everyone who keeps the Shabbat according to the Halakhah, even if he worships idols as did the generation of Enosh, it is forgiven him." Why does Shabbat contain such a powerful ingredient of atonement? Apparently, because Shabbat has in it certain endemic qualities of Jewish faith.

Firstly, the seventh-day rest is in imitation of God, who rested on the seventh day. Secondly, our observance of Shabbat is a public demonstration of faith: we trust in Him that even though we abstain from work one day a week, we will survive and He will provide. Thirdly, Shabbat strengthens personal belief in God by removing us from the physical universe, withdrawing us from the material, and causing us to live almost entirely spiritually for one day. Fourthly, the withdrawal from mundane affairs gives us, in a practical sense, time to sense and appreciate the presence of God, as well as to pray, listen, and study the words of His Torah.

Thus, Shabbat, because it builds faith in God and deepens it, turns out to be an atonement and an antidote to idolatry, for it undoes the work of idolatry.

This explains why, in Exodus 35, when the Shabbat laws are placed alongside the instructions for building the Tabernacle, Shabbat is mentioned first—whereas several chapters earlier, in Exodus 31, where Shabbat is also paired with the Tabernacle, the Tabernacle is mentioned first. In Exodus 35, it follows hard on the heels of the calf incident, and after a golden calf you must place primacy on the one mitzvah which is an antidote to idolatry, and that is Shabbat.

In our day, we have no real idolatry per se. But we do have our own substitutes. For idolatry is that to which we give our ultimate loyalty and allegiance. All of us have our own idolatries which move us away from the truths of God as sovereign.

Precisely today Shabbat is extremely important—for the proper observance of Shabbat mitigates the effect of all kinds of idolatry. It creates a temple in time, and in fact brings the peace and beauty of the Temple of old into our personal lives.

For those who do not yet observe it, it should be kept on the agenda as an ultimate goal. For those already observing it, an attempt should be made to enhance it, not to take it for granted. The day should not be frittered away. We have only fifty-two each year. It should be utilized for "soul raising," to help us better appreciate God's presence around us, among us, and within us.

The Purim Masquerade

ONE OF THE major differences between Purim and Hanukkah is that Purim represents the *nes nistar,* the "hidden miracle," while Hanukkah represents the *nes niglah,* the "open miracle." On Purim, all that happens seems to be natural. God's hand is hidden, concealed, unrevealed. On Hanukkah the miracle of the cruse of oil is an open miracle, obvious to all who witness it.

The very essence of Purim is hiddenness. The word "Esther" itself comes from the Hebrew word meaning "to hide"; God's name is not found in the Book of Esther; the saving events in the book seem to be ordinary coincidences, and the very presence of God working in the background is carefully concealed. And yet, when all is done, everyone could see in retrospect that God was fully in control at all times.

Perhaps this is the reason that the Jewish tradition specifies that in the month of Adar—more than any other month—one should "increase joy." When we come to the full realization that God is always present, that miracles occur to us daily though they are unseen, that even when God seems to have disappeared and to have abandoned us, He is nevertheless there: can there be a greater joy than this? Dramatic, sensational, heart-stopping miracles such as Hanukkah or the splitting of the Red Sea create awe and reverence, true; but the type of miracle that Purim represents creates real joy: on the surface it seemed that God was absent, on the face of things He seemed to have abandoned us; it was "obvious" that He cared nothing about us, that He had lost contact with us. And then, with a flash of insight, we suddenly realize that He has been there all along. Therefore, "increase joy."

People say: "I love Purim with its masks and costumes." You approach someone under a mask: who are you? He is a stranger, unknown to you, hidden. Later, when he removes the mask, the shock of recognition: "I should have known all along. If I had looked more closely I would have noticed certain signs."

So it is with God. Often He hides behind a mask, and even when we come face-to-face with Him and He looks right at us, we do not recognize Him. Later comes the shock of recognition: "I should have known all along. If I had looked more closely I would have noticed certain signs."

It is these "certain signs" that Purim would have us look for. The Purim month of Adar is a good month to notice these signs. The cold of winter begins to recede, nature comes out from under its cover, the sun rises a bit earlier, sets a bit later, there are stirrings and renewals all around us.

But the "certain signs" are found not just in the spring or in the seasons. We see, hear, think, feel, talk, laugh, cry, walk, sense. Being alive is the greatest mystery, an expression of the words in our prayer "and Thy miracles which are with us every day." But these are not dramatic miracles, and are thus not seen by us.

Purim is the holiday which celebrates the ordinary and demonstrates that the ordinary can be extraordinary. And that is why Purim is a time to look behind the masks and disguises and to increase our joy.

Part II

The Jew and His Land

Israel, Torah, and I:
Musings of a Temporary Resident

I AM WORRIED about Israel. And it is the Torah that makes me worry.

Presently, I am studying the Book of Judges, *Shofetim*, and it is evident here—and in so many other parts of the Bible—that we have never been promised Israel as a blank check. There are simply no guarantees from God which ensure continued and permanent existence for the Jewish people in *Erez Yisrael*. The mere fact of our sovereignty over the land of Israel at any one period in history has never implied that we would be eternally sovereign over it. On the contrary, it is a major teaching of Torah that the Jewish people has to *earn the right to dwell in the land*. And whenever Jews stop earning this right, Jews stop living in the land.

I find the tenth chapter of Judges particularly disturbing, because it is a paradigm for today. Israel turns away from God and worships foreign deities, and God turns from them and gives them into the hands of the enemy. And for eighteen years life is utterly miserable for the Jews. There are raids from all sides, and the enemy even crosses the Jordan River to terrorize them. The Jews finally cry out to God and confess that they sinned by abandoning Him. And God, in effect, replies: *I am a little tired of constantly coming to your rescue. I have saved you from Egypt, Amalek, the Philistines, and from others in the past. And still you abandoned me for strange gods. I will no longer save you. I suggest,* continues the God of Israel, *that henceforth you cry out to the new gods you have chosen for yourselves. Let them come to your help in your present troubles.* "Let them deliver you in the time of your tribulation" (Judg. 10:14).

I live here in Jerusalem, and I watch carefully the life about me. It is Jerusalem, and it is holy, and it has more portions of physical and spiritual beauty than any city on earth. It is Jerusalem, and it is a dwelling place of the Jewish soul, and in many ways one can see that it is an earthly reflection of *Yerushalayim shel ma'alah,* that heavenly capital of God of which this place is but a mundane shadow. But I live here. I ride the buses, shop in the stores, drive on the streets, buy petrol, walk, listen, absorb. And because I live here I cannot theorize or idealize, or give fund-raising pep talks. And about Israel and Jerusalem one must speak the truth even if it means chastising that which you deeply love.

I live here and I must confess that, as much as I love the city and the land and the people, occasionally I despair at what I see. For twenty-five years Israel's dominant leadership—political, social, educational, military—has followed a fundamentally areligious way. Israel's Declaration of Independence contains no direct mention of Israel's God, and in 1975 the New Year message of Israel's President also omits any reference to Him. This leadership has opted for the strange gods of secularism. They wanted a new generation unfettered and unencumbered by the albatrosses of God, Torah, mitzvot, observances, which were after all—it is by now a discredited cliché—only designed for the *Galut* Jew to keep him conscious of his Jewishness, but were no longer necessary in an independent Jewish state. And so they made the dominant school system a secular one. And now, twenty-five years later, having exposed an entire generation to the Bible as a book of literature and poetry and history but not as the Book of God, they have a youth whose personal commitment to the state can no longer be taken for granted, and which occasionally actually questions Israel's own right to live in the land. A professor at Hebrew University palavers with the PLO and "understands" them, and a small but alarming number of students say, "Yes, we are the aggressors, and we have stolen this land from the Arabs." And when all is said and done they are pitifully consistent: if the land was in fact not given to the Jews by God, and if the first Rashi in *Bereshit* is totally unknown to them, then they really have no more right to it than the so-called Palestinians. The logic of their position is unassailable. So they question—and the Minister of Information issues a revealing statement to the press: We have not lost our youth.

Illusions are punctured daily in Israel. They wanted a land *ke-khal ha-goyim,* "like all the nations," but having become like all the Goyim, they now find that the Goyim despise them as before. That which individual Jews around the world have long ago learned—that you can change your noses but not your Moses—is now being painfully relearned on a national scale in Israel. They wanted a state of their own in order to put an end to anti-Semitism, but having created the state, they find that the endemic anti-Semitism of the world is now directed against the State of the Jews. Little by little, the dreams and illusions of the secularist founders disappear like a mist.

They have raised a generation of socialists who are hard-eyed materialists; a young generation of "cultured" secular Jews who, according to a newly issued government report, know little even of the secular culture of the land—not the history, not the geography, not the literature. They wanted to be like the nations, and much of its youth lives for the now and has little commitment to anything beyond its immediate needs—just like the youth of the nations. They sought desperately to be accepted into world society, wanted to be normal like any other country—but so fearful were they that their own traditions would make them less acceptable and that their own uniqueness would make them less normal that they threw the wheat with the chaff to the winds, and now they possess neither the tradition, nor the normalcy, nor the love, nor the respect of mankind. Instead they have become the most lonely and most isolated and most forlorn among the nations, in ironic fulfillment of that very Bible which to them is not godly: "It is a people which dwelleth alone and is not reckoned among the nations" (Num. 23:9).

And now the land yields her bitter produce: there is precious little idealism in the country; "Zionism" is an epithet, a term of derision flung disdainfully by young people to describe pie-in-the-sky or worse; youths in unconscionable numbers are abandoning the kibbutz in droves and after coming to the cities they leave them in droves and join the thousands of *yordim* who have gone down to America and Canada, where the cars are bigger and the living easier. And when they happen to wander into a synagogue in the lands of their self-imposed dispersion, they embarrass themselves and their land and their *Galut* brothers by their inability to recite an elementary *berakhah* over the Torah.

The leadership wanted total secularism without religion, wanted to demonstrate that you don't need God in order to be a *mentsch*. But having rejected *Göttlichkeit*, they have begun to lose *Mentschlichkeit* as well. Elementary courtesy or consideration or kindness by members of the bureaucracy (how it hurts to say it openly) is less common in Israel than in the lands of the Goyim whom we imitate so much: rudeness and insensitivity are not as extraordinary as they should be, so that an occasional act of decency by a public official is a subject of a grateful letter to the editor. They wanted a *mentsch* without God, and in the past year major corruption has rocked the land: thefts of millions of dollars by officers of certain Israeli banks; scandals in major corporations like Zim, Solel Boneh, the Israel Corporation, Amidar. And a young Israeli *yored*, interviewed in the newspaper *Davar*, says that his parents came to Israel forty years ago and gave their all to the land, and now the fat cats at the top profit at their expense. So why bother, and why not live in Canada instead! And now comes the final report of the Agranat Commission, the blue-ribbon investigation of the Yom Kippur War, and it declares that the last bastion of Israeli elan and efficiency—the military—had been affected by the carelessness and self-centeredness which plagues civilian life, and that this accounts for much of the initial failures of the war. A quarter-century of secularism has revealed a moral, political, economic, and social dead-end, calling to mind the very last sentence in the Book of Judges: "In those days there was no king in Israel: every man did what was right in his own eyes."

After the Six-Day War, General Yitzchak Rabin, then Chief of Staff, rose up on Mount Scopus in Jerusalem and declared that there were no miracles and that the victory was a result of courage, planning, tactics, strategy, bravery. He omitted any mention of God. The near-tragedy of Yom Kippur, 5734, should have been an object lesson in the efficacy of tactics and strategy. But one year later, Prime Minister Rabin comes to Herzl Military Cemetery in Jerusalem to memorialize the twenty-five hundred war dead for whom planning and bravery were not enough, and again he speaks of Israel's might and valor, and again he makes the same incurious omission. A brilliant man, sincere and good—but in eight years he has learned nothing about the God of Israel. Secularism dies hard.

This is what worries me: in the times of the Judges, Israel was at least *aware* that there was a God above them. They turned to strange idols, but never really lost sight of their own God. They knew He existed despite their penchant for more tangible deities, and in times of distress they cried out to Him. But today we have transcended our idol-worshipping ancestors, and in our distress we call on our strength, our will, our arms, our courage, our allies (who are they?)—on everything but our God. We are not even aware that we have One of our very own.

Perhaps it is good that we do not call on Him. Were we to do so, we might hear what our forebears in Judges heard: "*I am a little tired of coming constantly to your rescue. Egypt, Syria, Jordan—I have saved you from them in 1948, and in 1956, and in 1967, and even more miraculously on Yom Kippur of 1973. And still you do not recognize Me. You want the Arabs to recognize your existence. When will you recognize My existence? At least de facto. No, I will no longer save you. I suggest you call out to your generals, to your cabinet ministers, your politicians, your tanks, your planes—to everything which you have granted your ultimate allegiance. Let them help you in your present trouble.*

We in Israel today are in the most serious straits since the establishment of the state. The shock of Yom Kippur will not soon fade away, for then it was finally perceived that the strange gods to whom were ascribed so much power were not at all omnipotent and had almost been responsible for Israel's doom. We are in serious straits, and the most serious of all is that, our idols having failed us, we have no one to whom to cry out, nothing in which to believe. Even the belief in the continued existence of the state—even this bulwark of Zionist ideology has lost its currency.

These are difficult times for nonbelievers. If I had been raised on secularism and did not believe in the divinity of the Bible and knew nothing of my historic right to this land and the eternity of God's promises and of the destiny of the Jewish people, and then saw my enemies growing stronger every day and our friends ever weaker, I too would see little hope for the future, and I too would be one of the tens of thousands of *yordim* today. Why sacrifice anything for a piece of geography whose only claims upon me are some vague folk-legends about mountaintop suicides and young warriors with sling-shots?

Let us be completely truthful: there are strong pockets of Jewish idealism left. Ironically, they are found primarily among the young people who were not raised on heavy doses of Zionism, but on heavy doses of Torah—in which love of Zion is an integral part. They are called *dati, benei yeshivah,* the religious youth. It is they who believe passionately in the land; it is they who are the best soldiers, it is they who spearhead *hitnahalut*—the attempts to create new settlements in dangerous and uninhabited border areas of Israel— and who are dedicated to the Land of the Torah. For it is from this Torah that they know their Israel and its meaning. It is they whom the generals have labeled the finest type of soldier in their command during the Yom Kippur War, and it is they who formed the core of the brigade which crossed the Suez into Egypt in 1973. It is they whom Ephraim Kishon—Israel's acid-tongued satirist and hardly a pious Jew—calls the only hope for the future of Israel because their vision remains unblurred and their idealism untainted. And it is they who know they belong in the land and that the land belongs to them. Nor is it a coincidence that the only meaningful aliyah from the West in the past decade has been not from non-religious Jews but precisely from committed and observant Jews, specifically the Orthodox.

And let it also be said that in certain circles Torah flourishes in the land. Yeshivot of all types are powerful generators which are producing a force of Torah scholarship and piety which, no less than Israel's physical defense forces, sustains the land and her people. All is far from black.

But if these are very difficult times for non-believers because they have very little left, these are also difficult times for believers, for they know the soul of the land, and it is a sensitive one. *Erez Yisrael* is *erez ha-kedoshah*, "the Holy Land." It is also the Land of Holiness. It cannot be lived upon like any other land. This land has its own special soul, its own life, and is so constituted that, like a delicate organism, it cannot tolerate strange and foreign ways within its borders: the God-filled land cannot suffer the efforts, conscious or casual, to empty it of God and to replace Him with nothingness. And in the fullness of time the land spews out that which is offensive to it. The same Torah which promises Israel's return to her ancestral land also promises that this land cannot endure profaneness. Is it not possible that the same God who before our very eyes is fulfilling the first may also choose, once again, to fulfill the second? These are difficult times for believers as well.

For a believer who daily recites the *Shema Yisrael*, certain passages in that testament of faith are very disturbing. I tremble when I become fully aware of the meaning of *hishamru lakhem*, "take heed lest you turn aside and serve other gods and worship them . . . and you will perish quickly from the good land which He gives you." I tremble because this has already been fulfilled several times in Jewish history. And when my Jerusalem neighbor goes off to a discotheque on Friday night and plays raucous American music on his stereo on all of Shabbat, I despair. Not so much because Shabbat should not be abandoned in Jerusalem, but because what he is doing is so imitative of a culture foreign to us; and because he is ignoring himself, his essence, his innate Jewishness. In his innocence and Jewish ignorance, this product of Israeli secularism barters sanctity for banality and is unaware that he lives in a land that is holy. (I hope that God will be patient with us: with my neighbor for ignoring Him, and with me for being intolerant of him who serves in the army and who is willing to lay down his life for me.) But my neighbor makes me think: *have we earned the right to live in God's land?*

It is time to permit Him to reenter His land, to turn to authentic Jewish modes of thinking and behaving.

It is time to take the Land of Israel out of *Galut*, and to stop whoring after false gods.

It is time to turn off the fourth-rate American rock music and to begin listening to our own rhythms.

It is time for the Land of the Bible to take its Bible more seriously.

It is time that Israel understands that Jews expect more from her because she is what she is, and to understand that she is failing the Diaspora, and to begin to consider another path.

The secularists have had their day and have amply demonstrated the insufficiency of their ways. *The single most convincing testimonial in favor of the religious life is the present bitter fruit of a quarter-century of secularist labor in Israel.* It is time the religious way be given a fair chance.

Israel is in deep crisis, and not UJA drives, or Bonds, or American aid, or Senate resolutions can solve this crisis. Only Jews can solve it. By becoming Jewish Jews.

What worries me most about Israel, the land that I love and the people that is mine, is the Torah. This too is mine.

Epilogue: This essay was written a year after the Yom Kippur War, in 1974. When it was published in Tradition *Magazine, the reaction was explosive. It prompted numerous rather heated letters to the editor, rejoinders, and countless personal letters to me. Some of the responses accused the writer of being anti-Zionist and anti-Israel. During a subsequent convention of the Rabbinical Council of America, one rabbi, an acquaintance of a quarter-century, said that I sounded like a* sone Yisrael, *a "hater of Israel," an epithet reserved for anti-Semites. To make matters worse, the article was reprinted, without authorization, by elements of the militantly anti-Zionistic Neturei Karta. It appeared, also without authorization, in Hebrew and Yiddish translations. I did receive certain favorable reactions, also heated, from people who thanked me for describing things as I saw them. Clearly, the article touched a nerve both among the right and among the left.*

Stadiums and the Ultimate Galut

NEWS ITEM: *The eleven Israeli athletes killed in Munich will be memorialized by the construction of sports stadiums in their names, to be built in Tel Aviv and Jerusalem.*

On first blush it seems appropriate. Olympic athletes, stadiums: there seems to be an equation. But on second thought I submit that it is rather inappropriate.

The Israeli athletes were not killed in Munich because they were athletes. They were killed because they were Jews. They did not give their lives to perpetuate the ancient Greek Olympic rite; they died because they represented, in their own persons, the living embodiment of that which the world hates: Jewish religion, Jewish life, Jewish historicity, Jewish continuity, Jewish eternity.

They were not shot because they were muscular or rhythmic or graceful. They were shot because of their ancestors—because one of their forebears was an Abraham, another an Isaac, another a Jacob, another a Moses.

To memorialize them by building a stadium is an act of Jewish insensitivity. Is it not a vestige of the *Galut* mentality to take a secular, worldly, non-Jewish symbol like a stadium and use it to perpetuate Jewish heroes? This is yet another symptom of a malady which afflicts Jews both in and out of Israel: the malady of *imitatio Goy*—of imitating the nations of the world rather than looking within for our own Jewish distinctiveness and uniqueness.

The eleven who died at Munich were martyrs who, like all those in our bloodstained history of martyrdom, were killed because they were different, not because they were the same as everyone else. Their memorial should be a tribute to this difference and to their

164

different Jewish souls, not a monument which will declare to the world that we think in non-Jewish terms.

Must we really be like all the nations, sending athletes to the Olympic Games? Did God bring us back to our holy soil after two thousand years of wandering in order that we should be able to tell the Goyim who tried to destroy us that really we are not so bad, we are deep down just like you, and see, we too memorialize athletes by erecting stadiums? To live in Israel and to think in non-Jewish categories: there is no greater Exile than this.

Has anyone thought of a school in their memory? A synagogue? a yeshiva? A loan fund for needy people? A scholarship fund for needy students? A foundation for worthy institutions and charities?

Anything—anything but the ultimate symbol of spiritual *Galut:* a memorial stadium in Jerusalem.

How Jerusalem Got Its Name

THE CENTERPIECE OF Rosh Hashanah is, of course, the Akedah. Interesting that God does not tell Abraham exactly where Moriah is, where the sacrifice will take place: He simply says, *al aḥad he-harim*, "on one of the hills."

What is this place Moriah, and why is it chosen?

One thing we do know: it is not the first time that great and shattering events have taken place there. Ten generations before Abraham, Noah survived the Flood and built an altar and offered up a sacrifice of thanksgiving to God—and the tradition tells us that it took place on this very same spot.

Nine generations prior to Noah, the sons of Adam, Cain and Abel, offered up their own sacrifices to God. One was accepted, one was rejected. But these sacrifices also took place on this same spot, Moriah.

But even before Cain and Abel, at the very dawn of history, the very first sacrifice of man was offered there. Adam, we are told, offered up an offering to God when he was created, and it also took place on this hallowed and sacred ground. And when God created Adam from the dust, where did He take the dust from which he formed Adam? He took it, says Maimonides, reflecting an ancient Jewish tradition, from this same mysterious place, later to be called Moriah (*Beit ha-Beḥirah* 2:2).

Clearly, this place towards which Abraham is walking with his son Isaac, thereupon to offer up the sacrifice, is not an ordinary geographical location. It is charged with ancestral associations, with memories, with anticipations.

For this place will later be called Jerusalem. The Temple will be built on this site out of which "the word of the Lord will go forth, and the Torah will go forth." From here will emanate God's teachings to mankind. This will be the Holy City, the source of the spiritual power of Am Yisrael, the earthly abode of the *Shekhinah*, the city beloved of God. It will be the scene of Israel's most tenacious battles, it will see exile and siege and destruction—and also rebirth and restoration and redemption. It will be fought over by the most powerful nations in history, but it will always belong to the children of Abraham. It will be a city which even in the last half of the twentieth century—some four thousand years later—will still be in the daily headlines, and will still be the first in the consciousness of its people, the holy people Israel.

And Abraham and Isaac are now about to give it its greatest moment: the Akedah.

This place was not always called Jerusalem. It had other names before it was called Jerusalem. From whence comes this, its final name, the name by which we have known it for several thousands of years? (For in the Torah, a name is not accidental. From a name we derive the essence of an object or a person.) What is the essence of the Holy City, this generator of our spiritual power?

A fascinating Midrash: this place had already been given a name by one of the sons of Noah, whose name was Shem. Shem was the forerunner of the Shemites; he lived nine generations prior to Abraham. Shem was the ruler over this particular area where so much had already transpired. He is identified as the "Melchizedek king of Salem," of Genesis, and he gave it a name of his own: he called the place *Shalem*, meaning "perfection."

The Midrash continues: Abraham, too, gave it a name of his own. He called it *Yireh*, meaning "he will see."

"Then the Holy One wanted to give it a permanent name. Said He: 'Shem called it *Shalem*. Abraham called it *Yireh*. Shall I call it *Yireh*? Shem will be offended. Shall I call it *Shalem*? Abraham will be offended. I will therefore combine the two names. I will call this holy place *Yireh-Shalem*' "—from which we derive the name of today, *Yerushalayim*, Jerusalem.

What is this story all about? What did Shem intend to convey with the name *Shalem*? What did Abraham intend to convey with the name *Yireh*? What did God Himself intend to convey with the name *Yerushalayim*?

Shem called it Shalem. Who was Shem? There is an interesting and relatively unknown tradition: he was the very first student and scholar and teacher of Torah learning. He founded the first school of divine learning. The disciples would come to learn the mysteries of Creation from him, the hidden aspects of holiness; they would delve into the ways of man and God that only later were to be embodied in the Torah. Shem was known as the bearer of godly teachings that began with Adam. He was known as *kohen gadol shel olam*, "the high priest of the universe." He delved into the teachings handed down to him by his forebears, and he himself became a teacher and a scholar par excellence.

Now Shem, this great teacher, knows that this is an extraordinary place. He knows that this particular place contains all the holiness and mystery of life, the hidden secrets of contentment, of meaning, of fulfillment. For Shem, the teacher and scholar and student, the ultimate purpose of mankind is to *know* God, to understand God, and to attain wisdom by study of His word and through this to become perfect and complete.

This place will become the source of all Jewish learning and wisdom, and therefore it shall be called Shalem, which means "fulfillment" and "perfection." It shall represent for all time man's striving for perfection and fulfillment through study of God's word.

What Shem is saying is that the essence of being a Jew is attained primarily through an intellectual process; that is, through understanding, thinking, and knowing. For Shem, it is primarily through the *mind*, the intellect, through man's cognitive qualities that one arrives at ultimate truth—as Shem himself was doing. Other qualities are important, granted. But the *prime ingredient* in becoming a Jew, and in relating properly to God, is the mind. A God-given mind will help us know God and become Shalem, as *He* is Shalem.

Abraham names the same place *Yireh*—"God will see or show." It is a peculiar name. What does this name represent?

A review of the Akedah narrative indicates several uses of the root *ra'ah*, to "see," or to "show." On the way to the Akedah, the innocent son Isaac says to his father, "You have all the implements for a sacrifice, but where is the lamb for the offering?" Answers the father: *Ha-Shem yireh lo*, "God will show the lamb." Later, when Abraham is poised with the knife to slaughter his son, his hand is stayed, and instead the ram, caught in the thicket, is sacrificed. And the narrative ends, "and Abraham called this place *Ha-Shem yireh*, 'God will see,' as it is said, 'in the mountain of the Lord, God will be seen.' " (And we must remember that at the very beginning of God's revelation to Abraham, in the twelfth chapter of Genesis, God tells him to leave his birthplace to go "to a land that I will *show* thee.") These are all very strange passages.

What does the word *Yireh* mean? Literally, it means "God will see or show." That is, *we* may not see, *we* may not comprehend, but

God does see, and ultimately God does show us why certain events take place and certain things are done.

This is what Abraham is saying. The essence of this holy place, the essence of being a Jew, lies not primarily in study, not primarily in striving to know, not primarily in the mind. The essence of our eternal faith lies in the heart, in total reliance upon God, in submission to God, in giving over the heart to God. *Be-yadkha afkid ruḥi,* "in Thy hands do I place my spirit": do with me as you please; I am your servant.

This view of Abraham's is not intellectual nor fully rational. This is an attitude of total surrender to God, even when it goes against all logic. But who better than Abraham knows the meaning of surrender? Says the Midrash: "and we will worship and then we will return to you" (Gen. 22:5) means that Abraham returned from Mount Moriah only *bi-zekhut hishtaḥavayah,* "because of his ability to bow down and to humble himself."

Many sacrifices were made prior to Abraham: Adam, Cain, Noah. But until Abraham no one had truly surrendered all: his son, his future, his destiny, his logical understanding of God. All this Abraham is ready to surrender. *Yireh:* we mortals may not see the future or the present: it may be dark, hidden, covered in shadows, lying behind thick clouds. It makes no sense to go on, no sense to do as we are bidden, it goes against all our knowledge, our mature, sharply honed minds. But we trust wholly in Him because *yireh*—He sees. And I—like a child—must put my total and ultimate trust in Him.

Yireh shall be the name of this most holy of places, for the essential ingredient of the Jew is not the intellect, not the sophisticated mind. The essence of being a Jew and a member of the holy people Israel is to become a *child.* A child trusts his mother completely and has absolute faith in his father. A child accepts innocently all that God asks of him, all that God offers and does not offer, all that He demands and all that he expects. It shall be called *Yireh,* "He will see, He will show," because not through Torah study primarily, but through *avodah,* through service primarily—not by becoming a mature adult but by becoming a young, helpless child—is the essence of Moriah and the essence of Torah and the essence of being a Jew achieved.

What is the difference between study and prayer, between the two great pinnacles of service, of Torah and *avodah?*

Study is not a matter of trust; scholarly research takes nothing on faith. You examine critically, analyze, challenge, confront. This is as

true in the laboratory of science as it is on the pages of the Talmud.
Nothing is taken for granted. One can achieve great heights through
study: the mind becomes disciplined, you learn to think precisely,
logically, the mind achieves clarity: the proper use of the intellect is
the pinnacle of achievement of the human being.

But Prayer, *avodah*, is not of the mind. Prayer is of the heart.
Prayer is faith and trust. Who prays best? A child. Because a child is
not ashamed to weep, not ashamed to plead, to use the emotional
language of the heart. Why do we sound the shofar on Rosh
Hashanah? Because the shofar is the ultimate, wordless prayer. The
shofar sobs and weeps. We are not always able to weep before our
Father in heaven, and so the shofar, that reminder of the ram
sacrifice, sobs and weeps in our behalf, begging to be admitted to
His presence. Prayer does not analyze, examine, deduce, question.
Prayer is not a process of the mind but a process of the heart.[1]

Shem calls it *Shalem:* man must become perfect through study
and mind and thought and analysis of Torah.

Abraham calls it *Yireh:* man must become faithful through prayer
and devotion and surrender.

And, concludes the Midrash, the time comes for God to name this
place. Shall He name it *Shalem?* Abraham will be offended. That is,
Abraham's thesis, that the childlike quality of prayer is primary, will
be shunted to the side for all time. God does not want it to be cast
aside, for childlike surrender and love are the key to the Jews'
relationship with Him.

But shall it then be *Yireh?* Shem will be offended. That is, Shem's
thesis, that the approach to God is an intellectual, rational process
developed by study of Torah and God's wisdom, will be cast aside
forever. This cannot be, says God, for it is through Torah study that
My will is discovered.

It cannot be Shem alone, it cannot be Abraham alone. Both are
primary. Both are co-equals. I will call it *Yireh* and *Shalem.* For this
city shall be a symbol of the people of the heart and the people of the
head. The people of prayer and the people of study. *Avodah* and
Torah. Warm love and cool logic. Innocent, childlike trust in God,

---

1. On Jerusalem as a source of Torah and of prayer, see Rashi's comment on Gen.
22:2. Referring to Moriah (later to become Jerusalem), Rashi says that it was called
Moriah because "from there *hora'ah* ['teaching'] goes out to Israel"; and Onkelos
translates, "Because from there the incense service which contains the spices of *mor*
went out to the world." All this indicates that from Moriah both Torah and worship
emanate.

accepting and surrendering, and the people of the intellect, sophisticated and analytical—questioning, examining, challenging.

And so it was that this source of our faith, this place from which Adam was created and on which the Akedah of Isaac took place, this earthly dwelling of the *Shekhinah* from which emanates our entire existence, received its name and molded our souls as Jews and made us into that unique people of world history: the people combining study and knowledge of Torah, together with faith and love and trust in God in the performance of His mitzvot.

For who has a greater intellectual tradition than we? Which religion other than Torah emphasizes study and knowledge of God? In which religion other than Torah is God called a rebbe, a *melamed*, a teacher, *ha-melamed Torah le-amo Yisrael?* In which religion is there an idea of the world-to-come as a *bet midrash*, a study hall? In which religion is the true aristocrat the scholar? Which faith has as its greatest mitzvot the study of texts, of Torah? Which faith has never withheld knowledge from the masses in the fear of what they might do with it? For which people is learning and education and knowledge an end in itself? We are truly the people of the mind.

But which people also knows better the limits of the mind and the dangers of the intellect? Which people has suffered more at the hands of the arrogance that results from the conquests of the mind? Which people has known more the cruelty and savagery and bestiality that can emanate from a total reliance on the head and that all but eliminate the heart?

We in our century have witnessed the results of people of culture and science and philosophy, untempered by the restraints of heart and feeling and love and emotion, who almost brought utter destruction to the world, and brutally murdered one-third of our people.

No, says the Jew, the mind alone, the intellect alone, is insufficient. It must be softened by feeling, by emotion, by affect.

Yes, we should be disciplined, mature adults—but we must also be like little children. For we are helpless, like nothing; we are here today and gone tomorrow. We are like *ḥeres ha-nishbar*, a "broken potsherd."

Technological conquest? Journeys to Saturn and Jupiter? We are as nothing. We know nothing. We see nothing. Only He sees: *yireh*. One misstep and we are gone. One blow to the body and we cry out in pain. One skip of the heartbeat, one wrong turn of the wheel, and we are finished, and all our proud, intellectual conquests are as of naught, *ke-ḥalom ya-uf*, "as a dream that vanishes."

But the heart alone also does not give us total dominion. For love and feeling and emotion unsupported by learning and unbuttressed by discipline, without knowledge, without work, without study, end in vague, fuzzy, pseudo-religious sentimentality which is at best without substance and at worst can be just as dangerous as mind alone. For we Jews have suffered mightily for two thousand years at the hands of a religion which preaches love and heart and turn-the-other-cheek, but gives its followers no mitzvot, no demands, and no disciplines.

And so our holy Jewish task is to merge the two: adulthood and childhood; maturity and innocence; sophisticated wisdom and naive trust; Torah and *avodah*; *yireh* and *shalem*; the analytical, logical, disciplined, probing, challenging mind, and the yearning, sensitive, longing, eager, enthusiastic, dreaming heart.

Although God is a teacher and his favorite is Moshe, He particularly loves the child and the qualities of children: *Ha-ven yakir li Efrayim, im yeled sha-ashuim*, "Is Ephraim a darling son unto Me? Is he a playing child?" (Jer. 31:20). And Jeremiah adds: *zakharti lakh ḥesed ne'uraich*, "I remember the kindness of your youth."

This merging of the two qualities is seen in the *Shema*. There is childlike surrender: "with all thy heart and with all thy soul"; and there is also the emphasis on the intellect, the mind: "and thou shalt teach them to thy children diligently." That is, love God, trust Him, and know Him; and study God, do His mitzvot, and know Him. We are great: We can create and build and conquer the universe. And we are nothing, we are as dust and ashes.

What makes a Jew? His knowledge and the discernment when to make the mind primary and when to make the heart primary. When to be precise, sophisticated, logical, adult; and when to be a trusting, relying, innocent child; when to challenge and confront, and when to accept and submit.

When it comes to our task as Jews the performance of mitzvot is primary. Here we should not confuse the mind and the heart. We must ask, inquire, analyze, examine, try to understand all that we can—but we must not permit analysis and challenge to disturb our performance. Shabbat? Where is it found in the Torah? What are the rules? Why this and why not that? The history of Shabbat, the practices of Shabbat, the categories of Shabbat—all need to be known. But when Shabbat appears, we must observe it in a childlike fashion, in complete love and outreach to God. Similarly with mezu-zot, similarly with tzedakah, similarly with any of the mitzvot of the Torah. We are an amalgam, a mixture, a blend, a merging of the two. We are powerful, we can walk on the moon. And we are as nothing: fragile, vulnerable, "For the wind passes over it and is no more."

Mourning for Jerusalem

TISHAH BE-AV IS not everyone's favorite Yom Tov, but it is one of mine; not because it is enjoyable, but because of what it represents.

I like Tishah be-Av because of what it says to me about the Jewish people. I am comforted by the knowledge that we are a people which remembers—and a people which remembers and knows its past has a future.

No one weeps for Rome. There are many more Italians in the world than there are Jews. Do thousands of people gather at the Roman Forum to weep and lament and pray?

There are many more Greeks than Jews. The Acropolis and the Parthenon are tourist attractions—but does anyone mourn because of their destruction?

Babylonia, Persia, Assyria, ancient Egypt's glory—who remembers, who sheds a tear, who cares?

I like Tishah be-Av because only a people who knows how to weep will someday learn how to laugh.

And I like Tishah be-Av because I need it.

In the midst of all the plenty and affluence and creature comfort, I need to remove my leather shoes, to have the lights dimmed.

I need to fast and not to indulge myself.

I need to read Lamentations and to weep for my people.

I need to focus outward and not inward—on my people, on my martyrdom, on my bloody history, which in the United States I tend to forget because God has blessedly spared us the wrath of the world.

I need it because it reminds me of what it is to be a Jew, and that Esau hates Jacob, and that Pharaoh oppresses Israel, and that Haman wishes to destroy us, and that the empires of the world abhor the Jew because he is *am levadad yishkon*, "a nation that dwelleth alone."

I like Tishah be-Av because it teaches something profound: that,

174

for Judaism, historical events are not merely historical, and not merely events. "History" and "events" take place at some point in time, but in Judaism, once an event occurs, it does not cease: it becomes a constant part of us—because they are not merely events: they are an awareness, a cognition, a perception, a new consciousness. And this is continuous, ongoing, and does not end.

When you suddenly achieve a new insight, it is always with you and always part of you. On certain days in our history the awareness of joy as an element in life (Sukkot), or the awareness of Godliness (Rosh Hashanah), or the consciousness of nearness to God (Yom Kippur), or the insight of freedom under God (Pesaḥ) enters the universe. On Tishah be-Av the elements of tragedy and of disaster were first introduced to us.

A man said to me once: "Why bother with an event like Tishah be-Av that took place two thousand years ago? Why mourn, why sigh? We have modern Israel, let us be joyous." But we know now, even in modern Israel, that modern Jewish joy vis-à-vis Israel is ephemeral, and how cold and distant the world can grow, and how rapidly it can rush into the arms of feudal Arab dictators when there is the slightest threat to its well-being.

No, there is a good reason for Tishah be-Av. It reminds us that occasionally it is good to bemoan, to bewail, and to remember.

And, finally, I like Tishah be-Av because it contains a message of profound hope and faith. On Tishah be-Av, our sages tell us, the Messiah was born. How suggestive, how profound an insight, how ironic, how just. On the very day of destruction, on that very day the element of redemption also began. On the very day of the end, the beginning. "Give us joy in accordance with the days of our suffering," says the psalmist: *samḥenu ki-yemot initanu* (Ps. 90:15). Thus it is the day of hope, a day not only of the past but also of the future.

On the Shabbat preceding Tishah be-Av we read the first chapter of Isaiah, the chapter of rebuke. On the next Shabbat, we read the fortieth chapter of Isaiah, the chapter of comfort: "comfort ye, comfort ye, My people." That is to say, just as the tears are real, so will the comfort be real. We may cry today and weep for the ancient glory of Israel, but we know that tomorrow God will redeem us.

Is it any wonder that I like Tishah be-Av?

Whatever Happened to Jewish *Sekhel?*

THE ANNOUNCER ON the six o'clock news was saying that the program would feature an intimate look into the real Moshe Dayan. Fine. I stayed tuned to learn more about this fascinating person.

Dayan was showing the reporter around his native kibbutz. "Jews should be farmers," he said. "A return to the soil is good. Your chicken lays an egg, the egg hatches, a chick pops out, it's almost as if you are a partner with God." Not bad: "partner with God." Considering Dayan's secular upbringing and background, not bad at all.

He then showed the viewers around his home, especially his collection of archaeological finds. (With characteristic Dayanesque modesty he declared, "This is one of the best collections in the world, not only in this country, but in the whole world.") The interviewer spoke of the return of the Jews to Israel, the rebirth of the Jewish state. Dayan replied: "The Jewish people has an historic destiny in this land. It goes back to antiquity." I loved every word of it.

But then it happened. Dayan backed away. "I am not religious," he continued. "I am not Orthodox, I do not go to synagogue, I do not pray. We have rebuilt this land because of our will, because we wanted to, not because it is a commandment of God." *(Moshe, who asked about your religion? Methinks you protest too much.)*

Moshe, Moshe, how could you? How could as brilliant a tactician as you not see the tactical blunder you committed with this gratuitous and unnecessary comment? Don't misunderstand: we don't expect you to be a pious Jew. We realize the embarrassment which many Israelis feel about being labeled "religious." And, frankly, we are not concerned with your personal religious philosophy or lack of it. That intellectual currents have passed you by; that you are still dressing your arguments in the secular fashions that went out of vogue twenty-five years ago, and in categories which went up in the smoke of Treblinka—this is forgivable. The Dayans of the world are paid not to be philosophers but military generals.

The problem, however, is that a brilliant military leader begins to take himself so seriously that he finds himself spouting philosophy. Which is harmless and occasionally even humorous posing. But, for heaven's sake, for Israel's sake, not on CBS television with forty million Goyim looking on! Moshe, as a man with some of the world's best archaeological artifacts, you should have known better. With your background, we don't expect you to be a pious Jew; we don't expect you to wear tefillin every day. But we do have a right to expect a brilliant man to have *sekhel,* ordinary common sense.

Your Zionist forebears, such as Theodor Herzl and Chaim Weizmann, had *sekhel.* When they approached the chancelleries of the world to plead the cause of a Jewish national home in Palestine, they won their case because they appealed to the truth and to the one grain of Jewish sympathy imbedded in Christian hearts: the Bible. They convinced the Prime Ministers and Sultans and Premiers and Presidents that the Jewish claim to the land was part of God's unfolding destiny, that the land of Abraham, Isaac, and Jacob was by historic Biblical right a Jewish land, and not a Moslem satrapy, nor a British colony, nor a Turkish fiefdom.

This was not only good politics and good strategy; it was sound history. Because if Jews have no Biblical, Godly claim to this real estate, we might as well have settled Uganda in Africa or Birobidjan in Russia—as the great powers once wanted us to do.

So, my dear General Dayan, as much as I admire your battlefield heroics, as much as I personally am in debt to you for saving our lives, I must say that on CBS this week, before forty million people, you blew it. Instead of stopping after you made your point, you kept on moving into treacherous territory. And you may have inadvertently struck a blow for those enemies of Israel who proclaim that the Jews have no right to be there at all. Once you remove the Bible from Jewish claims to Israel you have no claims; once you remove divine destiny as the factor you remove a powerful argument for the Jewish resettling of the land.

General, I have an offer for you which you should not refuse: If you promise not to deal with theology, philosophy, and religion, I will promise not to deal with tanks, fighter planes, or the tactics of desert warfare.

The Gust of Wind

IN THE SPRING of 1972 the Chancellor of West Germany, Willi Brandt, paid a visit to Israel. During the tour of the Negev, Mr. Brandt was helicoptered to the Massada mountain. Upon landing, a ferocious wind almost carried the helicopter and its passengers over the precipice. Only at the last moment was the helicopter prevented from going over the side. The incident prompted me to deliver this piece to my congregation on the following Shabbat.

And it came to pass in the year 5733
that the leader of West Germany came to visit
the Holy Land in the week after Shavuot.

Now this leader of the Germans
had not done evil in the eyes of the Lord.
But in the eyes of all Israel
he was the head of the cruel nation
which had attempted to annihilate
utterly
the children of Israel
twenty-five years earlier.

And men cried out
with angry words and bitter.
And it was deemed necessary that he come,
and so he came.

And it came to pass that wherever he journeyed in the Land,
he evoked awe and wonder and fear and terror
in the hearts of those who saw him.

178

And when he spoke in the tongue of the Germans—
of the SS men and the Einsatzgruppen and the gas chamber
  guards
who tended jolly red roses and played Bach
while inside the grim gray buildings
Jews gagged and died—
and the words themselves,
the sounds, the rhythms, the gutturals, the umlauts
so harsh and so thick and so unlike
the soft melodies of Psalms in Hebrew,
echoed other days
and other places
and other German leaders.

And on the last days of his journey
the German leader went to Massada
the great mountain stronghold on the Dead Sea
where two thousand years ago a small band of Jews
withstood for years
the onslaught of the armies of Rome.
And when the warriors of Rome
were about to overrun Massada
the zealous defenders took their own lives
and were not led into slavery by the conquerors.

A great helicopter flew him to Massada the mountain
whose summit is flat as a field
and then drops off thousands of feet to the ground below.
And as the huge machine descended to the top of the
  mountain
a sudden gust of wind came forth
and pushed the giant craft
towards the brink of the mountain and the edge of the
  precipice.
And the pilot applied the brakes,
and strong men outside tried to hold it in place,
but the great bird with the German inside
moved inexorably towards the edge.
And it came to pass at the very last moment before catastrophe
that the wind stopped
and the German leader emerged without harm.

And men asked: From whence came that sudden gust of wind?
And men answered: It was only a wind, an ordinary wind.
But they did not know.
For it was not an ordinary wind.
It was the breath of the defenders of Massada
who still live.
The breath of the hundreds
who gave their lives for their Torah in days of yore
speaking to the leader of the Germans, saying:
You whose people tried to silence our echo,
you shall not alight onto my soil with an easy smile,
you shall remember Massada for the rest of your days.

And the wind had come from yet another place.
From the air above Europe which is polluted
and hallowed
by the human dust which seeped forth from the chimneys of
    Auschwitz
and which hovers forever
in our air.

And together with the breathing souls of Massada
they were that sudden gust of wind
which spoke to the leader of the Germans
and to the world, saying:
You whose nation came perilously close
to destroying us all in the twentieth century,
know that we still live
and haunt
the very air you breathe.
You shall tremble the fear of the dying
and know a moment of terror
as you slide perilously close to the precipice
before you set foot upon this holy mountain.
You shall remember Massada.
Oh, that you were wise and took heed
and brought these words to your nation
and the other nations, saying:
The breath of the people of the children of Israel
is an eternal breath,
for I have felt its power.

And those who would snuff it out
shall beware
of the quick gusts of wind which rise
from the caverns of the earth
and descend suddenly from the heavens above.

Part III

The Jew and the Nations

The Jewish experience in America has brought out the best and the worst in us. The best: the Jew's ability to carry his Torah wherever he is, to create sanctity under conditions not always receptive to anything beyond the physical and the vulgar. The worst: to fall under the sway of the majority culture, whether it be the naked races of the ancient Greeks or the mindless excesses of contemporary Western life.

Some of the essays in this section deal with the positive manifestations of the Jewish American experience. Other selections attempt to limn the differences, philosophical and practical, between what is Jewish and what is American, and to warn about the pitfalls that are created when we take on the coloration of the world around us.

The American and the Jew

Equation or Encounter?

ONE OF THE paradoxes of the American Jew is the fact that despite his freedoms and his ever-widening vistas of opportunity, he lives under a nameless tension. In a country which offers him freedom to live as he desires, he is basically ill at ease. In an environment which permits him to live, act, and think as his non-Jewish neighbor does, the Jew, beneath the facade of apparent conformity, is not completely comfortable. Even as he conforms to the patterns of American life he feels himself the perpetual outsider.

The causes of this phenomenon are many, but basic to them all is the fact that there is a fundamental divergence between that which is characteristically Jewish and that which is characteristically American, a polarity of views which cannot quite be reconciled.

Of course, there are constant attempts at reconciliation. This is perhaps the fundamental raison d'être of the dissenting Jewish religious groups, and certainly of the secular agencies. From them there issues forth a constant clatter of "Judeo-Americana": Judaism and Americanism are really very much alike; each is democratic, freedom-loving, believes in social justice; even the Founding Fathers looked upon themselves as the chosen people in a promised land; the Liberty Bell contains a Biblical inscription; and so forth *ad infinitum*. Because of this, we are told, we have a great share in America. We really do belong.

To this, Torah Judaism, as I understand it, submits a demurrer. For over and above its insistence on maintaining halakhic standards and mitzvah way of living, it states frankly that the typically Jewish and the typically American are quite dissimilar. It would be more fruitful to ascertain what the two cultures have to say to one another rather than force them into an equation. In truth, it is precisely because they are not alike that an intelligent encounter between them is possible.

185

Orthodox Judaism would offer a fresh and healthful approach, one that would clear the fog of misconception by recognizing the diverging paths of the Jewish and the American *Weltanschauung*. These are many and on all levels. We will briefly sketch here a few of the more fundamental ones.

The most obvious difference between the two traditions is that of national origins. The beginnings of Judaism are as old as history itself, whereas the sum total of American yesterdays reaches 200-odd years, a total which in Jewish history amounts to only a page and which to the Jewish consciousness is absurdly small. While it is true that America's roots antedate 1776 and can be found in Greece and Rome, it is equally true that in conduct, thought, and character, America is distinctive and unique. For despite the variegated roots of American civilization, a homogeneous national character has emerged which is peculiarly a product of the New World. And the beginnings of this national character are quite recent.

This historyless character was observed by Thomas Hardy, who wrote, after his visit to America:

> I shrink to see a modern coast
> Whose riper times have yet to be;
> Where the new regions claim them free
> From that long drip of human tears
> Which people old in tragedy
> Have left upon the centuried years.[1]

Hardy could have been thinking not only of British but of Jewish history when he spoke of "the long drip of human tears" of "a people old in tragedy."

From this contrast in the origin and type of history stems an entirely dissimilar worldview. It cannot be said of the American tradition, for example, that it has a real sense of tragedy. Fortunately, it has not been burned in the crucible of martial fire. Except for the War Between the States, it has largely been spared agony and suffering. Quite the contrary, in fact. Observers have noted that "the history of America has been an epic continuity of almost unbroken success."[2] This, at least in part, accounts for an America which is "unwilling to confront a life experience which includes penalties as

---

1. Thomas Hardy, "On an Invitation to the United States" in *Collected Poems* (New York: Macmillan, 1926).
2. Max Lerner, *America as a Civilization* (New York: Simon & Schuster, 1957), p. 947.

well as gains, failures as well as success, tragedy as well as happiness."[3] If success is the goddess, it follows that failure is the devil. It is simply not supposed to happen.

It has been the dynamic of the American tradition that progress is inevitable, success a foregone conclusion. This condition was true of the frontiersman hacking a new civilization out of the forest, and it certainly obtains in modern American life. Witness the cults of Positive Thinking, of Confidence in the Future, of Optimism At All Costs. Vance Packard has shown how business growth and political campaigns are based on the premise that any form of pessimism is evil, and that a climate of confidence must be maintained at all costs—even when things are going badly.[4] It is true that we have a Melville, an O'Neill, and a Faulkner in our literature. But the very universal attention given them is perhaps in itself an indication that they are not typically American: the interest in them is less due to what they have to say than to the fact that these are Americans who are saying it.

A people old in tragedy is more realistic. The drip of human tears has given Judaism a keener insight into the life experience and a deeper awareness of the profundities of human existence. It is incongruous for Judaism to attempt to force itself into the mold of this ebullient forward-march. To do this is to twist and distort Jewish history. The attempts of fundraising publicists of Israel to picture the young state as a miniature United States, with its own pioneers and frontiersmen and cowboys, are often comically pathetic. The efforts of Jewish apologists in America are similarly grotesque. Jewish patriarchs were not frontiersmen; we reckon Jacob and not Daniel Boone among our forefathers. And Judaism knows that life has tragedy and failure—Job is more than a literary image—and that man has the power to transcend tragedy and failure into a higher and nobler life.

This contrasting length of the two histories accounts in part for their disparate time-view. A civilization whose past is measurable has a more restricted view of time than one whose traditions reach into prehistory. For Judaism, the future follows the way of the past, distant and infinite. In America, too, future is like past: brief, measurable, and immediate. Thus we find America operating on a short, hurried time scale. It is more concerned with the here-and-now than with the hereafter, both in the practical and the teleogical

---

3. Ibid., pp. 949, 951.
4. Vance Packard, *The Hidden Persuaders* (New York: David McKay, 1957), p. 230.

sense. There is no patience for eternity. By contrast, the Jewish time scale is long and far-reaching. The Jew has time. This has been celebrated in our folklore, our humor, and even in the classic Yiddish aphorism, *A Yid hat zeit*. He is patient, as one who has come from the dawn of history and now waits for the Messiah must be patient. The objects of his authenic ambition are sacred rather than secular, and he does not think only in terms of the immediately attainable. Time is not a commodity which must be used. God Himself is *mekadesh Yisrael ve-ha-zemanim*, "He who sanctifies Israel and the seasons." Time is holy. Speed in understanding all things, rapidity of movement for its own sake, short courses in learning and in scholarship—these are foreign to the Jewish tradition.

The Jew has time, and his Book is constantly expanded: Bible to Talmud to commentaries to supercommentaries *ad infinitum*. The American Book is quickened, shortened: novels to pocket editions to abridgements to condensations. Characteristically, the Jew has carried his Book on his shoulders: *ol Torah*, "the Yoke of the Torah." The American carries his book in his hip pocket.

This impatience manifests itself in the American compulsion to change for its own sake. Young, with no deep moorings in the ancient past, the American civilization has little respect for tradition, and this rootlessness accounts for her frenetic chase after newness and experimentation. The very character of America, according to Frederick Jackson Turner's classic theory, was shaped and molded by the frontier experience and born out of the American forest. A frontier is always moving. It is restless, energetic, inventive, and there is a pervading sense of experimentation. In our day, Harold Laski has shown that the "spaciousness of the United States as a physical entity makes the idea of unlimited horizons, of constant discovery, of novelty that is always imminent, part of the background against which each American is set."[5] (How do Americans greet one another?—"What's new?") Even today the phrase "American experiment" is part of our daily vocabulary, for the character of the restless frontier did not cease to exist when the frontier was conquered. Modern American civilization still retains this restless experimentalism. "The characteristic American is always on the move. He is always willing to try something new. He is skeptical of anything that expresses itself as permanent or absolute."[6] And David Reisman has even viewed the American search for

---

5. Harold Laski, *The American Democracy* (New York: Viking Press, 1948), p. 5.
6. Ibid., p. 716.

newness as a modern manifestation of the explorer, and the suburbs as a counterpart of the old frontier town.[7]

Even the arts have been forced to keep pace with this constant motion and its search for infinite variety. Music, always an accurate index of any civilization, provides a characteristic illustration. The truest American musical idiom is found in jazz. This is America's most important national musical style, and reflects more than any other art form the experimentalism and the search for novelty of which we speak. It places a premium on improvisation. It is inventive, restless, mobile. It is the embodiment of an experimental literature, an amorphic architecture, a formless painting, a casual speech. It is, in a word, thoroughly American and a mirror of its innovating culture.

For Judaism, events are seen *sub specie aeternitatis*. For while Judaism is dynamic and moving, its dynamism is expressed in the key word *halakhah*, a "going," a movement along a certain path without constant forays into the backroads of experimentation and innovation. The structure of the Halakhah is absolute and eternal. But the key phrase of America is found in "nothing is here to stay." New structures have in them a built-in transiency and impermanence, and Detroit builds "dynamic obsolescence" into its automobiles.

For further contrast, consider the poets of the two traditions. Could any Jewish poet have written in the wild enthusiasm and self-deification of a Walt Whitman?

> I celebrate myself and sing myself,
> And what I assume you shall assume,
> For every atom belonging to me as good belongs to you . . .

Can any Jewish poet boast of his own land as Whitman boasts of America: ". . . born here of parents born here of parents the same, and their parents the same"? Conversely, could an American poet have written in the prophetic cadences of a Bialik, who was a contemporary of the modern Whitman and not an ancient?

> If you wish to know
> The eternal strength of my people . . .
> Seek out the *Bet ha-midrash*

---

7. David Riesman, *Individualism Reconsidered* (New York: Anchor Books, 1954), pp. 138 ff.

> And there you will see,
> Bent over the Talmud,
> A figure swaying, swaying . . .

Or consider the folk literature, in which a deeper split is found. Contrast the American folktale with its hyperbole and self-assurance (the "tall story") with the Jewish folktale and its understatement and self-deprecation. Jewish folk heroes are quite dissimilar from Paul Bunyan, logger de luxe, and Billy the Kid or Jesse James, outlaws. (Again the frontier is visible.)

The American spirit is the song of the open road. The past is known, the future charted. American history is clear, factual, documented. Perhaps as a consequence of this we find in American life little of mystery or symbolism. In truth, the very attraction which ritual and mystery hold out for Americans is an indication of its absence from daily life. Witness the fascination with which America observed the Queen's coronation ritual several years ago, or the powerful appeal of exotic organizations.

> To belong to a secret order and be initiated into its rites, to be part of a "Temple" with a fancy Oriental name, to parade dressed in an Arab fez or burnoose, to have high-sounding titles of potentates of various ranks in a hierarchy: all this has appeal in a nonhierarchical society *from which much of the secrecy and mystery of life have been squeezed out.*[8]

It has been suggested the United States Constitution is achieving the status of sacred symbol because the openness of American history has resulted in a society bereft of symbolism of a mystical nature.[9]

The Jew is rooted in something less open and tangible. His beginnings and his destiny are shrouded in the unknown, and Jewish life is replete with symbol, with ritual, and with mystery. We need only compare the respective holiday celebrations. Passover, for example, is taught to many Jewish children as the "Jewish Fourth of July." Externally, both occasions celebrate independence and freedom from oppression. But they are celebrated quite differently. Pesach is typically Jewish. It brims with symbol: matzah, *maror*, the Seder, the Haggadah. The Pesah cup of ritual runneth over. But

---

8. Lerner, op. cit., p. 635. Emphasis added.
9. Ibid., p. 30.

Fourth of July observances are frequently diluted into nothing more than noise, fireworks, and patriotic speeches.

Because of the intrinsic clarity of the American tradition, its thinking concerning some of the basic issues of life is expressed in the pragmatic: that is good which succeeds, that is evil which fails. There is a concurrent admiration for the concrete and particular as against abstract ideas. A leading American historian states that "the American felt instinctively that philosophy was the resort of the unhappy and the bewildered, and he knew that he was neither."[10] The authentic American is not a thinker, but one who gets things done. He believes in tangibles: intangibles make him suspicious, for, in Turner's words, "American democracy was born of no theorist's dream. God Himself, to the American mind, was not so much a supernatural Being as a kindly older brother." In Commager's words, "Americans naturalized God, as they naturalized so many other concepts."[11] The American is a technical man who is concerned with *how* and not *what* or *why*. His thought is therefore often tentative and fragmented, and he is "anxious to do rather than to be."[12]

Judaic thought, however, is based on concepts less utilitarian. To William James the "good is the maximum satisfaction of demand," but for the Jew the quest is not for the good but the holy. For him, that is holy which is godly, that is profane which is ungodly. His concern is not the satisfaction of a demand but the satisfaction of a command—God's. The Jewish concept is absolute and unswerving. Torah, prayer, Messiah are not useful in immediate life. Their value can be known only at some future point in eternity. But the American mind, rooted in the now, cannot wait until eternity for results.

We have attempted to point out several of the key differences in the American and Jewish experiences. Some of these differences, of course, obtain in any discussion concerning secular and religious traditions. But this is precisely the issue: that an equation between the two cannot be made. If some of the characteristics of the two traditions have been simplified, we have done so not to disparage but to present archetypes so as to crystallize our theme that America represents an unfamiliar rhythm and a strange tempo for the Jew. If Judaism has thus far been able to survive in this milieu it is less an

---

10. Henry Steele Commager, *The American Mind* (New Haven: Yale University Press, 1959), p. 9.

11. Ibid., p. 164.

12. Laski, op. cit., p. 39.

indication of the essential compatibility of the two than of the viability of Torah in all cultures.

This is not to say that the two are mutually exclusive, but simply that the issue should not be one of reconciling the two civilizations. This is not necessary, or even desirable.

The credo of authentic Judaism is this: creative Jewish thinking must do more than merely make feeble attempts to force Judaism's compatibility with every current doctrine. Apologetics are less important than self-understanding, and Judaism must be true to, and consistent with, nothing but itself. In so doing it best serves the majority culture in which it may find itself at any given time. Particularly is this true in America, where the unmistakable signature of the Jewish experience can serve as a benign control on some of the more disturbing aspects of living.

The constant clatter of Judeo-Americana serves only to confuse. America is open to all points of view, to the Jewish no less than any other. The divergent worldviews here adumbrated are an indication of some of the areas in which the American Jew, by being a standard-bearer of his own unique tradition, can contribute to the American experience and enrich it with his own perspective and heritage.

On the Publication of Rav Soloveitchik's Lectures

THE SCENE IS familiar: a large assembly hall, perhaps two or three thousand people in attendance. Present are young and old, men and women, rabbis with years of learning and experience in the pulpit, members of the academic community, Orthodox as well as non-Orthodox Jews. Tape recorders whir, pencils take rapid notes. On the podium stands a tall, lean, gray-bearded figure, delivering a lecture on the fine points of Halakhah and Jewish thought. Although his subject is complex and subtle, he will hold his diverse audience enthralled for several hours. The speaker is Rabbi Joseph B. Soloveitchik, known to his disciples by the appellation, both respectful and affectionate, of "the Rav."

What lies behind the veneration and awe in which he is held by his disciples and by the Jewish community at large? He is not, after all, a product of the kind of media hype occasionally found in Jewish circles: he grants no interviews, has no press agents; his words are not calculated to shock, intrigue, arrest, or attract. Nor is he a Hasidic rebbe commanding an automatic following by virtue of leadership of a particular sect. And although he is first and foremost a scholar and a student, he rarely publishes. Yet for the past several decades Rav Solovietchik, Rosh Yeshivah at Rabbi Isaac Elchanan Theological Seminary, has been perhaps the single most intriguing figure within comtemporary American Judaism. Born in Poland in 1903, scion of several generations of world-famous talmudic luminaries, beginning with Rav Ḥayyim Soloveitchik—the "Brisker Rav"—Rabbi Joseph B. Soloveitchik is recognized as one of the preeminent Torah personalities of this generation.

But despite this genealogy and his readily acknowledged erudition and brilliance, the phenomenon of Rabbi Soloveitchik goes beyond this. For our generation has been blessed with a number of rabbinic intellectual giants. And while each of them has had a deep influence beyond his circle of immediate students, it is fair to say that no one has attained as wide an audience among diverse groups within Jewish life as has Rav Soloveitchik.

When the surprising revival of American Orthodoxy in the twentieth century is finally recorded, historians will give due recognition to the various great *roshei yeshivot* and Hasidic *rebbeim* who, together with the newly arrived immigrant survivors of World War II, brought with them the stubbornness and the vision which were the catalysts for Jewish renewal in America. The schools they founded, the yeshivot they nurtured, the personal examples which they set, the attitude of self-confidence which they created—all resulted in the newly committed corps of Jews who are the vanguard of today's recrudescent Orthodoxy.

At the same time, the historian will have to understand a more subtle truth: that it was the unique approach and personality of leaders such as Rav Soloveitchik which provided the intellectual framework and model by which the secularly oriented Jew could find his way back to the tradition. He, perhaps more than any other, was able to demonstrate to a wide audience the intellectual rigor and discipline of halakhic categories as well as the profound worldview inherent in the apparently legalistic minutiae of daily Jewish life—a worldview which addresses itself not only to the mind but also to the troubled heart and soul of lonely, alienated contemporary man. This demonstration of the universality of Torah, presented with such clarity of mind and passion of heart, also contributed immeasurably to the strengthening of the Orthodox community, which was being intellectually buffeted on all sides. In particular, he has had a lasting impact on the American-trained Orthodox rabbinate, not all of whom studied under him at Yeshiva University, but many of whom have benefited from his teachings. Thus the historian will find that he was a major architect of the bridge upon which many marginal Jews were able to return, as well as a primary shaper of the thinking of much of the traditional Jewish leadership.

While these contributions of his are significant, they still do not account for the fascination which he holds for so many. Part of this is undoubtedly due to his gifts as an orator. His ability to hold an audience for hours-long lectures is a study in the use of voice, gesture, inflection, and language: a natural ability to create a connection with his listeners. And though he crafts his lectures meticulously, writing, rewriting, and editing mercilessly, his talks are marked by a spontaneous, incisive wit, by questions to the audience—particularly to an audience of rabbis—which are not simply rhetorical, but to which he often expects an answer from his listeners; by an affect and emotion which do not hesitate to bare his innermost soul; by anecdotes about how things were in his father's or his grandfather's house; by an unconcealed ardor for his subject. And when he talks, as he often does, about the relation of mind and heart, and the so-called emotional coolness of the approach of Brisk and the so-called emotional warmth of the Hasidic tradition in which he is also steeped, he is in actuality discussing the special intellectual and emotional qualities which are his own. He is, in brief, a consummate platform teacher, and in fact he constantly refers to the role of the teacher/rebbe in Jewish life as being the most significant figure in all of Jewish history: Moshe Rabbenu is the teacher par excellence and is considered superior to king and prophet in Israel.

His appeal may also be due to his independent and innovative persona. Elsewhere, he has written that he has "a liking for pioneers, for experimenters, for people who do not follow the crowd. I have always admired the first ones, the early ones, the beginners, the originators. Even in my *derashot* I prefer to speak about those who defied public opinion, disregarded mockery and ridicule, and blazed new trails leading man to God."[1] He is a traditional *rosh yeshivah* with a philosophy doctorate from the University of Berlin; a recognized talmudic authority who is *au courant* with contemporary thought; a preeminent authority on Maimonides whose restless mind also knows Kierkegaard and Heidegger. Intellectually, religiously, spiritually, and scholastically he is in the mold of the classic *rosh yeshivah*, giving regular *shiurim* in Talmud and relentlessly striving to teach his students the underlying logical core of halakhic discourse. But he eschews the traditional garb of the *rosh yeshivah*, the *capote* and the wide-brimmed black hat, which is perhaps symbolic of the maverick within him. While constantly upholding the clear supremacy of Torah learning in all of its forms and manifestations, and while emphasizing the strict, disciplined, and uncompromising allegiance to the totality of halakhic living, he does not hesitate to call upon the resources of secular thought and learning when they can underscore his message, thus apotheosizing the secular into the sacred.

---

1. Rabbi Joseph B. Soloveitchik, in *Rabbi Joseph H. Lookstein Memorial Volume*, ed. Leo Landman (New York: KTAV, 1980), p. 338.

In his recurring themes one also finds a key to his ability to make contact with the contemporary soul. The motif of alienation is sounded regularly in his work: we hear of "the dark night of the soul"; the meaning of death and mourning in human life; loneliness (Jewish prayer is a dialogue between the lonely Jew and the lonely God); defeat; the absurdity of existence without God; retreat, pain, suffering: the entire lexicon of modern existential thought. Whether it be in the touching eulogy for the Talner Rebbetzin or a theoretical excursus into the metaphysical realm of the role of authority in Jewish life, the listener is caught up short by the recognition of his own hitherto inchoate vexations and anxieties. It is only the saving quality of Torah and Halakhah which makes it possible for absurd and lonely man, whose life without God and Torah is inherently pathetic and tragic and whose physical end is in the grave, to reach out confidently to the King of Kings and to make contact with Him. Thus Rabbi Soloveitchik gives expression to his own genuinely religious personality, for whom Torah is not an abstraction, but the *leitmotif* of all of existence and the prism through which God's presence is apprehended.

In addition to this ability to strike responsive chords within contemporary man, the mystique of the Rav involves his remarkable use of language. Whether he speaks in his adopted English or his native Yiddish, his use of words is at once precise, felicitous, dramatic, eloquent, and poetic. While the world of Torah scholarship can boast of a profusion of great intellects, what is altogether rare is the corresponding gift of articulation and communication—without which the most profound and incisive scholarship remains unshared, unknown, and untaught save to a select few. This fusion of rigorous thought and language is at the heart of Rav Soloveitchik's power, and makes him a teacher par excellence. In fact, he has often said of himself that he is not a professor, not a philosopher, but primarily a teacher.

Clearly, the appearance of any book which attempts to capture and transmit the thought of such an intriguing figure is an occasion of great interest. Particularly so since Rav Soloveitchik's teachings have been transmitted primarily not through the written word but the spoken word. Articles and essays by the Rav are so rare that they rapidly become collectors' items. He clearly prefers to teach Torah *she-be-al peh* rather than a Torah *she-bi-khtav;* and, to be sure, his rare oratorical gifts are eminently suited to the podium and platform. Although several of his lectures were reconstructed and published in Hebrew or in English,[2] there had for many years been no attempt at a definitive and thematic reconstruction in English. However, in *Reflections of the Rav: Lessons in Jewish Thought* (Jerusalem, 1979), Abraham Besdin, long a disciple of the Rav, filled this lacuna—and he filled it extremely well.

Because of the nature of the materials, it is a difficult task to transpose the spoken work to the written page. Choosing not to present us simply with literal transcriptions of taped messages, Rabbi Besdin has wisely and expertly organized and reconstructed the salient themes of a number of seminal lectures in order to make the major concepts of Rav Soloveitchik's thought more available to a wider audience. In many instances, the reconstructions of lectures are so redolent of the original that one can hear an echo of the Rav himself as he uttered the words. Besdin has deliberately abbreviated much, encapsulized much, shortened much, but he has done so judiciously and with sensitivity. Whether the reader is new to the thought of the Rav or whether he has been a student for decades, he will greatly profit from this text. And while the subject matter is often recondite, Rabbi Besdin transmits the lessons with a light and gentle touch, so that even the heart of the novice can be engaged and his mind be taught. Here we find Rabbi Soloveitchik's classic lecture on the rebellion of Korah in the wilderness, his moving discussion of prayer as dialogue, the incisive analysis of the religious centrality of *Erez Yisrael;* the relationship of God, man, and the Jewish people, and much more.

The volume is divided into twenty chapters, thematically arranged under six overarching themes. Its value is enhanced by helpful footnotes and by a full listing of Rabbi Soloveitchik's available publications in Hebrew and in English. The essence of the Rav's teachings is found here in convenient form, and serious English-speaking Jews are in great debt to Abraham Besdin for his efforts in bringing forth this significant contribution to twentieth-century Jewish thought. One would hope to see more of Rav Soloveitchik's essays in their pristine form, written and edited by him alone. Until the day when the Rav's oral Torah is transformed into his written Torah, this type of summary reconstruction will serve us well.

---

2. See *Tradition* 17, no. 2, which is devoted to five major lectures of Rabbi Soloveitchik.

Relatively Jewish: Einstein as a Religious Personality

SOMEONE ONCE ASKED Dr. Albert Einstein about his formula for success. He is said to have replied that his formula was: A + B + C = success. When asked to elaborate, he said that A equals hard work, and B equals play. "What," he was asked, "is C?" "C," he said, "is knowing when not to speak."

I stand before you to discuss a great scientific mind, but I am not a scientist nor the son of a scientist. Instead, I am a rabbi, the son of a rabbi, and I should know when not to speak. The nearest I can come to the success in Einstein's formula is to limit my remarks to those elements of his thought which are in some way connected with religion and with Judaism, and to present a response from the perspective of Jewish tradition.

Let us at the outset define the framework within which we will be functioning.

I believe it is fair to say, though it is admittedly a broad generalization, that one of the fundamental differences between science and religion is that science deals, in general, with that which is seen and is verifiable, while religion deals with that which is revealed, with faith, with matters of belief.

If God is scientifically verifiable, he is hardly God. And if the microscope's results are revealed from above, it may be quite miraculous but hardly scientific. Science seeks to understand the world through observation and experimentation. That which stands outside the courtyard of observation and experimentation—that which cannot be measured—such as prophecy, revelation, God speaking to man—is not part of scientific discourse. Religion, on the other

198

hand, is at bottom nonobservable, nonmeasurable, and ultimately above rationality.

In science, truth is arrived at as a result of man-made hypotheses and theories which explain certain facts. In religion, certainly in Judaism, truth is arrived at as the result of prophecy, tradition, faith. The beginning of Judaism is that God is: "In the beginning, God . . ." There is no question as to who, why, or what He is. He simply is.

This is not to suggest that a religious Jew has it revealed to him on faith that he must be in eternal conflict with science. On the contrary, he believes that God the Creator has given us the intellectual tools with which to understand observable phenomena; that God wants us to explore His Creation and through this to explore Him; that implanted within our soul is a yearning to know the universe and to know the Creator of this universe.

Of course, there was a time in the history of mankind when it was considered blasphemy to inquire into the workings of nature. God made the universe in His wisdom,, and it was not up to us to question His work. Physical instruments used for experimentation were discouraged and looked upon with suspicion. Roger Bacon, the English monk of the thirteenth century who was an excellent physicist and who discovered the laws of optics by physical experiments, spent many years in prison because he was suspected of black magic and of questioning the handiwork of God.

Judaism recognizes that man's mind is inquisitive, and Judaism has by and large been spared the classical science versus religion battles which have bloodied the pages of religious history. Alvin Radkowsky points out that according to Talmudic tradition, "Abraham arrived at his belief in a single universal invisible God by scientific observation, starting with the regularity of appearance and of departure of the sun, moon and stars." Abraham discerns and analyzes the laws and phenomena of nature and arrives at his conclusion that there must be a God, an Author. In fact, Adam himself is commanded to master the forces of nature: he is told to "fill the earth and subdue it," which implies the acquisition of a knowledge of nature and of science. And the Master Builder of the Temple, Bezalel, was required to be a man who was able to penetrate the mysteries of the physical as well as of the spiritual universe, since the Temple was to incorporate the secrets of both worlds. Maimonides follows this pattern by citing the importance of scientific study as increasing man's awareness of God's greatness.

Throughout Jewish history, then, a good case can be made for the remarkably reciprocal relationship that exists between science and Judaism.[1]

I do not imply that science and Judaism have always gone hand in hand: the disparities have been great and remain great. But in the ultimate sense, Judaism has never felt threatened by science. And in the person of Albert Einstein we have a figure who perhaps came closer than any other scientist to overcoming some of these disparities. Whether he actually did so is the question to which we will address ourselves below. But that in certain major elements in his thought and his life he came close to doing so—of this there can be little question.

The total effect of twentieth-century science, particularly of physics, has been to impart a sense of wonder and awe at the universe around us, a sense of our finitude, a sense of humility. Probably his greatest contribution to the history of twentieth-century thought was not his world-shaking paper of 1905, but rather the restoration of this sense of awe and wonder into all inquiries into the universe. In Einstein's hands science meant an almost religious reverence for the all-pervading unity and lawfulness and logic which manifests itself in the universe. He was more than a sober scientist. He was filled with rapture and ecstasy for the creation. He listened to the "music of the celestial spheres." He was throughout filled with reverence and inspiration for the magnificence of creation. His reach was audacious: he wanted to know what makes the universe tick. The more he saw the more humble he became. "The most incomprehensible thing about the world is that is is comprehensible," he said. Like the psalmist, his work sings the praise of the One whose work is awesome: "How great are Thy works, O Lord, how profound are thy thoughts" (Ps. 92:5). In Albert Einstein's hands, the handiwork of God is truly great and truly profound. So much so, that in the eyes of his colleagues he had changed from a physicist to a metaphysicist, to a man searching for ultimates.

And well might they have so felt, for here was a physicist who was capable of saying that "the finest emotion of which we are capable is the mystic emotion. . . . Here again lies the germ of all art, all true science.[2]

Here was a rational scientist, trained in the laboratory, who was

---

1. "The Relationship Between Science and Judaism," *Bulletin of the Association of Orthodox Jewish Scientists* 2 (1967): 151 ff.

2. H. Cuny, *Albert Einstein, The Man and His Theories* (New York, 1939), pp. 157 ff.

able to say that "anyone who is not capable of wonderment . . . is a dead man."[3] Certainly it is not an ordinary physicist who can say, "to know that what is impenetrable for us really exists, and manifests itself as the highest wisdom and the most radiant beauty whose gross forms alone are intelligible to our purest faculties . . . this knowledge, this feeling . . . is the core of true religious sentiment. In this sense, and in this sense alone, I rank myself among profoundly religious men."[4]

Although he was not religious in the formal sense and in his early years was even hostile to structured religion, what he did possess was an intuitive insight into certain fundamental religious truths. Basic to this, of course, was his vision of the oneness, the unity behind all of nature. He showed us that nature is not hostile to ideas, nor is it impenetrable, nor capricious. Nature is a mystery, but it wants to be known. It is covered with many veils, it is very subtle, very sophisticated, but it does not play games with mankind; it is not malicious; it operates according to certain rules. There is a unity in nature, just as there is a unity in an apparently diffuse symphony.

Now, if we substitute for the word "nature" the word "God," we find Einstein making a profoundly religious statement: God is One, He wants to be known, He is not malevolent, He is good, He is covered with many coverings. He poses many difficult questions and apparently insurmountable problems. He wants His creatures to come to know Him, to study Him, to see His godly smile. As Einstein put it in a rather playful way, but in a typically precise way: "God does not play dice with the universe." God does not leave the universe to blind chance. There is nothing random in the universe. Everything is according to a definite mathematical law, verifiable by observations. There is rule, there is logic. This was the subject of his first paper in 1905 and was really the origin of the concept of atomic energy. Like Kepler and Newton before him, he had a profound faith in the rationality within the structure of the universe, and he was excited at the possibility of perceiving but a glimpse of the rationality that existed within the world.

Here again, he is in intuitive consonance with a basic Jewish teaching: that although all the commandments of the Bible seem unrelated, there are in fact unexpected relationships between them, and they form an unbreakable whole. Torah and its traditions have

---

3. Ibid.
4. Ibid.

always sought to demonstrate the consistency and unity of all of its discrete parts. The Talmud is in fact a search for unity in the Torah, just as science in Einstein's hands was a search for unity in the universe.

He was driven to understand, in the Biblical spirit of *be-khal derakhekha da'ehu*, "in all thy ways, strive to know Him" (Prov. 3:6). In an autobiographical note he tells how, at the age of four, he was shown a compass. The behavior of the needle made a profound impression upon him. "Something deeply hidden had to be behind things."[5] And this yearning for the mystery was the leitmotif of his science. In 1921, sixteen years after his revolutionary paper on relativity, he told a fellow physicist in Berlin: "I have no interest in learning a new language, or in food, or in new clothes. I'm not much with people, and I'm not a family man. I want to know how God created this world. I am not interested in this or that phenomenon, in the spectrum of this or that element. I want to know His thoughts; the rest are details."[6]

The audacity of this statement has a certain Biblical ring to it: it is in a way reminiscent of Moses demanding to know the essence of God; of Jacob demanding of the stranger with whom he wrestles, "What is thy name"; that is, What is your essence? Never mind that "My thoughts are not thy thoughts" (Isa. 55:8). The yearning of man to know his Creator will not be denied.

And so he asked the questions to which there are no easy answers: "Why does the world exist? Why does life exist?" The thought of these mysteries caused a kind of mystic exultation within him as he marveled at the strange harmony of the world which was demonstrably mathematical.

Einstein's habit of referring to God on a regular basis confounded his colleagues and even enraged some of them. While we will see below that Einstein's concept of God was hardly the traditional one, his constant references to a deity were highly unusual for a physicist. For science seeks not only greater accumulation of knowledge, but also more and more systematic knowledge. A philosopher of science has defined it in this way: "System is no mere adornment of science, it is its very heart. . . . it is an ideal of science to give an organized account of the universe."[7]

When you posit a deity which operates above and beyond things as

---

5. Paul A. Schlipp, ed., *Albert Einstein* (Evanston Ill., 1949), p. 9.

6. R. W. Clark, *Einstein* (New York, 1971), p. 18.

7. Michael Slote, "Religion, Science and the Extraordinary," in *Studies in the Philosophy of Science* (Oxford, 1969), pp. 197 ff.

we see them, you posit an entity that does not fit into the framework of science, for this entity, this deity, may operate by different laws entirely. Furthermore, the relationship of this entity to other entities is not clearly understood. Thus, when a scientist inserts a God in his universe, he is doing violence to the very nature of scientific inquiry, which is to arrive at some systematic unity of knowledge about the universe.

But along comes someone like Einstein who sees extraordinary things in nature and is not afraid to posit something extraordinary behind these extraordinary things. For him, unlike other scientists, scientific unity is not an idol which is to be preserved at all costs. For others it is much more reasonable not to posit any entity which may do violence to the nature of scientific inquiry. That a God does not fit neatly into already accepted scientific theories is for Einstein no reason not to postulate the existence of a God. He was not afraid to say that there may be realms of existence which are outside the scope of science.

This is because his was in essence a universal mind. He saw things in a total setting, and the compartments that for lesser mortals divide religion, philosophy, art, and science into separate chambers did not exist for him. Instead, he saw all of these in one grand hall of human heart and mind, and that which was a contradiction to the ordinary mind did not for him exist.

Am I saying in all that precedes that he was thus a religious Jew with a distinctively Jewish outlook? I could not argue that. His God, firstly, was not clearly a personal one. Despite Einstein's familiar and almost playful attitude about God and his desire "to know his thoughts," there is no clear basis for believing that the Einsteinian God was one who is self-conscious, who has "thoughts" or possesses will. One cannot find any evidence that his God was one to whom, for example, a human being might pray. Einstein senses the "intelligent smile of the Universe God," and he recognizes in this intelligence a true friend, one who works according to rules and laws, and so in brotherliness and friendship Einstein smiles back in his piquant way. But his God is more a Spinoza God than a traditional Jewish one. On one occasion he says explicitly that he "believes in Spinoza's God who reveals himself in the orderly harmony of what exists and not in a God who concerns himself with the fate and actions of human beings."[8] (Spinoza, by the way, would have been surprised at an independent reality who does or does not play dice.)

Similarly, it is not certain that Einstein's God is He who created

---

8. Schlipp, op. cit., p. 103.

the universe. Like Spinoza's God before him, the God in Einstein's lexicon is the independent reality and the intelligibility—the impersonal rationality—of the universe. This is the God of the philosophers, but it is not quite the God of Abraham, Isaac, and Jacob. He may be in nature, yes. But is He in history? Does one have faith in such a God? In the Jewish tradition God has on his crown the seal of *emet*, "Truth." This God could also be the God of Einstein. But the tradition also speaks of the God of Life, *Elohim Ḥayyim*. Whether Einstein's God has independent "life" is an unanswered question.

Einstein would admit that the world of nature testifies to a divine movement behind it all, but is there a real dialogue between God and man? Does the God of Einstein meet man in prayer? The chances are that he does not, for man may or may not be God's creature. Nor is there in the Einsteinian/Spinozian God a human sense of personal dependence upon God. Einstein has a God, surely, but He is far removed from the Biblical God who demands and loves and listens and is concerned and is a father and a friend.

Yes, Einstein was stirred by the more poetic elements in the Jewish tradition, by its strong ethical impulse, its emphasis on life, its strong universality. But some of his views on Judaism have about them a certain innocence and naivete. Thus the fact that he was born into an assimilated family, that he did not receive Jewish instruction until he was well into high school, and that at best his exposure to Jewish thought was sketchy and haphazard[9]—all this becomes apparent when we encounter some of his views of Judaism.

The undeniable fact is that when we move from Einstein the physicist to Einstein the Jewish thinker, we move from a bold, imaginative, precise, and inventive mind to one which contents itself with generalities and platitudes. Perhaps it adds a human quality to this giant among men to note the intellectual inconsistency which on the one hand was able to discard the clichés which had controlled scientific discipline for centuries, and on the other was unable to discard current clichés about the nature of religion in general and Judaism in particular. That a figure of such gigantic proportions could make ordinary, commonplace statements about religion, and that a mind which rejected accepted notions could readily accept the prevailing pieties of his time about Judaism, is somewhat surprising. Statements like "in the philosophical sense there is no . . . specifically Jewish point of view," or "Judaism seems to me to be concerned almost exclusively with the moral attitude in

---

9. Cf. Philipp Frank, *Einstein: His Life and Times* (New York, 1947), p. 14.

life," or "Judaism is not a creed . . . and is an attempt to base the
moral law on fear," or "Judaism is not a transcendental religion, but
is concerned with life as we live it and as we grasp it, and nothing
else," or "no faith but the sanctification of life in a supra-personal
sense is demanded of a Jew."[10]

Such comments from a mind as subtle and sophisticated as
Einstein's are puzzling. They reveal a total disregard of basic elements of Judaism as creed, faith, system of law, and a discipline
governing every facet of life. Certainly sanctification of life, for
example, is a key factor in Judaism, but to state that this is its
exclusive teaching is to ignore a system in which there is a Commander, the *meẓaveh;* a commandee, the *meẓuveh,* and, most
importantly, a commandment, the *miẓvah,* about which Torah
teaches that there are no less than six hundred and thirteen—one of
which is the commandment of faith in God. (And according to some
authorities this is not a commandment at all but a statement of
faith.)

The fact of the matter is that today even the secularized Jew must
read these comments on Judaism with a sad realization that in this
area the great mind of Einstein—never exposed to the depths of
Jewish thought—had quite simply fallen victim to the prevailing
sentiments of the day. He lived in a time, after all, when it was
accepted that religion had outlived its usefulness. This was the
meliorism of the early twenties, the optimism that was convinced
that all progress was inevitable, that things will turn out well if only
we learn to live moral lives and love one another. Much of this went
up in the smoke of the European crematoria chimneys. It may still
be true that things will turn out well, but we apparently are having
more difficulty than we thought in learning how to love each other
and live moral lives. We are finding it not quite so simple, and there
has been a flight from the airy optimism of the early twentieth
century to the more realistic and sober present, and in such a time
the teachings of traditional religion and traditional Judaism, which
hold that religion and its discipline is a way by which mankind can
learn to love each other and live in peace, which hold that religious
acts and disciplines and ceremonies—holy acts, mitzvot—are not
empty rituals but are in fact physical and symbolic manifestations of
the yearning of the human soul for God—all this takes on new
significance after the Holocaust. Today religion is undergoing a kind
or recrudescence, and the easy optimism of the past, and the glib

---

10. Cited in Schlipp, op. cit., pp. 144 ff.

dismissal of religion as being merely a series of ethical guidelines with no specific *Weltanschauung*, has been swept away as the morning mist. History, as is its disturbing, inevitable habit, has caught up with these neat, comfortable simplicities.

All this has a rather humanizing effect on the great man. If inconsistency is the hobgoblin of little minds, Einstein's mind is far from little. And, after all, is it a denigration of a great scientist to say of him that his insights into his religion were not on the same profound level as his science, any more than it is a denigration of a great religious scholar to say of him that his insights into science are not as profound as his religious learning?

Perhaps, in justice to this great and good man, there is a hidden reason for these apparently superficial views on Judaism. I would suggest tentatively that these views can be ascribed to a basic facet of Einstein's personality. Perhaps the inner compulsion which drove him relentlessly to seek the answer to the unified field theory; which drove him to a pacifism seeking the unity of all mankind; which pushed his physics towards the concept that all emanates from one single, unifiying, common source—perhaps this same obsession with unity among all things and among all men obfuscated his vision of the uniqueness of Jewish thought. For the pattern which emerges from all his comments about Judaism is this: Judaism is humanistic, it is ethical, it believes in the sanctification of life. Judaism is not a creed, it makes no specific demands on its adherents, there is no specifically Jewish point of view on life. In effect, he is saying that Judaism is not different from any other faith system, that it is not apart, that it is not separate or unique. Nor are the Jewish people in any way chosen or endowed with a special mission or purpose.

Is it possible that this "world government" view of Judaism was an outgrowth of his complete absorption with the universal, his antagonism to that which separates and his fascination with that which binds? Thus his view of Judaism was one in which all that is separate and unique is discarded, and only universal tendencies are emphasized. That an emasculated Jewishness emerges from this is beside the point. For Einstein was unable to accept a world-view that tended towards apartness—and he rejected aspects of Judaism which saw it as apart and holy and unique. He could not accept the Torah's dictum that Israel is "a nation that shall live apart" (Num. 23:9).

All this makes his battle for Jewish rights, and his Zionism, all the more remarkable. For it is clear that his personal identification with

Jewishness ran very deep—and this we see in that one aspect which endears him to most freedom-loving people and certainly to Jews: his spirited battle, in the twenties and thirties, for the idea of a Jewish National Homeland long before it became fashionable to do so. Intellectually, he may have been the universal man, somewhat estranged from classical Jewish thought; but on the deep, emotional, spiritual, "gut" level, he responded as a Jew. The stirrings of anti-Semitism in Europe in the twenties and thirties deeply shook him as a man. Unlike some of his rank and stature, never did he attempt to deny his origins or to sell his birthright. Constantly did he take his place with the rank and file of the masses of Jews who were becoming the victims of pogroms and persecutions. And the idea of a homeland in Zion awakened his dormant Jewishness and fired it and quickened it.

He saw in Zionism the only movement capable of creating unity—again the theme of unity!—among the Jews.[11]

One cannot fail to be deeply touched as this quiet, self-effacing, truly humble man lashes out against those terrorists who committed atrocities against Jewish settlers in Palestine in the 1920s. Einstein's verbal attack on the Grand Mufti of Jerusalem, who had "accused" Einstein of demanding the rebuilding of the Temple on the site of the Mosque of Omar, is a model of controlled fury. The gentle scientist calls the Mufti a "young political adventurer . . . an utterly irresponsible and unscrupulous politician . . . exercising his evil influence, garbed in the spiritual sanctity of religion, and invested with all the temporal powers that this involved in an Eastern country." Only a man whose Jewishness goes very deep could write in the following way about an attack of Arab mobs on defenseless Jewish settlements in Palestine: "In Hebron . . . the inmates of a Yeshiva, innocent youths, who had never handled weapons in their lives, were butchered in cold blood; in Safed the same befell aged rabbis and their wives and children. . . . Arabs raided a Jewish orphan settlement where the pathetic remnants of great Russian pogroms had found a refuge. Is it not then amazing that an orgy of such primitive brutality . . . has been utilized by some of the British press for propaganda not against the instigators of brutality but against their victims?"[12] (These lines were written in 1929; today the press and media still make heroes of terrorists and call their victims intransigent.)

---

11. Frank, op. cit., pp. 151 ff.
12. Albert Einstein, *About Zionism: Speeches and Lectures* (London, 1930), pp. 60 ff.

Here one sees a glimmer of the inner passion that was kindled when he toured Palestine and envisioned the noble idea of Jew and Arab living side by side, each contributing to the welfare and betterment of the other, each profiting and benefiting from the peculiar talents of the other.

To return to our original question: we said earlier that Einstein came closer than any other scientist to overcoming the disparities between science and religion. Did he in fact do so?

What we can say is that Einstein brought to science certain important and basic religious attitudes and sensibilities: a sense of awe, a familiarity with God, an overpowering yearning to know the secrets of the universe, a recognition of the wonder and the mystery. What he did was to restore the equilibrium, [13] but the living human soul is not yet addressed by Einsteinian physics, even though in the wondrous construction of the universe we do begin to apprehend a living God.

And in another, very major way, he also intuited a major Jewish truth. His insistence on order in the universe strikes strong Jewish echoes. What I mean is this: the early sages tell us, in a particularly striking Midrash, that before He created the universe, God looked into the Torah and used the Torah for His blueprint in Creation. The Torah, thus, is the Book of Order, the Book of Unity, the Book of Law. And the universe, according to this, was constructed in accordance with Torah and in accordance with principles of law—not out of some capricious, haphazard chaos. In the beginning there was logic and law and mathematical order. In the Bible, the first day of Creation is not "and evening and morning, the first day," but "and it was *one* day." That is, the day of the One. The day of unity. The world begins in unity, it begins in order, it begins in law.

All this Einstein sensed intuitively, as he did so many other truths. He probably never heard of that Midrash, but he would undoubtedly have smiled quietly and enjoyed its imaginative and poetic echoes. And the new openness of many present-day physicists to the very idea of Creation is in large measure due to the new vistas opened by Einstein.

This is the way the world begins, and this is the way the world ends: in unity, in oneness. "In that day," says the prophet, "God will be One and His Name will be One." That is, God will not only be recognized as the Source of all, the One behind all of nature, but all

---

13. Henry LeRoy Finch, Introduction to *Conversations With Einstein*, by A. Moszkowski (New York, 1970), p. xxii.

will be One—in the sense that that which seems contradictory today will not be contradictory in that day, and all questions and problems and contradictions and inconsistencies will be reconciled in that day of One.

But in between that first day of the world's beginning and that last day of the world's fulfillment, it is the task of man to search, to discover the unity that is at once the ground of the universe and its destiny.

And for this we are indebted to the great Doctor Einstein.

American Yeshivot at a Crossroads

IT HAS BECOME orthodox to study the Orthodox.

The phenomenon of a resurrected Orthodox Judaism in America long after observers of the American scene had delivered its eulogies has engaged the interest of contemporary historians of Jewish life. What were the forces which helped transform the dormant and hopeless old-world Orthodoxy of the first half of the twentieth century into the self-confident movement of the eighties? Studies and symposia on contemporary Orthodoxy appear regularly these days, examining Hasidic sects, Orthodox synagogues, Orthodox scholarship, Orthodox strengths and weaknesses.

A gaping lacuna in this renewed interest has been the study of the role of the yeshiva in American Jewish life. Although there have been a number of brief investigations of the yeshiva in its various manifestations, a full and carefully researched work has to date not been available. This, despite the fact that virtually all Orthodox rabbis and day school teachers receive their training in such institutions, and that the yeshivot are virtually the only vehicles by which Jewish learning and tradition at its most intensive levels are transmitted.

In a superb work, William Helmreich now fills this gap with his *The World of the Yeshiva: An Intimate Portrait of Orthodox Jewry*, a thoroughly researched, carefully documented, and sensitively presented examination of one of the least understood and appreciated institutions of American Judaism.

The subject matter presented a challenge of gigantic scope to the author, particularly because of the paucity of written records of the early yeshiva period in America. As a result, Helmreich had to conduct hundreds of personal interviews with yeshiva students as well as with heads of yeshivot, faculty members, and administrators.

Clearly, this kind of study could only have been conducted by one who is familiar with yeshiva life from the inside and who is perceived by its leadership and students as a friend. Helmreich, an experienced sociologist, fits this requirement well: an ex-yeshiva student himself (and author of the semi-fictionalized account of yeshiva life, *Wake Up, Wake Up* . . .) and an observant Jew, he reenrolled in a yeshiva during the course of preparing this study. As a result, his words carry the authenticity that comes from direct observation. Although he applies objective analytical and statistical techniques to his work, it is evident that he is a very sympathetic and understanding observer. These sympathies do not cloud his judgments, however, and he does not withdraw from an occasional critique of the yeshiva world. He is bent neither on ridiculing the yeshiva world nor on offering a public relations release for them. He describes things as they are.

The description is an absorbing one: the courage, vision, energy, and passion of the European *roshei yeshivah*, such as Rabbi Aaron Kotler, who came to the United States during and following World War II, after having lost their own families, institutions, and students in Europe, and stubbornly, tenaciously, and heroically replanted their institutions in the untilled soil of America. Not only did they redevelop their own yeshivot from the ground up; at the same time, they galvanized the dormant Orthodox community on these shores which was still traumatized from the shocks of the European destruction. There were yeshivot in America prior to World War II, of course. But the postwar newcomers demonstrated that the intensity of the European yeshiva could be translated even to "treiffe" America, and they showed that American Jewish students, like their European counterparts, would respond positively to a serious quest for holiness, to uncompromising spiritual and scholarly demands, and to rigorous intellectual honesty and discipline. The yeshiva community became the generator of ever-increasing commitment and devotion, until gradually the Orthodox community halted its retreat and stood its ground with self-assurance.

The *roshei yeshivah*, whose entire world had been destroyed, had managed to salvage one thing from the fire: the fire. They were driven by a profound zeal to create anew that which had been destroyed, despite the overwhelming burdens and negative conditions which militated against new beginnings in America.

This is a story of a world within a world—one with its own norms, values, and mores; a value system separate from the society around it—separate even from Jewish society—with its own taboos, manners, and value system. How this inner world of the yeshiva has been able to insulate itself from the often hostile forces of the outside world; how a system which teaches Torah knowledge for its own sake has competed with a society which stresses utilitarianism; how effectively the yeshiva world has impressed its own values upon students whose roots are in that outside world—these are the elements of this fine study.

There are only five thousand young men studying in post–high school yeshivot in America—not a remarkably large number, but an extremely significant number who are willing to forgo the luxurious conditions of ordinary college life for a life of long hours, strenuous discipline, and serious study seven days a week. Helmreich captures the spirit of this elite corps and their mentors: the *roshei yeshivah*'s drive for ever deepening intensity; the quest for God through a deeper understanding of the sacred texts; the relentless search for the divine will as revealed in the performance of mitzvot; the pursuit of Torah knowledge as the highest sanctity; the love of learning, even after the student leaves the yeshiva.

Nor does the author neglect the problem areas. He points out that the normative American yeshiva, based on the intellectual Lithuanian model, pays a serious price for its traditional emphasis on the superior student: those of average intelligence often look back on their yeshiva experience with some resentment at not being noticed, and with disappointment in their inability to relate personally to their admired teachers. More seriously, the heavy stress on intellectual achievement can result in a de-emphasis on creating authentically spiritual personalities—with serious implications for the future of the entire Jewish community. Thus he notes that because the Talmud's depths and intricacies require full-time study, few students are exposed to systematic courses in areas such as Bible, Prophets, Jewish thought, Jewish ethics. Similarly, he notes the shadow-boxing with the question of secular learning. On the one hand, institutions like Yeshiva University—which itself has moved to the right in the past decades—maintain that secular learning is not merely a compromise with necessity, and that all learning can be an instrument in a fuller understanding of God's unfolding will in nature and in history; on the other hand, institutions like Telz in Cleveland or the Beis Medrash Gavoha in Lakewood feel that since Torah is the repository of all truth, secular knowledge is necessary only to the extent that it is useful for a livelihood. Most yeshivot tend towards this latter view, while at the same time permitting—though not encouraging—their students to attend secular colleges on a limited basis. But philosophically, the issue has been shunted aside rather than confronted.

Helmreich leaves no aspect of yeshiva life untouched, from admission procedures, to dormitory life, to dating practices, to pecking orders. In addition, he offers the reader a number of important insights. Among these are a brief but valuable history of the yeshiva movement from its inception over one thousand years ago. He explains the subtle differences between the Lithuanian-model yeshivots—with their emphasis on intellectual discipline and careful analysis of textual material—and the Hasidic yeshivot; we learn the differences between the "Strict Orthodox" and the "Modern Orthodox" in American Judaism; and we find fascinating historical nuggets about familiar names such as R. Bernard Revel, R. Moshe Soloveitchik, R. Shraga Aryeh Mendlowitz (the famous "Mr." Mendlowitz of day school fame), and, *yebadlu le-ḥayyim*, R. Moshe Feinstein and R. Joseph B. Soloveitchik.

One of the more touching sections deals with the multifaceted role of the yeshiva *mashgiach*. At once personal counselor to the students as well as disciplinarian and spiritual guide, he attempts through his personal warmth and example to help young students in the difficult task of integrating heart, mind, and soul. The *mashgiach* is one of the least-known figures of the contemporary yeshiva; but an effective *mashgiach*, more so than the normative faculty, often makes the difference between a good yeshiva and a mediocre one. Normally, he does not teach formal classes per se, but spends his days and evenings in the beis medrash (study hall), available to students for everything from impromptu conferences and questions on the text to the personal and intellectual crises which beset young men in their post-high school years. More than any other single yeshiva personality, the *mashgiach* has the potential of molding and shaping future lives on an intensely personal level.

Also unappreciated is the fact that, in general, yeshiva faculty are grossly underpaid. It is often their personal idealism alone which forces them to continue in positions requiring great energy and long hours, and in which wives often must work out of necessity. Helmreich's lucid description of the intricacies of Talmud study, how it differs from other disciplines, and how a Talmud class in a yeshiva actually functions, gives us an insight not only into Talmud, but into the delicate meshing of intellectual and personal qualities which is required of the successful *rebbe*. That such *rebbeim* and *mashgichim* stay on the job despite the poor conditions is a tribute to their sense of commitment and dedication to the Jewish future; that such conditions prevail is a reflection of the myopia of the Jewish community at large.

The World of the Yeshiva is not truly "an intimate portrait of Orthodox Jewry," as the author claims in his subtitle, but it is an intimate portrait of a major element of Orthodox Jewry which, as we shall see, has the potential of influencing the total Jewish community. Lucidly written and thoughtfully presented, Dr. Helmreich's book has given us a valuable instrument for the understanding of contemporary Jewish life. The bibliography itself is a mine of information for the student of Jewish life who wishes to follow up subjects such as the tension between reason and faith, mind and emotions, religion and intellectual knowledge. This study transcends mere sociological analysis, and will surely become a classic in the history of American Judaism. It is required reading for all who seek an understanding of twentieth-century American Jewish life.

By definition, an objective study does not deal with matters beyond the present, and can only conjecture whether present trends will continue into the future. But one lays this book down worried about that future. What will be the impact of the yeshivot on the world around them in the coming decades? In truth, some impact has already been felt. Most of the day schools in the United States were spearheaded by communal rabbis who are graduates of the yeshivot, and have been staffed by *rebbeim* who stem from these same yeshivot. And the prime catalyst of the day school movement itself, Torah Umesorah, was the handiwork of the *roshe yeshiva* and their disciples who have immeasurably enriched American Jewish life by their visionary zeal. The unarguable fact, however, is that while Orthodox Jewish life in America has grown more energetic and more powerful because of the yeshiva's direct and subtle influence, the larger community of Jews has been suffering the traumas of runaway intermarriage, assimilation, and universal Jewish illiteracy. As far as Jews in general are concerned, the yeshivot exist on a different planet. Is there a role which the yeshiva can ultimately play in the total Jewish community?

In truth, the same question can be asked concerning the Orthodox community outside the yeshiva. Here too there is much room for *tikkun*. One hopes that years of exposure to the most gifted of *roshei yeshivah*, *mashgichim*, *rebbeim*, to ideals of sanctity and of intellectual honesty, will ultimately seep down into the Orthodox com-

munity-at-large. And if the rigors of the rabbinate, Jewish education, and Jewish communal service are (regrettably) rejected by the
majority of yeshiva graduates, it is to be hoped that though they may
opt for medicine or law or accounting or computers, they will
nevertheless be able to inspire the Jewish community by their
personal example of religiosity and spirituality.

It is a pity that, to date, yeshiva graduates have kept these
qualities to themselves. Preferring to be among their own kind, they
have virtually abandoned the Orthodox synagogue as an institution
in favor of their own small *minyonim* and *shtiblach*, and thus have
lost an opportunity to have an impact on large numbers of Jews,
and have permitted the synagogue to be weakened as a central
institution of Jewish life. In fact, Helmreich himself sees the decline
of the "establishment-type" Orthodox synagogue as we have known
it—at least in the major Jewish centers like New York—and suggests
that the future will find (a) small groups of yeshiva graduates
banding together under the leadership of scholarly rabbis whose
main task will be to teach Torah to those who have a yeshiva
background; and (b) a concomitant increase in the appeal of the
scholarly teaching rabbinate as a career. Which could be a positive
development—if the vast majority of Jews who have not attended
yeshivot are at the same time not hopelessly cast adrift.

Nor, as yet, has the yeshiva movement's higher standards of
spirituality had a major impact on the Orthodox community's religious life. It is not unfair to say that in its enthusiasm for material
things, the non-yeshiva Orthodox community often seems no less
self-indulgent, ostentatious, and hedonistic than the society around
it. Orthodox weddings, for example, in the world's largest and most
observant Jewish community, are only occasionally the models of
taste, restraint, and discretion which might be expected from those
who punctiliously observe Shabbat, kashruth, and mikveh; and the
writers of the ubiquitous invitations which vigorously remind one
and all to dress modestly in accordance with Jewish tradition
frequently forget that Jewish tradition requires modesty not only in
sleeve lengths, but in Viennese tables, expenditures for flowers,
twelve-course meals, and exaggerated outlays of money to TV and
camera crews. Orthodox organizational functions are often unable
to resist the grotesque selling of honors and "man of the century"
awards to the highest bidders; intra-Orthodox disagreements are
not always restrained in their incivility and vituperation; *zeniut* in
dress does not always extend to *zeniut* in word. This is not to
suggest that the non-Orthodox are not as guilty of hedonistic excesses. But one has a right to expect more of an Orthodox commu-

nity which claims to be Torah-oriented, and in these areas, some of the integrity, disicpline, and asceticism of internal yeshiva life could profitably be transferred to the outside.

Another question mark about the future concerns the development of extraordinary leadership. Despite the heavy emphasis on producing outstanding Torah scholars, the American yeshiva—while developing very competent scholars—has not yet produced the giants of Halakhah and of creative Jewish thought of the breadth and depth that were once produced by the European yeshivot. It is possible that it is too soon, and that indigenous religious authorities will yet emerge from the American yeshiva movement. It is also possible that the materialistic ambience of American life is so pervasive that our soil remains hostile to truly prodigious Torah scholarship. Perhaps the future will yet produce an American-trained and universally acknowledged halakhic authority to follow in the footsteps of those who, like R. Aaron Kotler, fueled the yeshiva movement itself.

These are some of the issues which Helmreich's volume brings to mind. While they are not wholly within the parameters of the book, the questions remain: we have seen a surprising reversal of trends in the field of advanced Jewish learning; will the future see a similar reversal of trends in the larger community as a result of the yeshiva movement? Helmreich notes that in the future "the Orthodox community is likely to have increasing power with respect to policy making, organizational influence, and politics, particularly because Orthodox Jews are increasingly better educated and more prosperous. A more powerful Orthodox community will obviously increase the influence and impact of the Yeshiva upon Jews in general" (p. 310). The question is whether this influence will transcend policy-making in politics and truly become a spiritual influence. It may yet be possible, in our infinite genius for miracles, to find ways to replicate the windows of the ancient Jerusalem Temple: to prevent outside influences from affecting the internal workings of the yeshiva, and at the same time to permit the holiness of the internal yeshiva to seep outside.

Great things have been accomplished within the world of the yeshiva in the past thirty-five years. Perhaps in the next several decades William Helmreich will be able to study the Jewish community outside the yeshiva and will be able to tell the story of a community which reversed the tides of assimilation, illiteracy, self-satisfaction, and hedonism to become, despite itself, a holy community.

"Creative Services" and Davening

I HAVE BEEN studying two recent "creative worship" booklets: *Shalom, A Contemporary Supplementary Service for Rosh Hashanah*, and *Haggadah for Today*, by Baruch Raskas. I find the material among the best that has been done in contemporary Jewish liturgy. One senses in it a positive Jewish commitment and a genuine desire to reach outward and inward during worship. At the same time, the work is a kind of metaphor for all that is legitimate and all that is problematic in this genre.

The fact is that we are faced in our time with grievous problems of prayer. For one thing—and this is everything—few Jews are praying, much less davening. The awful and awesome neglect of prayer, the almost universal conviction that traditional Jewish prayer is without meaning, the gap between the Jew desiring to talk with God and the prayers on the printed page: these have given creative liturgy its impetus. We need to find some means by which to teach a neophyte davener that he need not be afraid of reaching up to God; some way to give him security and confidence as he stands at the threshold of a new experience. For those who do not, cannot, will not, or know not how to daven, we seek a bridge, a road back. Certainly these are some of the considerations which have motivated the writers of innovative liturgy.

But these new services make promises they cannot keep. The very names which have been given this genre—"creative," "affirmations," "relevant," "contemporary," "celebrations" (rather pretentious names incidentally—and names which unfortunately reinforce the gullible impression that the Siddur is uncreative, stilted, irrelevant, and somehow unworthy)—offer visions of new horizons of religious experience, of encounters with the One of the universe and with one's own mighty soul. But these soaring hopes are dashed when the innocent worshipper opens the colorful creative booklet and discovers, amid dismembered traditional prayers, an anthology of readings by a mélange of poets, philosophers, and "famous men" which are often moving and genuine but which speak not to—or of—the *melekh malkhei ha-melakhim*, Who is hiding, and Whom we desperately seek. For example—and here I am citing creative services in general—Walt Whitman on the miracle of being alive is beautiful, but is it prayer, and is it uniquely Jewish? Moshe Dayan on Jewish faith is mildly interesting—but how does a definition of faith which entirely omits God fit into a book of worship? Is it prayer, and is Dayan on faith authentically Jewish? Aphorisms of life by Henry Ward Beecher are harmless, but are they prayer, and are they uniquely Jewish? Is there anything here that could not be equally shared by a Buddhist or, for that matter, an atheist?

Even more disquieting are those readings in which a conscious attempt is made to be Jewish and contemporary. Concerned news bulletins about Southeast Asia, ecology, and California Lettuce serves to keep heaven informed and remind one and all that we are Relevant, but, in all frankness, some of these readings smother us with so palpable a Sincerity and Honesty that they get in our way.

Another roadblock: the creativists, ironically, leave nothing to the imagination of the worshipper. The essence of prayer is *avodah she-ba-lev* ("service of the heart")—the thousands of sparks which a single word may kindle within us. "Is not My word like fire, like the hammer that breaketh the rock in pieces?" (Jer. 23:29). The *Shema*, the *Amidha*, *Borkhu*, *Kedushah* may touch the soul in a hundred unarticulated and unverbalized ways. But the creativists insist, with their lengthy and ubiquitous meditations, on telling us how to feel and what to think at every opportunity. They destroy the implicit with their explicit.

To make matters even more difficult, these home-made readings reveal serious deficiencies of grace and style. Even in the better examples these problems are endemic. A few concrete examples taken from *Shalom:*

1. Its commentary on the Akedah states: "Singing unifies the soul, the mind, the body, and the spirit of the human being. It truly gives voice to the totality of man's feelings and aspirations. This very thought is expressed by the phrase, 'and the two walked on together.' " The congregation is then exhorted to "sing together and . . . walk together to a greater and a greater responsibility to other human beings and a greater feeling of serenity." This is Noble

Sentiment, but if a man has no ear or voice for singing, shall he go home? And, really now, is this what is meant by *va-yelkhu she-neihem yaḥdav* ("and they both walked together")?

2. The "innovative" introduction to the Musaf of Rosh Hashanah:

> Rebel O Jews / Against the rubble
> of the ghetto / Against the gaberdine
> [*sic*] of the mind / Which substitutes
> linguistic rapidity / For ethical
> concern. / The Siddur is not a book /
> To mumble as a charlatan/spouts
> some abracadabra . . .

To which one is tempted to reply: A creative service is not the place / to polemicize / against traditional Jews / who do not write / innovative services. How do pejoratives like "mumble," "spout," and "charlatan" fit in with calls for peace and justice and ethics? And do slow Hebrew readers have more "ethical concern" than those who read fluently?

3. The majestic *Nishmat* prayer is introduced by an attempt to depict the Creator's greatness: "Lord, how can there be . . . / so many color combinations . . . / We cannot comprehend / Your creative spirit / Your endless imagination / Your sense of beauty." And then we find: "God is the conductor of creation and the whole universe is orchestrated in a great symphony of splendor." It is this attempt to gild the lily which is so characteristic of innovative liturgy. Why not let *Nishmat* stand on its own merits? In every way—religious, stylistic, emotional, theological—what it says is "right." Talk of His "endless imagination and creative spirit" is embarrassing.

Now if petulance, affectation, and sheer overwriting can creep into one of the better examples of contemporary innovative liturgy, how much more so for others less committed, less genuine, less knowledgeable.

Certainly I do not deny that within the traditon there is a place for personal and spontaneous prayer. Does not Maimonides say that any prayer to God—formal or spontaneous—fulfills the mitzvah of *tefillah* ("prayer")? But today's creative liturgy is not a spontaneous burst of prayer. It is spontaneity codified: printed, bound, formalized, given a pretty and attractive wrapping, and not at all a match for the traditional formality it seeks to replace.

My point is that the creativists, having recognized that there is a prayer problem, have approached it from a side door. They are apparently working from the unfortunate premise that prayer/ davening is essentially a matter of words, phrases, sentences. And since the words of the traditional Siddur are apparently irrelevant/ noncontemporary/out of tune, new formulations have to be devised.

But this is precisely the problem: davening is not merely a matter of speech, of outward expression. It is primarily a matter of using words to create a mood of inwardness and of openness to God. And a mood of listening. To what God has said and is saying; to what some great spirits like King David said and are saying; to others, and to our own soul which also tries to speak to us. Davening is an attempt to attune our selves and to open our selves in order to be able to participate in this eternal colloquy of God, man, Israel, past, present, and future.

Our *bobbes* and *zeides* didn't affirm, innovate, or celebrate: maybe that's why they occasionally wept when they davened. Authentic Jewish worship, I submit, is more than a verbalization of vague, private feelings, no matter how touching and solemn and genuine. Sincerity and good will are fine qualities, but it takes more than these to become a Shakespeare or a Beethoven or a Chagall—or a composer of prayers. Jewish worship involves an encounter with the Lord of Israel, with the Jewish past, with our historic destiny as a people. Love, peace, celebration, universality, community, meaning, mankind, fellowship—these are lovely words. But using them in reverent categories and printing them in"poetic" form do not necessarily constitute a search for the Lord of Israel who is the ultimate object and subject of *tefillah.* An innovative service is here today and, by a click of the loose-leaf spiral, gone tomorrow. This is eternity?

Perhaps it is time to reevaluate and seek a different way. Perhaps we ought to take seriously Psalm 65: "To Thee, silence is praise." In place of the frenetic search for newness, it might be well for the creativists to be silent in the face of the traditional *matbe'a* ("form") of prayer, and to look at it anew. Instead of emasculating the Siddur it would be well to innovate by lovingly exploring the subtlety and beauty of the traditional liturgy. Before updating cavalierly the tradition, it might be intellectually honest to accept the challenge of teaching Jews how to appreciate and respond to the awesome grandeur of the Rosh Hashanah liturgy; the delicately precisioned daily *Amidah;* the subtlely woven Psalms; the carefully wrought themes and rhythms of *Pesukei de-Zimra;* the glow and the elegance of the Shabbat evening service; the grace and vigor of the festival davening; the power and majesty of the Yom Kippur liturgy. We teach music appreciation; let there be prayer appreciation.

Of course there is a difficulty in this: the celebrants want an experience without preparation, without knowledge, without a heart attuned to the idea of praise or humility or worship, and they want it now. So we give them loose-leaf current events scrapbooks, complete with psychedelic covers and lots of sincerity, under the rubric of "creative service." The truer way is to begin to teach what prayer was and is.

We are confusing the road with the destination. By accenting new prayer forms when the old have not been tried, we are blocking the very bridge we want to open. The way to God does not lie in an emphasis on techniques; the strolling cantors and the electric guitars will not lead us to *kavvanah*. The way to *tefillah* is *tefillah*. The way to *kelal yisrael* is *tefillah*. Why not emphasize the idea that davening joins a Jew with a hundred generations of Jews who have davened before him, and joins him to his fellow Jews today in Russia, Israel, Syria, Mexico, Turkey, Australia, who may also be davening at that very moment. Davening thus transforms the individual into an integral part of a mystical faith community. Why not utilize the traditional liturgy as an aid in teaching us how to approach God and how to pray.

The chances are that an exposure to the wealth of meaning and suggestion and association—intellectual, emotional, historical, psychological—of the traditional davening, davened in the traditional way, will make it clear why even sincere attempts at prayer-writing seem inevitably to result in hollow echoes.

Such an approach, led by people who have the courage to sacrifice a touch of immediacy for a touch of eternity—and who are themselves daveners—has not been widely attempted. But where it has, it has elicited a surprising response. Witness the burgeoning *ba'al-teshuvah* movement.

A personal note: As a practicing rabbi, I too have been troubled by a congregation who knew not *tefillah*. For years on end we followed the tried—and untrue—pattern of late Friday services, "creative" English readings, Birthday Shabbat, Youth Services. People came sporadically, but remained essentially unmoved. Then we began to "innovate." The Friday night late show was eliminated (cries of anguish from the "traditionalists" who had never heard of not having it), and the Shabbat morning davening was reinstated—and resuscitated—as the focal point of the week. We eliminated all tricks and gimmicks. We even eliminated English other than in the sermon—and even the sermon is not a regular aspect of the service. We began, in many different ways, to teach our people to daven. They responded to what they recognized as an honest attempt to restore the tradition without gadgetry. It took a number of years, but now, in this young (and Orthodox) congregation of five hundred families, well over three hundred people are in shul every Shabbat—davening. And we are rather proud of our youngsters who go off to school or get married and cannot find themselves in any other type of service—even in "creative" ones—because they long for the authentic tradition of davening which they felt here.

We must rethink innovative prayer because: we have no poets to equal the poets of the Siddur, and our sincerest efforts often result in counterfeit; temporary substitutes tend to become permanent fixtures, and the original coin of prayer is denigrated and ultimately eliminated in favor of the counterfeit; we are being unfair to the young, who will soon tire of the inauthentic and, having confused it with the genuine, will reject both. We have stressed techniques over content and have achieved a vacuous newness which lacks unique Jewishness; we have not demonstrated an understanding of the role, purpose, and function of Jewish worship.

We should reevaluate, and call a moratorium on our new words which we take so seriously. Let us create a stillness in which we can listen to what others, wiser and holier than we and more attuned to Him than we, have to say to us. Perhaps then we will find Him. Which will be creative. And an innovation.

The Case for "Out-of-Town"

EVEN TO THE cursory observer, it is apparent that Orthodox Judaism in New York City has in the past decades made dramatic forward strides. There seems to be an air of intensity in the Orthodox community, a zeal in Torah living, a pride in observance of mitzvot, a dedication to learning. This is undoubtedly a reflection of the newly developed sense of sureness and confidence which has been injected into the mainstream of New York Orthodoxy by the maturing graduates of the many yeshivot and day schools, and by the increased influence of the dynamic Hasidic communities. Where once observant Jewish living was the exception, today in many areas of New York it is the norm. Glatt Kosher signs abound, yeshivot proliferate, beards and *peiot* are common, and *sheitlach* have become big business.

New York Orthodoxy takes all of this luxury for granted. It also takes for granted that outside of New York no Jews and no Judaism exist.

For New York Jews there are only two cities in the United States: New York is one; the others is that vast area stretching from the Atlantic to the Pacific, from Maine to Texas, known as "out-of-town." New York is Jerusalem; out-of-town—New Yorkers like to call it "the hinterlands"—is *ḥutz la-areẓ*. And the unspoken implication is that New York Jews are Jews, and out-of-town Jews are not.

For all of its vaunted sophistication, New York Orthodoxy lives in a vast, provincial insularity. Its *glatt* becomes *glatter*, its *kanaw'us* more intense, its *ḥalav* more Yisrael: an admirable state of affairs when taken by itself. But when it implies a repudiation of the millions of Jews who live in the rest of the country this is unfortunate, for by so doing New York Orthodoxy is neglecting the opportunity to be an inspirational force and influence on American Jewish life.

223

This rejection of "out-of-town" is partly the result of the fact that the New York Jew and the American Jew do not speak the same language. They use the same words, the same phrases, but they do not mean the same thing. For example: "I'm very strict with my daughter." In the Orthodoxy of New York this means that the daughter must wear modest clothes, must daven, and must attend the most pious of girls' yeshivot. But in a typical southern town, this proud statement by a Jewish mother means that the daughter is not permitted to go to a dance until she is twelve, nor date until she is thirteen, and that she must be home by 1:00 A.M.

Hopes and dreams take on a different character. In New York, observant parents hope that their daughter will marry a *talmid hukham* who will continue to learn and study, and that their sons will marry girls who are pious and learned. Out-of-town parents who have some commitment to Judaism have one hope: that their child will marry a Jew. For this they pray, of this they dream.

Even the word "religious" bears different meanings. A religious Jew in New York is one who keeps the mitzvot. A religious Jew out of town is one who occasionally attends the late Friday services in English.

"I sacrifice for my child's Jewish education" means, in New York, that the child is sent to an intensive yeshiva at which he will study from eight to four daily, six days a week, and for which the father must pay a high tuition; out of town, the same words mean that a Jewish father in a tiny hamlet will get up at 5:00 A.M. every Sunday in order to drive his child to Sunday School sixty miles away. The sacrifice of the out-of-towner is perhaps no less than the New Yorker's—it is certainly more poignant—but do the two fathers speak the same language?

Although we live in an age where we can know instantaneously what is happening in the Congo or in China or in outer space, New York Orthodoxy knows little of what is happening in the Jewish communities a few hundred miles away. This is a form of the curse of the *dor ha-pallagah*, for what else but lack of communication is *bilbul ha-leshonot*?

The New York Jew, for example, finds it hard to believe that there are Jewish communities out of town in which a Sabbath observer is a rarity and in which a minyan for Shabbat morning cannot always be expected. And out-of-towners find it hard to believe that it is not uncommon for 150 Jews to come to *Minhah* on a Shabbat afternoon in New York or that there are entire districts where every shop is closed on Shabbat.

Similarly, New Yorkers are not fully aware of the great and crucial battle which is being waged out of town by a small handful of committed Jews, against overwhelming odds, for the preservation of Torah and mitzvot—a battle which is the more heroic because it is a lonely one.

There is, for example, the young father living in a town which has a total of three Jewish families in a population of a thousand, who teaches his five-year-old child and the children of the other families three nights a week; they learn to read Hebrew, to daven, to make berakhot.

There is the young couple who, after much soul-searching, decide to observe kashruth, shabbat and *taharat ha-mishpaḥah;* they do this despite the raised eyebrows of their friends and the open mockery of their acquaintances. They persist, they study, they begin to shake the smugness of their friends and to win them over.

There is the college freshman who defies campus opinion and convinces his Jewish fraternity brothers to have a kosher banquet for the first time in twenty years. He is subject to obloquy and scorn and charges of hypocrisy. But he prevails.

There is the heroic ongoing struggle throughout the United States to establish and maintain day schools. The daily chapters of dedication and sacrifice in maintaining a network of hundreds of such schools in this country are an untold story.

These are not isolated cases. They are repeated constantly in one hundred different forms by individuals in whom there still burns the *"pintele Yid."* But New York Orthodoxy knows nothing of this, and apparently cares nothing.

For New Yorkers do not have to fight a hostile environment. Even if an immediate neighborhood should be non-observant and antagonistic to Torah, there is within reach a yeshiva for one's children, there are friends, there are rabbis, there are monumental Torah institutions, there are *Gedolei Yisrael* who can be seen and heard, and there is the concomitant sense of a certain security in one's spiritual life. The Torah Jew in New York is not alone.

He is not alone, and so he remains in New York. He looks with horror at the suggestion that he live and his children be raised in any other city. And when such opportunities arise he rejects them out of hand.

So pervasive is this mood of unconcern that even those traditional bulwarks of Jewish idealism, our major yeshivot and metivtot, find themselves inadvertently fostering it. Numerous are the students who express a disdain about entering the active rabbinate. Better to remain in New York, they say, as a teacher or as an accountant or as a businessman, than to enter a rabbinate which entails living out of town and which may tarnish one's pure, pristine piety.

And this is true: one's piety can become tarnished; but it may also be purified. It depends how we translate the Rashi of *Im lavan garti ve-taryag mitzvot shamarti:* did Jacob keep the mitzvot *despite* the fact that he lived with the evil Laban, or did he keep them *because* he lived with Laban?

In any case, the result is that our finest *musmakhim* and our ablest and most talented minds do not enter the lists to do battle with the forces of anti-Torah, and are content to make Shabbat for themselves in a secure environment. Is not New York City filled with young and competent Orthodox rabbis and teachers who might have had an impact on American religious life if they were to live elsewhere? Similarly, we must confess, is not "out-of-town" replete with rabbis and teachers whose greatest desire is to live in New York?

The opportunities for productive and influential work for Torah have never been greater; we have unlimited and untapped resources; and yet we do not utilize them, ironically, because of a misguided piety. It was Rabbi Yisrael Salanter who said of the young men of his day who were learning in order to become rabbis, that "there is no greater *lishmah* than this." But today, instead of vigorous and idealistic rabbis and educators who might save Torah in America, we have Rabbi X the accountant, Rabbi Y the insurance agent, Rabbi Z the computer expert.

Certain things should be said about New York Orthodoxy. One occasionally gets the impression that in certain circles Orthodoxy has become a kind of status symbol. Piety has apparently become a commodity in the marketplace of acceptance. Some seem to be concerned not with the state of their relationship to God and Torah, but with the state of their personal *frumkeit* in relation to that of their neighbors. Competitive piety abounds. Out-of-towners may boast: My car is bigger than yours, my house better, my lawn greener; New Yorkers occasionally seem to be saying, My piety is deeper than yours, my shul is more kosher, my praying more intense. Torah living, which is designed in part to develop man's concern for his neighbor seems, in New York, to have turned inward unto itself. It is possible to detect a certain smugness, a satisfaction with self, a lethargy and a contentment which are disturbing. Disturbing, because the religious personality by definition cannot be self-satisfied, and is rarely at peace. His soul aches at injustice and at cupidity, and his mind and heart cry out against selfishness and greed. He is in constant struggle against his own self, against his baser instincts and drives and appetites; and he is ever striving to improve his dealings with his fellow man. Smugness and self-satisfaction are furthest removed from the truly pious. God, Torah, one's own personal observance of mitzvot—these are never taken for granted.

In some respects it is the non–New York Orthodox who most characterizes these aspects of the religious personality. Contentment and smugness are luxuries which he can ill afford. He has no spurious peace of mind; his is a constant struggle against the environment; his is the honest commitment to a way of life for its own sake; his the decision to uphold Torah and mitzvot though it means no status and no honor for him and at times the very opposite. Here at least Torah and mitzvot are not taken for granted.

One cannot help but speculate that more contact with the non–New York Orthodox would be of great benefit for New Yorkers. It would strengthen their own way of life and perhaps stretch their religious horizons. And, since the bridge has two lanes, the presence of new observers would be of untold moral and spiritual support to the embattled few out of town, as well as a step towards creating a true community of Orthodox Jews in the rest of America.

Although it is not the purpose here to present definitive solutions—sometimes an understanding of the problem is part of the solution—certain tentative suggestions can be made.

We must begin with the greatest source of our strength, the major yeshivot. These institutions are the citadel of Torah devotion and idealism. Is it a whim to hope that these yeshivot might systematically encourage senior students to give six months a year to a given hinterland community—as rabbis or teachers? The benefits accruing to Torah would be staggering to behold: the communities would begin to realize that the centers of Torah are concerned with them and care about them; they would have the benefit of zeal, enthusiasm, and dedication; and for the student this could be an invaluable experience, a kind of internship which is otherwise not available today.

Is it an idle speculation to anticipate a period in which our ever-growing Orthodox intelligentsia—the Association of Orthodox Scientists is an example—will set the pace in their willingness to accept posts away from New York, and that, once they are out of town, they will curb their natural disinclination to become involved in Jewish communal matters? They have the potential of teaching a profound lesson by their very presence; let them enter the strife.

Is it visionary to contemplate a time when our Orthodox national rabbinic and lay organizations will concern themselves with a full and ongoing program for American Jewry which goes beyond the sponsoring of conventions, and that the genius, talent, and vast apparatus which is manifest in the leadership of these groups be directed towards the specific issue of a deepened Torah living in America?

Perhaps these are nothing more than dreams. But this in itself may be a sign of good tidings. For when God returns us to Zion, *hayinu ke-holmim*, "we are like dreamers" (Ps. 126:1). Perhaps we are at the crossroads leading back to Zion in its profoundest sense, and therefore a dream or two can be forgiven.

Part IV

A Jew and Himself: A Personal Notebook

Reminiscences and
Recollections

Memories of Kiev

I SHARE WITH you here a very personal incident that took place during the several weeks I spent in Russia, an incident which stirred me more deeply than anything I can remember. When it happened, I did not think I could ever repeat it to anyone, and I found it impossible to talk about it for several months after my return from Russia. But as time went on—and it was on my mind daily—I gained a new insight into the event and began to realize that the story did not happen just to me alone, but happened to every single Jew in the world.

Let me tell it to you as it took place. It happened in Kiev. I had by then spent ten days in Russia, had been exposed to much spiritual suffering, had seen Babi Yar, the ravine outside Kiev in which one hundred thousand Jews had been gunned down in World War II and which today is marked by a small, well-kept garden, with roses and poppies and trees, and a small marker to the memory of the "anti-Fascists" who perished there.

I remember how I felt as the taxi drove out towards Babi Yar. I recalled the whole history of that massacre. For two weeks in September, 1943, posters had appeared on the walls of Kiev, placed there by the Nazis who had taken the city. All the Jews in the city were ordered to gather at a particular railroad station or at a certain schoolhouse. From these staging areas, one hundred thousand Jews were marched down a five-mile stretch of road to a ravine in a forest outside the city. There, Nazi gunners were waiting. The Jews were neatly lined up on the edge of the ravine, gunned down systematically, buried with bulldozers, and then the next group, and the next group, and the next group.

When I was in Kiev, and as we drove out to Babi Yar, and as the guide in the taxi pointed out the railroad station and the school-house, I realized with a sudden sense of horror that I was physically on the same road that my own fellow Jews, my brothers and sisters, had walked three decades earlier on the way to their deaths.

I looked at the railroad station. I could see the thousands of Jews swarming there thirty years earlier. They were still milling around, frightened, confused, carrying their few belongings, holding their infants wrapped in blankets. The Germans were telling them that they would be transferred to another, "safer" area, away from the front lines of war.

Two blocks later, my taxi passed the schoolhouse in which the Jews were processed prior to their death. I looked into the building as we drove by. It was summer, July: not a soul was to be found there. But for me the building was teeming again with the cries of babies, the weeping of women, the silent, helpless sobbing of strong men. I felt as if I myself were standing there, waiting to be processed.

I looked back out the rear window of the taxi, down that street of history. I was with my fellow Jews in that railroad station; I was with them in that schoolhouse. I was in that procession of Jews ten abreast across the wide thoroughfare marching out into the countryside, out to the ravine. I and the others were lined up at the edge, we were told to remove our clothing, we were ordered to fold them neatly—and then we were shot down, and we fell forward into the ravine—my brothers, my sisters, and I; and the bulldozer came forward, dumped tons of earth over our heads, and we moaned a final moan, and there we died.

Perhaps in retrospect all this was an extreme reaction on my part. But this was how I felt: at that point, their fate and mine were one. They and I were Jews, and what had happened to them had happened to me.

I lingered a while at Babi Yar. I said a quiet *Kaddish* and whispered a memorial prayer. The day was unbearably beautiful, the birds chirped in the trees. And then the taxi drove me back down that same road that led from 1943 to today.

All this is by way of background to the incident I want to relate.

I was scheduled to leave Kiev the next morning, but I also wanted to attend the morning minyan. The synagogue was quite far from my hotel, down in the Podol section, and I knew that I was taking a chance on missing my plane entirely if I went to services at the shul. But I had a strong compulsion to get to that minyan. Possibly never again would I be able to daven in such a shul, with such a minyan, with such Jews.

I went to the shul, and davened *Shaḥarit* with a small group of ten or fifteen old men. I sat near the rear, and here is where my story begins.

Near the beginning of the service, I heard a whisper behind me: "Menachem ben Yosef." Menachem ben Yosef? I was stunned. That is my Hebrew name, that is how I am called to the Torah. But today was Wednesday, there was no Torah reading, and besides, how could anyone in Kiev be calling me by my Hebrew name?

I looked around me. Behind me there was an elderly Jew, with a white beard, eyes closed, swaying back and forth, reciting the *Kaddish*.

I said to myself: It is your imagination; these have been difficult days, emotional times, you are physically exhausted, forget it.

I continued to daven and heard nothing more. And then, towards the end of davening, at the *Aleinu* prayer, there it was again: "Menachem ben Yosef." It was a whisper, but it was not my imagination: someone was calling me. The thought chilled me; I physically trembled. Who in the USSR, in the middle of the Ukraine, in the city of Kiev, would know my name, much less my Hebrew name and my father's Hebrew name?

Again I looked around, and again the same white-bearded Jew was saying the *Kaddish* after the *Aleinu*. This time, I resolved to keep my eye on this old man. I had to know if I was completely losing my mind in this God-forsaken country.

I looked at him. His tallit was over his head, his eyes were still closed, he was swaying to and fro, totally oblivious to me, reciting the psalm for Wednesday. I remember how appropriate I thought that psalm was: "Lord, how long shall the wicked triumph? They crush Thy people, O Lord, and attempt to destroy Thy heritage. They say, the Lord will not see, He is not aware."

I watched him carefully. The reader pronounced the last words, *ki el gadol,* which was a signal for the mourners to begin the final *Kaddish*.

And then the old man, his eyes still closed, pronounced my name again and began saying the mourner's *Kaddish!* For a terrible moment, it seemed that he was saying it for me, and I trembled a great trembling. And then I quickly realized how foolish I had been, and what it was that he was really doing. He was only saying the mourner's *Kaddish* for a friend, or perhaps for someone who had left no children, and when you say *Kaddish* for someone who is not a relative, you must have that individual's name in mind, and you therefore whisper the name prior to the *Kaddish*. In effect, you are saying, "I am reciting this *Kaddish* in memory of—" This old man was saying *Kaddish* after someone whose name happened to be Menachem ben Yosef.

The mystery was solved, but it did leave me shaken, and I trembled again as he said the *Kaddish*, even though I knew that it was, thank God, not for me.

But was it not for me? Had I not felt, just one day before, as if I had been killed? Had I not died at Babi Yar? Had I not been shot a hundred thousand times at that scene, fallen forward a hundred thousand times, been shoveled over a hundred thousand times? Had I not died in Auschwitz, Bergen-Belsen, Buchenwald, Dachau, Treblinka; had I not died six million times? And was I not, at this moment, now in danger of dying three million times in the USSR? Why could he not be saying *Kaddish* for me, Menachem ben Yosef, as well as for the rest of the Jewish people?

Of course, I knew that he was saying *Kaddish* for someone who happened to have my name. But I shuddered with horror, for on another level of meaning, I knew for whom he was saying the mourner's *Kaddish*. He had never seen me, he did not know me, he would never again see me, but he was saying *Kaddish* for me and for the whole Jewish people.

I left Kiev that morning. But that brief encounter at the synagogue just would not leave me. Weeks went by, and it remained in all its vividness. It would not evaporate from my memory. It had too much impact, force, and power. And so profound was that experience that each day since that July day I have thought about it and what its implications truly are.

But after returning home, and as the summer wore on, the incident began to give me a certain sense of comfort. Gradually, it dawned on me that in reality, I had not, by the grace of God, died at all in the Babi Yar ravine. I remember clearly driving back down that road, back down past the railroad station, on the road away from the mass grave, back towards life. And I had not died in the death camps of the Nazis. Jews had been murdered many times before—by Pharaoh, Haman, Torquemada, the Crusaders, Hitler, Stalin—they had murdered us, but I was not dead. On the contrary, they were all dead, and I, Menachem ben Yosef—I and the Jewish people—were all alive. We bore wounds and scars, but I was quite alive. Were I not alive, would they still be trying to murder me?

Fine, I said to myself, but if I am alive, why is that man in Kiev saying *Kaddish* for me? How can I be comforted when I know that every morning and evening before the mourner's *Kaddish* he whispers my name?

But the answer it clear: *Kaddish* is not necessarily a prayer of sadness. *Kaddish* is a paean of praise to God. It all depends on your point of view.

Kaddish is not necessarily a tragedy; *Kaddish* can also represent triumph. *Kaddish* does not mention death at all: it praises God. It is not merely a lament, but also a poem of joy in God: not only a eulogy, but a reawakening; not only tears, but a reaffirmation, a statement of man's faith in the living God of Israel.

The man who recites *Kaddish* with tears in his eyes at the grave of a loved one is in fact saying: "God, I do not fully comprehend Thy mysterious ways, but I reaffirm my faith in Thee, and I reawaken and restate my trust in Thee. May Thy great name be magnified and sanctified. I stand at the threshold of the great mystery of life and death, and though I suffer, Thy name is supreme." Thus, in the profoundest sense, *Kaddish* is a triumphant message of renewed strength and faith in the Almighty.

Now, if *Kaddish* can be either a lament or words of triumph, what kind of *Kaddish* is that old man in Kiev reciting? Is it a *Kaddish* of mourning and tears, or a reaffirmation of Jewish life? Is it a *Yitgadal* with a resigned sob: this is the end of Jewish life? Or is it a *Yitgadal* of the beginning of faith in the future?

There is no single answer to that question. If we live our Jewish lives casually, carelessly, without seriousness, then that *Kaddish* is a *Kaddish* of mourning for the demise of a people. If, on the other hand, we live our Jewish lives with concern, with attention to holy details, then that old man's *Kaddish* is a reaffirmation of life for the Jewish people. The problems of the Jews in Russia will not easily go away. What can we do to help? Obviously, letters, wires, protests are important. But there is one way that American Jews have not yet tried. We must not play into the hands of our enemies by neglecting our Jewishness, by allowing it to grow stale. When we grow estranged from our beautiful heritage, we collaborate with all the tyrants of history who want nothing more than to see the *Kaddish* of mourning recited over the Jewish people. Every rejection of Jewishness is a victory for our enemies. If the enemies of the Jewish people wish to forbid Jewish learning, close Jewish schools, close synagogues, and ban Hebrew we must not play into their hands in a land of freedom, not give them a victory here which they cannot achieve there. If they want all synagogues to become museums, we must not permit it over here. The synagogue must become a living place, breathing with the presence of Jews at prayer.

If they consider Jewish mitzvot to be contraband, and confiscate tefillin, *ẓiẓit,* and *mezuzot,* we must not do the same here.

The old white-bearded Jew in Kiev will be saying *Kaddish* today at the end of services. Will it be a lament for the dead, or an affirmation for the living God of Israel? By our actions, we can transform his chant into a song of triumph, and history can still show that all of us lived, and did not die, at Babi Yar in Kiev.

The Russian Tallis

THERE ARE ALL kinds of talleisim. Some are tiny as shawls, and would barely do as a scarf on a wintry day; some are as huge as blankets; some are made of pretty silk or linen: dainty, light, colorful, glistening; some are heavy wool, without any attempt at being colorful, stylish, or fashionable.

There are all kinds of talleisim in all kinds of places. Let me take you along with me on a journey to visit some talleisim I have known: some are in Jewish book shops; some are in synagogues; some are in customs desks in Moscow; some are in bureau drawers of the nicest homes; and some are seen only in death.

First, some definitions: a tallis is a four-cornered garment requiring fringes *(ẓiẓit)* to be attached to it; the ẓiẓit are knotted in such a form that they remind us of God. In Biblical times, the tallis had a cord of blue among the fringes, so that any four-cornered garment required eight fringes on each of the four corners, and on each of the four corners there was one cord of blue among the eight fringes (Num. 15:38). Clothing styles changed, but in order to maintain the mitzvah we don a cloak of four corners which in turn requires the fringes—which is why a Jew wears the *tallit katan* over or under his shirt, plus a *tallit gadol*, the prayer-shawl as we know it today.

A tallis has certain measurements, and except for Yom Kippur eve, is a garment required to be worn only by day. The wearing of the *tallit katan* is a very easy mitzvah and is an eternal reminder of one's Jewishness.

There are all kinds of talleisim. Let me tell you about some of them.

Firstly, there is the tallis of Bar Mitzvah. Proudly, lovingly, the mother and father buy their son his first tallis which he will wear to recite the *berakhot* expressing his loyalty to God and Torah. That tallis is usually quite small, rather colorful, often made of linen or silk, and it has pretty blue stripes. It is a lovely moment in the life of a family.

There are other talleisim. A tallis that a man begins to wear when he is married, the tallis that denotes that now that he has become a married man he is no longer half a person but a full person. And this tallis—sometimes the wife, sometimes the father-in-law presents it to him—is of course much larger, is made of wool, and covers at least half the body, as a real tallis should.

Occasionally it remains brand-new, tucked away in a bureau drawer, to be pulled out only on very special occasions. In some cases it is used constantly, and every few years, as it grows old and worn, it has to be buried and a new tallis is obtained.

Talleisim: "clothes make the man, tallis makes the man." In New York's East Side there is a Jewish bookstore with a sign outside: "Specialists in custom-made talleisim: WE TAILOR THE TALLIS TO FIT YOU." I went inside, and there was a man getting fitted into a tallis. It was almost ludicrous. It was as if he were buying a suit. It occurred to me that many of us do just that, without the aid of the bookstore tallis specialist: we have taken the tallis of our religion and cut it down to size, trimmed it here, improved it there, streamlined it, shaped it so that it fits our standards. I don't know who that man was, and I am sure that ultimately he got himself a beautifully fitted tallis. The sign, however, should read: WE TAILOR YOU TO FIT THE TALLIS. This is what Torah is all about.

Talleisim: there are talleisim which are forgotten in shul by their owners, who never come back to pick them up: apparently they never miss them. I wonder about these talleisim: don't they feel abandoned, neglected, unwanted?

And there are the public talleisim, the ones that hang in shul, worn by different individuals each week. I think about them, too. On some Shabbosim one of these public talleisim might be worn by a worshipper who davens and pours his heart out to God, who thinks and listens and absorbs; at other times it may be worn by a person who chatters throughout the davening, who strolls in and out of shul, nervously counting the minutes until he can remove the tallis and be on his way.

One of my sweetest memories of youth is the Simḥat Torah tallis, when we used to tie together the ẓiẓit of everyone's tallis. And, of course, kal ha-ne'arim, when all the children would gather under a huge tallis, as if under a canopy, and a sudden solemnity touched us as we recited the *berakhah*. It was long before Bar Mitzvah, and what excitement it was to be called to the Torah.

There is the tallis of death, as well. When a man dies, the Ḥevra Kaddisha prepares his body before burial, with special washing and clothing—and the final garment is a tallis in which he is wrapped as he is placed in his final resting place. An individual once told me, as he watched his father being prepared by the Ḥevra Kaddisha: "You know, I never saw my father in a tallis before."

Yes, some talleisim tell very sad stories, and who knows how many sons and daughters in America have never seen their fathers wearing a tallis, have never seen their mothers in shul, or their parents give tzedakah, or a kosher home, or their family life wrapped up in a living tallis—until it was time to say *Kaddish* and *Yizkor*—and then God and talleisim and synagogue—all strangers—suddenly converged on the scene at center stage.

There is a poem about man's eternal battle with grass: man cuts and works and weeds and trims the grass throughout his lifetime; but, writes the poet Louis Untermeyer, it is a losing battle: in the end, the grass is the victor, because man

> Having exhausted every whim
> He stretches out each conquering limb
> And then the small grass covers him.

A tallis is much the same. We may try to put it away in a bureau drawer, get it out of mind, ignore it, forget it—but in the end, the tallis covers us finally and completely.

There are all kinds of talleisim: decorative talleisim, talleisim that are really only scarves, talleisim that wrap you completely and embrace you; talleisim that are always worn, talleisim that are rarely worn, talleisim that are placed upon you when it is too late.

Let me tell you about four large talleisim at the customs desk in Moscow. Several years ago, on a visit to Russia, I carried in my baggage extra supplies of prayer books, mezuzot, tefillin, Bibles, Siddurim, and some extra talleisim—all the things that are in desperately short supply in the Jewish communities of Russia and which I hoped to give to those who needed them.

In Moscow, the customs man piled up a number of these religious items on the counter. He was very suspicious, and I had to account for each one. To whom was I bringing all this? I assured him that I knew no one, had no friends in the Soviet Union. I had to explain the tefillin, the Hebrew books, the mezuzot. Then he pulled out four talleisim, and with each one his anger increased: "What is this, and what is this, and what is this!" he demanded. I stammered out some reasons, but he interrupted me: "My dear man, how many of these prayer-shawls do you need? You only need one!"

Two answers went through my mind like a flash, but I did not utter them. Instead, I mumbled something innocuous to the effect that it never hurts to have an extra set in case one gets lost. He was not satisfied, but somehow he reluctantly let me through, warning me not to give anything to anyone, and ordered me to have them in my possession when I left the country.

I share with you the two replies that flashed through my mind at that time, the replies that I would have liked to have given to the customs agent.

How many of these prayer-shawls do you need?

> I will tell you how many I need.
> I need six million
> for the Jews of the Holocaust who are buried
> without benefit of tallis.
>   I need another three million
> for the Jews of your Russia
> who cannot buy a tallis
> in the workers' paradise.
>   And, sadder yet,
> I need four million talleisim
> for Jews in the United States
> who are able to wear a tallis,
> who live in freedom and can afford to have one,
> but who know
> nothing about a tallis
> nothing about tzitzis
> nothing about Torah
> nothing about tradition
> about mitzvot,
> who are innocent and well-meaning,
> who have never been taught Torah,
> and who are assimilating and intermarrying
> in frightening proportions.
>   I need at least four million talleisim
> for the Jews of America
> who have never seen their fathers

in a tallis before.
I need, my dear customs agent,
descendant of the Cossacks,
representative of a regime which hates Jews and Israel,
I need, dear sir,
something like thirteen million talleisim.
You ask me, sir,
how many of these I need?
I brought only four.
I need thirteen million.

That was one answer that coursed through my brain. There was
another.

How many of these do I need?
I need only one,
You are right.
Just one is all I need.
In the ultimate scheme,
That's all anyone needs
and that's all anyone gets,
finally.
One lonely, solitary tallis.
This is my problem, this is my confusion.
As a Jew,
I need millions of talleisim.
As a Jew,
I need
only one.

A Holocaust Encounter

MILLIONS OF US were deeply moved by the recounting of the destruction of our people in Europe during the film *Holocaust* on TV. Whatever the merits of the program, it served to awaken within us that sense of history, memory, and shared suffering and destiny which is the stuff of our people. It was difficult for us to relive, even if we did not actually live it the first time, and painful to see how mankind, left to its own devices, can become a beast.

(I do not know what was worse: watching the recapitulation of the horror, or watching the juxtaposition of the commercials between the horror. The ads for deodorants and dog food and cleansers, juxtaposed with mass-murder scenes and views of mass graves, gave it all a surrealistic quality.)

But during the week in which the film appeared, a less public event occurred to me, one that actually caused me more pain than the film, and which in a real sense is connected with the film.

It happened on the day before the series was about to begin. I had an appointment with a young lady who was about to marry a non-Jewish man. Her parents, frantic, had asked me to talk with her.

I had never met the young lady, I did not know her family, she was from another community entirely. She came in, we spoke. She was a student at college, had met a non-Jewish boy whom she "loved" and with whom she became involved, and she was now about to marry him: the usual sad story of an intermarriage. And, of course, today, by our standards, when you are "in love" nothing may stand in the way: not reason, not concern for one's family, nor for one's heritage, nor for two thousand years of Jewish history.

I expected the next question to be: "Rabbi, will you convert him to keep peace in the family?" But it soon became apparent that she had different ideas. This girl was on the verge of abandoning Judaism altogether. "Why not believe in Christianity?" she asked me. "Why

244

should the crucifixion and the moral qualities of Christianity be foreign to us? Why are Jews so stubborn that we refuse to accept Christ as the Messiah?"

I was taken completely by surprise. Not only was she ready to marry out of the faith, but here was a new breed: she was ready to leave the faith entirely and was parroting to me the superficial arguments of the missionaries.

I spoke with her for over one hour, and it was clear that she knew nothing about the Torah, Jewish life, Jewish tradition, Jewish beliefs, Jewish practice. She had never studied, never learned anything about Judaism. I tried to appeal to her emotions, to her sense of loyalty: that we are a people of martyrs, saints, who gave our lives for Torah and God, and was she ready to turn her back on her own suffering people? That she is part of the line of tradition that began with Abraham and Sarah, and that now, voluntarily and deliberately, this line would come to an end with her, that her children and grandchildren would not be Jewish for the first time in four thousand years. She cried a bit, and we decided that we would talk again. I also suggested to her that she make certain to watch the Holocaust film.

I do not know how much good I did her, how effective our conversation was. I felt as if I were involved in a Mephistophelian struggle for her soul. But I do know that she affected me deeply. I remember having to attend a committee meeting right after talking with her, and I recall that I could not concentrate on the deliberations, so shaken was I by our encounter: here was a fine, sweet Jewish girl who was ready to throw it all overboard.

And why? There was nothing in her background to indicate that she would abandon Judaism. She came from a nice family; they had an annual Pesaḥ Seder; they went to synagogue on Rosh Hashanah and Yom Kippur and for *Yizkor;* she had gone to Sunday School, had been "confirmed." Her mother and father occasionally gave some money to Israel, they were active in Jewish organizational life, they "love" being Jewish, they eat bagels and lox and gefilte fish; and on Pesaḥ they eat no bread.

They were, in a word, a typically Jewish family. Of course, there was nothing extreme about them: nothing like kashruth in the home or Shabbat or even Yom Tov—simply a typical Jewish family.

Why, then, was this great tragedy about to befall this typical American Jewish family?

The question answers itself: when you live the life of a typical American Jewish family, when your standards are those of the non-

Jewish world, when your children see no sense of dedication or commitment to Judaism; when there is no sacrifice, no strength, no Jewish study, no learning—such tragedies will befall such typical American Jewish families as surely as night follows day. It is the children of such typical American Jewish families who make up the latest statistics of a fifty percent intermarriage rate among Jewish young people in America.

It is such typical families who, according to a recent demographic study from Harvard, will be responsible for the American Jewish community population one hundred years from now, which may have a maximum of four hundred thousand Jews (from today's over five million!) and possibly as little as ten thousand—because we will lose the rest through intermarriage, assimilation, and an abysmally low birthrate.

And when I spoke to that young lady, I saw not only one, but hundreds of thousands of such wonderful young people, innocent and ignorant, who, because their parents simply went along and were "typical" and not different, are creating in America a Holocaust of our own. And that is why I found my conversation with her even more painful than watching the drama on TV.

For we can resist the enemy. We can resist him spiritually and we can outlive him—when we know who we are. The question that gnaws at me is this: can we resist the enemy when the enemy is us?

And the enemy is us when we live by the standards of the world rather than our own. The enemy is us when we have Jewish schools in our community—day schools and yeshivot—and we send our children elsewhere. The enemy is us when our way of life, our style of life, is measured by the standards of the world around us—what will *they* think, how will *they* react?—rather than by the standards of eternity. The enemy is us when every study and survey demonstrates that the Torah-oriented family suffers fewer breakups, less intermarriage, and has more stability than any other. And the enemy is us when we choose to ignore these facts.

We have seen what the values of the world are. We have experienced in our lifetime where it leads. We have seen that there can be Christmas trees and "Silent Night" and Bach and Beethoven and pretty roses right in front of the crematoria. Culture, sophistication, worldly ways: we have seen where these can lead. Are we now going to go over to their side and live by their values and turn our back to the one civilization and culture in which man and woman have not become animals, and which has not brutalized humankind?

What we saw on TV in *Holocaust* was the inevitable result of that very Western Christian civilization which we think is so important that we cast everything overboard just to be accepted by it—and just a few decades after the Holocaust.

To my great sadness, I occasionally find that certain parents will accept with more equanimity the marriage of their children out of the faith than the prospect of their child becoming Jewishly observant. They may find the presence of a yarmulke and ẓiẓit on their children more unsettling than the presence of a non-Jewish daughter-in-law. A kosher home, Shabbat, *mikveh*, true Jewish commitment—are often fought with more vigor than intermarriage and assimilation. We have met the enemy and he is us.

We are a heroic people—not because we resisted in the Warsaw Ghetto, but because we are faithful to a dream and a memory and an ideal; because we are stubborn, because we are spiritual heroes. We are the heroic, martyr people who resisted all the blandishments of the Pharaohs and Hamans and Torquemadas and Stalins and Hitlers and have—at least until now—emerged triumphant.

Will we now voluntarily slip out of the camp, go AWOL over to the enemy, and live by his standards?

Have we come to this in America—that we will voluntarily surrender to those who would destroy us?

We suffered and moaned as we saw the *Holocaust* film; we were repelled with horror; we shed tears. But we are witnessing in the United States a Holocaust of our own doing.

A Man Touched by God: A Walk with S. Y. Agnon

SHMUEL YOSEF AGNON was out for a stroll in the afternoon sun of Jerusalem, brilliant even in February, and he asked me to join him. There was no hint in his appearance—short stature, ruddy complexion, unobtrusive bearing—that here was a Nobel laureate. Only his luminous blue-gray eyes and sharply etched nose suggested the extraordinary.

Well known as he has been in Israel for so many years, he was surely accustomed to the rigors of fame. But had his new international recognition affected his life in any way?

"I am not a young man. The papers say I am seventy-eight, and I suppose they are right. For months now I have been doing nothing but giving interviews and greeting well-wishers. This is my first walk in a long time. The prize gave me much honor, but it is an honor wrapped in much trouble. From morning to evening they come to my door—professors, neighbors, students. Can I say no to them? Tourists come with their children, ask me to step outside and pose with them. They snap a picture and they disappear. I am trying to do my work, I am trying to answer all my mail, but I will need twenty years just for that." Abruptly he turned to me and said rather briskly, "Well, what can I do for you?"

Off guard, I chose the wrong question: why had he changed his name to Agnon many years ago, and did this have any connection with the title of one of his early stories, "Agunot," which means "alone, bereft, isolated"? "Yes, there is a connection," he said, and walked along silently, obviously unwilling to elaborate.

I turned to his craft. Does he deliberately write in the symbols and metaphors which the critics see in his work; does he in fact read the critics at all?

"Critics say many things, but I want you to know that I don't read the critics. First of all, I certainly don't read the foreign critics, because I don't know their language. And even in Israel I tend to ignore them. Critics are not always reliable. I've never been one to give out details of my life—I have written no autobiography—but they write things about me as if they were facts. Totally untrue things. Now I understand how history is made. Everyone writes what he pleases—or what pleases him. It's all very subjective, even when it comes to cold facts that are not matters of judgment.

"There are writers who are greatly influenced by critics and by what they say, and there are others who are not. I, in general, am not greatly affected by my surroundings or by what is said about me. I live in the modern State of Israel, and I love it, yet I write very little about it. Everyone about me speaks modern Hebrew, yet I don't write in modern Hebrew.

"As for the symbols they find, different people will see different things. Look over there. Some will say, 'The sun is setting beneath the earth.' Others might say, 'The evening is rising from the earth.' Who is to say which one is right? They are both right. Or take the *Aleinu* [the concluding prayer of each of the three daily services]. We are so familiar with it, we say it so often that we just mumble it quickly without giving it much heed. But comes Rosh Hashanah and Yom Kippur, and what happens to the poor *Aleinu?* It becomes the focal point of the services. The entire congregation rises, they open the Holy Ark, and they read the *Aleinu* as they prostrate themselves, and the cantor chants every single word slowly. What has changed? The *Aleinu* is the same. Why suddenly all the fuss and bother? The answer is that we are different on those days. Take different attitudes and different approaches, and the same words mean different things. Especially in Hebrew. Every word has thousands of shades and nuances. Whatever a man sees in my writing—if he has a trained mind and an attuned heart, that is in my writing." And then, almost as an afterthought, he added with a smile, "The word that God puts into my mouth, that do I speak."

Agnon knows the Bible too well not to be aware of the undertones of this last remark: it is a quotation from Numbers 27:38, and is uttered by the heathen prophet Balaam. This is a typical Agnonism and reveals his mastery of original sources as well as his sense of irony about himself. Although the world makes much of his ability to call easily upon the resources of the Bible, Agnon exemplifies many Jews for whom the Bible and its accompanying literature have since childhood been natural components of daily vocabulary. Perhaps it is in the puckish quality with which Agnon clothes the source material that part of his uniqueness lies. Later, when I asked his son about his father's constant utilization of the supernatural in his stories, he replied, "You must understand that my father has a fine gift of laughter." It may be that the key to much of the dark mystery surrounding Agnon's use of metaphor and allegory is precisely in his ability to poke fun at himself and at the world around him, which in his eyes contains no border between the mysterious and the ordinary, and where there is, in Musil's phrase, "a sliding away of boundaries."

From Agnon's front steps, incidentally, one can almost reach out and touch the desolate hills across the Israel-Jordan boundary line. Every so often he would stop short, touch my arm, point to the hills, and say, "Look, just look," and we would stare across the border at the softly rounded slopes brooding in the strange yellow light of the afternoon sun. I thought of Leah Luria in his "The Betrothed," who is so deeply moved by the sight of the moon on the sea that she can only call out, "Girls, girls, just look! Look!"

How does one put into another language the subtle rhythms and cadences, the artlessness, the archaic tone, the radiance and lyricism of a prose that is really poetry? Did Agnon think he could be adequately translated or understood by anyone who was not oriented in the nuances of Jewish life and learning?

He smiled. "The Nobel Prize Committee members do not read Hebrew, they were not brought up in Judaism, they do not study Talmud. But apparently this did not bother them.

"I will tell you. I don't know French, yet I read Flaubert in translation and appreciate him. I don't know Russian, yet I read Dostoevsky in translation and appreciate him. Certain aspects of writing are evident even in a translation. I can take any story, in any translation, read any two lines and know if it's trash or worth reading further. I don't think Edmund Wilson knows Hebrew, but a long time ago he proposed me for the Nobel Prize."

Agnon looked up at the sky. "Come, it grows dark and you must be getting cold. Let us go to my house." I protested that I had already taken enough of his time. "No, no. It's chilly and you must have a cup of tea before you go." He guided me up an unpaved street to an old, pleasant-looking cottage surrounded by an iron fence. He carefully scraped his shoes on the concrete walk. "My wife has no helper, and when I come in with mud all over my shoes I just cause her extra work."

Inside, Mrs. Agnon was darning his socks at the dining-room

table. "Get him a cup of tea right away, my dear. The poor man is freezing." Dainty and graceful even in her seventies, she nodded knowingly and disappeared into the kitchen.

"She is a good woman for putting up with me. I am a totally disorganized person. I save every scrap of paper; my workroom is always a shambles. There is no *seder*, no order in my life—even in normal times. And now I get fifty letters a day, and I try to answer them all. Each one took the trouble to write me. Shouldn't he get a reply?

"Nelly Sachs has sent me everything—books, manuscripts, poems. She is a kind soul. I have sent her nothing yet, I've been so busy. But she has been busy too. My son helps me a little. He is an engineer, so he should be a little more orderly than I am.

"It is interesting. People keep telling me, 'Agnon, you are the glory of all Israel.' Why am I the glory of all Israel? Because the nations now approve of me?"

I asked permission to take a snapshot of him. "Go right ahead." As the camera snapped he said playfully, "Not good; you'd better take it again. My eyes blinked." Was he twitting me? I wasn't quite sure but I took it again. "Pictures," he said, "pictures, the whole world is pictures. What is it about a picture that is so fascinating?"

He rose suddenly from his chair. "You must excuse me for a moment. It's practically nightfall and I've almost forgotten about *Minḥah* [the afternoon prayer]." He went into the next room. Agnon adheres scrupulously to such traditional practices as blessings before and after meals, morning and evening worship, strict observance of Sabbaths, holy days, and dietary laws. While he goes about these duties in a natural and unostentatious way, they are not merely perfunctory acts but part of an intricate pattern of a life that is pervaded by the past.

For example, when asked what he considers his greatest literary achievements, he likes to reply, "*Yamim Nora'im* and *Attem Re'item* [*Days of Awe* and *Ye Have Seen*] plus some additional tales and novels." Each of these books is a compilation of ancient homilies and anecdotes, one based on the High Holidays and the other on the Sinaitic Revelation. For Agnon to select these anthologies as his best work may be a whimsical joke on his public, but it is more likely that it underscores his preoccupation with the tradition.

In view of all this, would Agnon classify himself as a religious writer? The answer seems obvious, but he evades it: "I am a writer. I do not need labels." What is clear is that he is far from being the simple man of simple faith he tries to project. The European Jewish

Holocaust and the apparent hiddenness of God left their mark on him and his craft: his Galician town of Buczacz, so endemic to his work, is the *Everyshtetl* whose caftans and earlocks went up in smoke—and only Sinai (God reaching down to man) and the Days of Awe (man reaching up to God) remain intact. This may account for the classic Agnon character who embodies, in Edmund Wilson's phrase, "the granting and withholding of divine grace."

Agnon himself is the prototype of this ambivalence. On the one hand is his anguished awareness of a God who is able to withdraw from the affairs of man; on the other, despite his air of a man who does not take himself too seriously, is his apparent view of himself as having been touched by this God. In his Nobel acceptance speech he claims to be "of the lineage of the Prophet Samuel." He continued:

> In a vision of the night I saw myself standing with my brother Levites in the Holy Temple, singing with them the songs of David, King of Israel. . . . The angels in charge of the Shrine of Music . . . made me forget by day what I had sung by night, for if my brethren were to hear, they would be unable to bear their grief over the happiness they have lost. To console me for having prevented me from singing with my mouth, they enabled me to compose songs in writing.

This is poetry, but his phrase "the words that God puts into my mouth" is apparently more than banter.

The alternately hiding and speaking God is part of the complexity of Shmuel Yosef Agnon. Perhaps this is why he is open and innocent, yet elusive and melancholy; congenial and friendly, yet lonely and brooding; gentle, but capable of a sharp retort; reaching for others, but himself unreachable. His friend Professor Gershom Scholem describes Agnon's frequent conversations with others as "actually walls guarding his loneliness."

Agnon calls to mind his own story "Tranquility," in which the just and God-fearing neighbor of Moses asks the lawgiver to do him a personal favor when he goes up to Sinai: would he kindly ask the Lord to grant him a little tranquility? Moses promises to do what he can. After his mission is done, Moses puts in a good word for his neighbor. And God replies: "Son of Amram, everything that I created, I created during the first six days; but tranquility I did not create." Agnon is that restless neighbor, still searching for that which he alone must create.

The Rock Singer and the Rebbe

IT IS ABOUT four o'clock in the afternoon. At noon the radio had broadcast the news that the man who lived on this particular street had died. The news was totally unexpected. The morning papers had mentioned nothing about it, and yet here they were—one hundred thousand people on the street, and according to some estimates close to a quarter of a million. They were from all walks of life. One could tell from their garb, from their manner. All had apparently come to this street to pay spontaneous tribute to this individual who had died. If you looked upward, on the balconies and rooftops, it was crowded with yet more people of all colors and hues. In the background, mothers with babes in their arms all came to pay tribute. And not just tribute: one could tell from the faces that they were not just spectators but fellow mourners grieving over an irreparable loss.

Who was this man who had died and who was able to muster up so much respect and love, for whom hundreds of thousands the world over were willing to weep, though they knew him not?

This scene that I describe is taken from the Israeli newspaper *Maariv*. It describes the death and funeral—not of the famous rock singer from Memphis—but *le-havdil*, the death and funeral of the Gerrer Rebbe, who died last spring in Jerusalem at the age of eighty-three.

I will tell you about the Gerrer Rebbe shortly. Suffice it to say that although his funeral attracted almost a quarter of a million people, most American Jews probably never heard of him or his funeral.

What we did and still do hear of is the other mass funeral that took place last month in Memphis for the famous king of rock and roll. There was a frenzy at his funeral; women fainted in the streets. It was a front-page story for weeks; he appeared on the covers of the national magazines; people wore black T-shirts in mourning; de-

253

mands for his recordings and memorabilia are still heavy. A woman interviewed at the airport on the way to the funeral in Memphis said, "Why, for me he was the next thing to God." Letters to the editor, months later, said, "I still can't get over it."

These two funerals are a remarkable study in contrast. We all know who the rock singer from Memphis was. Many of us were brought up on his music. We are aware of the revolution in pop music of which he was a beginner and a pioneer. He is part of the air we breathe, part of the ambience of our everyday existence.

But few of us know who the Rebbe of Ger was. His name was Yisroel Alter and he was the most recent of a family of saintly and scholarly giants who lived in Ger, also known as Gur, a small town in Poland. His great-grandfather, known as the "Rim," was the author of a compendium of Talmud still widely used. His grandfather was equally great and noble and saintly. His work, the *Sefat Emet*, is a basic text in Biblical commentary. His father, Avraham Mordecai Alter, was of the same genre. Upon the death of his father, he, Yisroel Alter, took over the dynasty. In 1948, after losing his wife and son and daughter, and having escaped the dragnet of the Nazis, he came to Jerusalem—which was itself under siege. R. Yisroel Alter, the spiritual leader of a hundred thousand Polish Jews who had looked to him for direction, took over the leadership of the surviving remnants of Hasidim who had been all but decimated in Europe. The few straggling survivors now in Israel were in despair, despondent, shattered.

I must confess that when the mourning for the pop idol from Memphis reached its peak, my mind went back a few months earlier to the death of the Gerrer Rebbe and his mass mourning. I was struck by the external similarity and the essential contrast: here were two diametrically opposing symbols: a *zaddik* and saint on the one hand, a pop idol and drug addict on the other; on the one hand, the Rebbe, saintly, pious, shunning publicity, quietly doing God's work on earth; on the other, the pop idol, dressed in sequins, with blue eye shadow and pink shirts and dozens of multicolored spotlights focused on him.

On the one hand, the Rebbe: living the godly life, denying himself, unconcerned with self and things and goods, devoting his days to the furtherance of Torah and saintliness in the world, appealing to the most spiritual instincts of his followers.

On the other, the singer: packaged, wrapped, hyped, amassing a huge fortune, symbolizing the body, the physical, the vulgar, appealing to the animal instincts in his followers.

On the one hand, a man who represents the spirit; on the other, a man who represents the body. On the one hand, heaven; on the other, earth. On the one hand, the future ultimate destiny of the holy people, against the now and the immediate. The one, who lived the life of simplicity, died at peace with himself and the world; while the other lived a tormented life in the midst of plenty, a life of personal unhappiness and fear, and drugs and guns and misery.

One represents the godly soul, the presence of God within a human being; the other represents the animal vitality and dynamism of the body and of the flesh.

One gave his life to others, and was constantly sought out by people; the other died a tormented recluse, shunned by those who knew him best.

And this is precisely the point. Each of these lives is a paradigm, a symbol of a particular way of life. One represents Jewish life as it has always been and was always meant to be: a life of meaning and fulfillment, of spirituality, of building, of spiritual triumph, of inner joy. And the other kind of life which we see about us is essentially godless, hedonistic, pleasure seeking, destructive of the self.

Each type of life has a certain power, and each has attracted passionate adherents. We ourselves live in a society which tugs and pulls us in various directions. Certainly if we were to ask which type of life in the United States is more powerful and has the most influence on our lives—the one represented by the pop idol or the one represented by the Rebbe, the answer would be obvious. The miracle is that despite the magnetic pull of hedonism, we still identify as Jews.

Why is the pop idol's attraction so powerful? Because it represents the power of nature in the raw, and nature in the raw is difficult to resist. It appeals to the animal within us, the beast within us, the appetites and hungers within us. And who can resist that—particularly when it was the enthusiastic approval of an entire society of hundreds of millions of people. And when everyone is doing something one way and you are doing it another way, when everyone is living one way and behaving one way, and you are moving and behaving in another, you get worn down, you get worn out, you begin to feel that they are right and that something is wrong with you.

We live in a wanton, orgiastic, hedonistic, pleasure-seeking society which insists on fun at all costs, pleasure at all costs, amusement at all costs: a mad pursuit of sensuality without limit. This is an age which regards all that is possible as permissible, which acknowledges no restraint in human appetites, which asks not why, but why not?

This is the magnet of idolatry, the attraction of paganism—and the Torah acknowledges its power. But the Torah says: we are not simply creatures of instinct and urges and appetites. The Torah says that God created nature and that God created us, and there is such a thing as discipline, there is such a thing as restraint. Yes, there is a place for the physical in our lives, there is room for the material. We do have to eat, we do have appetites. But the Torah supplies the wherewithal to live spiritually in a physical world.

The irony is that this world of pleasure and gratification does not really satiate or fulfill or satisfy except in the most fleeting, temporary way. It requires more and ever more just to stand in the same place. It requires constant seeking of new thrills, of new excitements, new varieties which themselves become instantaneously old, engendering again the never-ending search for something new. And the result is no real joy, no real excitement, no real verve; instead, there is misery, torment, anguish. We live in a society where life has little value, where moral pollution and the desanctification of life are the norm.

"I set before you life and death," says the Torah, "and you shall choose life." Why does the Torah need to command us to choose life? Is this not a natural human choice? The answer is that without the commandment, it is tempting to choose death—because on the surface death is attractive. Thus, says the Torah, I remind you to be careful in your choice. There is the glittering surface attraction of rock idols which looks like real life and happiness, and there is a life of Torah which appears like a denial of life and enjoyment.

The idols are dressed in sequins and pearls, they dance under a thousand multicolored lights, they glitter and they dazzle the eye, and they penetrate the brain and the heart and the intellect and the soul.

But this is not life, for beneath it all is tinsel, falsehood, artificiality, sham, fraud—promising everything, delivering nothing. Worse: it delivers emptiness, frustration, dashed hopes, wasted dreams, disillusionment. Therefore: "You shall choose life." Look at life around you and ask yourself if this is what you want for yourselves, is this what you want for your children: broken homes are the norm; selfishness is the norm; immorality is the norm; cheating is the norm; alcoholism is the norm.

The Rebbe and the drug addict: the choice is yours.

Jews and Blacks on Wabash Avenue

[This essay was written in 1954, before full integration came to Atlanta.]

WABASH AVENUE IS a quiet street in mid-Atlanta, Georgia, a street of well-mowed lawns, dogwood trees which bloom with a sudden whiteness each April, of neat houses with sloping red-and-blue asphalt roofs, of many birds which in the springtime sing from dawn until night. Cars are parked in front of most of the lawns: a '51 Plymouth, a few Chevrolets, an old Buick, one or two newer Fords.

The residents of Wabash Avenue: two Greek families with many children; a woman recently widowed; an immigrant Jewish couple who own a grocery store downtown; an elderly native-southerner Baptist lady who lives alone; several middle-aged couples; a rabbi. Most own their own homes. The street is clean, residential, and white.

But beginning one block south of Wabash Avenue, Negroes, seeping from the bottled crowdings of their South Side settlements, have in the past few years expanded their traditional boundaries northward. At Wabash Avenue they stopped, and the friendly folks on Wabash have since been living in a suspended state of hush and whisper.

In August, most of the talk on the hot summer nights, on the Wabash Avenue porches lit by yellow antibug lights, through the polite tinkling of iced-tea glasses and Coca-Cola, was about Mrs. Wasser, the recent widow. Some had heard that she was selling out to Negroes. "And why not," someone asked, "she's alone and she wants to move and she has to sell to *someone*." Someones, it was obvious, were hard to find, for Wabash Avenue had become a no-man's-land, with whites afraid to buy houses there because of the proximity to Negroes, and Negroes afraid to buy there because it was still white territory. And yet they felt that the widow, if the rumors were true, was somehow betraying the rest of the block. "If she has to move, why can't she rent to white folks?"

Rumors soon became facts. A "For Sale" sign appeared early the next month on her lawn. It bore the name of an obscure real estate agent. Scrupulous tracing by neighbors showed that he was colored. A similar sign soon appeared on the lawn next door, also with a colored name. At first there was disbelief that such things could be done, then deep resentment, then wishful waiting: it could never happen here on Wabash, no matter what; the neighborhood has to be zoned for colored before they can move in; even if a Negro does buy a home, he'll probably rent to whites; it's the northern interests who are buying the houses for them just to muddy the waters, but they can't move in just like that; and so on. But that same month it was said that Negro real estate agents had been ringing many doorbells, inquiring.

In the pale light of the late October afternoons the menfolks raked leaves into tiny hills in the gutters, leaned on their rakes, and chatted. They were certain that the colored would never go through with it. They had heard that the banks were being very careful with their loans, and that the prices asked for the houses were too high for the Negroes. A week later, however, signs appeared suddenly on four of the neat lawns. And in the evening, as the men burned the leaves, the large red letters on the signs were visible through the smoke. They were not real estate signs. They said:

This is WHITE Property
Not For Sale.

In December it was said that some of the white property owners had been visited by Negro prospects who were admitted through backdoors at night. This was denied. In January, Mrs. Wasser was seen showing several Negroes through her home. In February she moved. And on a sunny day in March a small green delivery truck stopped in front of the empty house, a Negro and his wife stepped out, and from the back of the truck four children came whooping. Slowly, systematically, they began moving in their furniture.

It was noontime, few people were at home. Those who were pulled aside curtains and from their darkness stared blankly. The two older boys were soberly helping with the furniture, and the little girls, beribboned hair jouncing, jumped in the garden, rolled in the grass, leaped around the house, touching, exploring, shrieking. Their father shushed them.

Across the street the signs stubbornly protested, "This is WHITE Property—Not For Sale." But their bold redness was faded now from the winter. Only the large WHITE was clearly seen, and even that would be washed away with the next good rain.

Negroes have now been living on Wabash Avenue for several months, but there have been no incidents. The white folks on Wabash are quiet, they do not throw bombs. A fire did break out one night in one of the houses which was about to be sold to another Negro, and the owner, asleep, was asphyxiated, and swiftly the rumors flew that the fire had been deliberate, that it was arson, and some said that it served him right for selling out, and the people clucked their tongues and said, "You never can tell what will happen." But the fire chief found nothing wrong, and people forgot about it. Of bombs there have been none; of talk there has been an abundance. When neighbor says hello to neighbor the inevitable question is: "Are you moving or are you staying?"

"I don't know," most will answer, "I put a lot of money into my house."

One or two, unlike their signs, are still spirited. They will stick it out. They feel it's a shame the street's going colored, such a nice street, too. They hope the neighbors will stick together and that nobody will move. They like Negroes, don't misunderstand, and they know the Negroes have to move someplace, but it's a shame that it has to be Wabash.

But everybody else is not so resolute. They are deeply troubled. They greet the new Negro neighbor on the street when they see him, and they are polite. But as he walks on they pause and look back at him and are puzzled, because he seems so refined and well behaved; his house is immaculate, the grass is cut, and the roses this summer seem to have splashed forth even more ferociously red on the bushes of his lawn.

To some it is a religious problem. They come to the rabbi for guidance. They sit in his study, and one woman blurts out desperately, "What should we do, what should we do? We feel we have to move, but is it right for us to go? They're God's creatures too—I suppose in heaven there won't be no special section for colored. But—you see I was raised in a small town in south Georgia. I lived around them all my life, and I know what it's like. Right now they're quiet and all, and clean, but you just wait, and soon they'll be all over the street and noisy and dirty and all. I want to do the right thing."

The rabbi replies that one must do what one thinks is right and that the decision must be made with one's self.

The woman's sign is now gone and she is moving. The Negro to whom she is selling, she says, is extremely nice, well mannered, and clean.

And so it goes. It is only a matter of time. The Greek families with their children, the rabbi, the immigrant Jewish couple, the widows, even the one or two who are spirited—all will go. Slowly, gradually, like sand seeping from a clenched fist, they will move, and Wabash will go colored.

The next street above us is Angier Avenue. We must go and visit the white folks on Angier. Find out how they're getting on.

After the End and Before the Beginning; Erev Rosh Hashanah

THERE IS A certain magic moment that comes only once a year, and that is the moment between the last *Minḥah* prayer of the old year and the first *Ma'ariv* prayer of the new. The last *Kaddish* of the afternoon is recited, and then the *Ḥazzan* mounts the center *bimah* to intone the first word of the first evening *Ma'ariv* of the new year.

If time must have a stop, it takes place at this moment just after the end and before the beginning. The sun hangs in the evening sky, unmoving; there is a hush in the world; God closes the book of the old year, puts it away, and opens up the book of the new year.

The last word of the old year: do you know what it is? The last word of the concluding *Kaddish* of *Minḥah*: Amen. The first word of the new year: do you know what it is? *Barekhu.*

Amen signifies agreement, acceptance, affirmation. We say Amen to His rule over us, to His guidance of our lives, to His dominion over the affairs of mankind. Amen was heard hundreds of times a day, every day of the old year.

Barekhu is an imperative: "you shall bless." It is a public call to worship. It is the keynote of the new year. *Barekhu* will be heard every night of the new year, and every morning, and every time the Torah is read.

Amen, the end; *Barekhu*, the beginning. And in between the Amen and the *Barekhu* is mankind, standing at the end of one adventure, and poised at the outset of a new one.

The end and the beginning happen just once a year. It is a mysterious, awesome, delicate instant, a moment when time stands still.

261

With Tongue in Cheek

Sometimes it is in his attempts at humor that the real person emerges. I offer to the reader in this section a small sample of some pieces which have entertained me—and a few others—over the years. Whether they are truly reflective of the rabbi who wrote them is not clear, but it is true that these offerings, perhaps more than some of the weightier ones in the other sections, accurately mirror the Jewish life of these past decades. Certainly pieces such as these have enabled me to vent my annoyance and occasional frustration at the foibles of the American Jewish community, its organizations— and disorganizations—its lay leaders, its rabbis, its pretenses, its superficialities—and thus to retain some semblance of my own sanity. That these brief notes have now and then caused people to smile, and in rare moments perchance to laugh, has been sufficient reward for me even when the conditions lampooned have failed to change one iota. It is a never-ending source of gratification that although I may have labored mightily over some of the essays and lectures in this collection, those which people remember most clearly and vividly are often these light thrusts at our own weaknesses. And so they are offered here with a wink, a smile, and a sigh.

The Dismissal: A Dramatic Tale of American Jewish Leadership

MR. JACK MOSESON was today asked to resign from the board of directors of America's leading Jewish organization: the prestigious International Council of the World's Greatest Jewish Leaders.

This was shocking news, for Moseson had always been a Jewish Leader, and had supported every worthwhile Jewish organization—and even some that were not worthwhile. In the past decade alone he had received twelve Man-of-the-Year awards, and been honored at seventeen testimonial dinners. He had been photographed with Moshe Dayan ten times, Menachem Begin three times, and Abba Eban eleven times. He had kissed Golda Meir on the cheek on two separate occasions (after having each time pledged $100,000 to the UJA), and his picture had been featured in the centerfold of the *Jerusalem Post* when he last visited Israel on the Prime Minister's Mission. The caption had said that "he was second only to Moses in his beneficence to the total Jewish people." (This was after he had pledged $250,000 to the UJA.) He was, in brief, the very model of a modern Jewish Leader.

But at today's meeting of the board of directors of the International Council of the World's Greatest Jewish Leaders, Moseson was asked to resign because of conduct unbecoming a Jewish Leader. The allegations against him were so serious that the other Great Leaders really had no alternative but to ask him to step down.

It all began when the International Chairman of ICWGJL (himself the possessor of twelve medals of honor from the State of Israel, and the recent recipient of the coveted annual Greatest Jewish Leader of All the Ages Award) stated that a member of the board had been conducting himself in a manner unbecoming a Great Jewish Leader, and that according to the bylaws, such conduct results in automatic dismissal from the board. "I regret to do this," he said, "but the integrity of this organization must be preserved at all costs. The eyes of the world are upon us."

"What did he do?" asked a member of the board.

"It is too painful for me to recount in detail. Suffice it to say that Moseson has caused great embarrassment to us all, and it simply does not reflect well upon the total Jewish community."

During subsequent questioning, it was shown that as of two months ago Moseson had willfully and with premeditation attended daily minyan in the synagogue regularly (though he was not a *Kaddish*-sayer), read eight Jewish books, transferred his children to day schools and yeshivot, worshipped in synagogue every Shabbat (even when there was no Bar Mitzvah), and had been giving less money to Jewish hospitals and Jewish defense agencies and more to Jewish educational institutions.

"Good grief," gasped a Leader, "next thing you know, he'll be trying to get us all to pray regularly!"

The Chairman arose: "Jack, you know that as Great Jewish Leaders, we are honor-bound to represent the Total Jewish Community. Your actions have offended part of this community. Furthermore, we have more damning evidence against you. We know, for example, that you have a daily schedule of study in which you read Bible, Mishnah, and *Shulḥan Arukh*. You also have been observing Shabbat strictly. My God, Jack, where is your sense of community? Where is your loyalty to this board?"

"What's a Mishnah?" whispered a board member.

"Look here," said the Chairman. "Our job is to help Jewish life, not to become a fanatic! Why couldn't you be mature about this thing?"

"Well, sir," said Moseson, "it's only that the Torah—"

"The Torah!" scoffed the Chairman. "Jack, this is a community organization. Don't try to confuse the issue."

"What's a Torah?" whispered a board member.

Moseson continued: "My rabbi says that the Torah—"

"Your rabbi!" said another Leader, who had recently been photographed shaking Shimon Peres's hand. "We love, respect, and venerate your esteemed rabbi, but he really ought not to meddle in communal affairs. When we need an invocation, we will get in touch with him."

And so it was that the board of directors of the International Council of the World's Greatest Jewish Leaders made its decision. For conduct unbecoming a member of the Total Jewish Community, Jack Moseson was asked to resign. A truck was dispatched to his house to pick up his plaques, photographs, Man-of-the-Decade citations, and Great Jewish Leader awards.

The next day the Chairman of the ICWGJL was quoted in the *New York Times* in a three-column spread: "It is the task of Jewish Leaders to have vision, especially when the principle of total Jewish communal cooperation is at stake. Our heritage teaches us that a Jew has to have the courage to take a stand." The article reported that Moseson was unavailable for comment, but that he was last seen entering a little synagogue in order to engage in a "*daven-mincha* ceremony." A *Times* editorial the next day applauded the "courageous action" of the ICWGJL, declaring that "it is questionable whether those who would engage in exotic rites such as Torah study and *daven-mincha* ceremonies can really be entrusted with the awesome responsibilities of Jewish Leadership."

At the subsequent World Convention of the ICWGJL, the International Chairman received the newly minted "Moses and Aaron Medal" for visionary dedication to the eternal principles of Jewish life.

Once Upon a Peace

PEACE CAME TO Israel that year with electrifying swiftness. The Arabs signed a mutual-aid pact with Israel, and as a gesture of solidarity with world Jewry, Russia granted full freedom of emigration to Soviet Jews. Israel's economy boomed, and she notified the world that it was no longer necessary to raise funds for her needs. The stunning tidings brought dancing to the streets of world Jewry, with mass demonstrations and prayers of thanksgiving.

But a pall hung over the offices of UJA, Israel Bonds, and a hundred local Federations. The clattering typewriters stopped, the clanging telephones were stilled, the bustle and excitement subsided. An army of executives, fundraisers, and consultants suddenly found themselves out of work.

In the ensuing weeks, Hadassah collapsed, Mizrachi folded, Israel Bonds closed up, ORT ceased operation, UJA toppled. The vast, complex, and talented bureaucracy, with nothing left to do, ground to a halt.

What does an unemployed Jewish leader do?

American Jews, after the initial joy subsided, began to exhibit withdrawal symptoms. Communal leaders were seen aimlessly wandering the streets in search of a meeting. In the evenings, with nothing to occupy them, they took to reading *Robert's Rules of Order*. In one midwestern town, a group of former committee chairmen began a weekly study group to analyze the details of organizational procedure and to reminisce about great parliamentarians they had once known. One enterprising ex-executive formed an organization called "Chairmen Anonymous." Whenever anyone felt the urge to go to a meeting, he would dial a number and listen to recordings which replayed the proceedings of past meetings, featuring points of order, committee reports, budget readings, motions for adjournment, and other highlights.

In New York an emergency conference wired Ariel Sharon: HUN-DREDS OF JEWISH PROFESSIONALS OUT OF WORK. THOUSANDS OF LAYMEN WITH NOTHING TO DO. AMERICAN JEWRY IN CRISIS. PLEASE ARRANGE FOR A SMALL SKIRMISH ALONG THE SYRIAN BORDER. The wire was signed by 350 unemployed Federation directors. But it went unanswered.

It was a time of triumph for Israel; it was a time of trial for American Jewry.

As time went on, those whose only Jewish identity had been loyalty to Israel started suddenly to ask who they were, and why. They began a desperate search for something to live for, some new way by which to express their Jewishness.

And then they found something they had never noticed before: themselves. They discovered that in their zeal to help Israel they had totally neglected their personal Jewishness. They had helped the educational needs of others, but had forgotten their own, and so it happened that Hadassah and Mizrachi took joint responsibility for the fundraising of every day school in the United States of America; UJA opened a network of twenty-five yeshivot throughout the country; ORT rehabilitated Jewish youth by opening fifty intensive Jewish summer camps. Fifty-two Federations voted unanimously to fund Jewish educational needs from kindergarten through university.

The entire army of executives, fundraisers, and consultants returned to work. The bustle and excitement were felt again in the Jewish offices, the stilled telephones began to clang again, the stopped typewriters clattered, and the vast complex, and talented machinery of American Jewry sprang to life—all devoted to one cause: a crash program to raise the spiritual level of Jewish life.

It was a time of joy, a time of laughter. Federations gave dinners to honor young Jews who committed themselves to Jewish learning and to mitzvot; UJA gave its Man of the Year awards to poor and unknown scholars; every day school and yeshiva in the country ended the year without a deficit.

That was the year the Messiah came.

Testimonials; or, I Can Get It for You Wholesale

AMERICAN JEWISH ORGANIZATIONS face a serious crisis. Unless something drastic is done soon, the time is rapidly approaching when Jewish organizations will run out of people to whom they can give testimonials. But this crisis is being ignored. On the contrary, if New York–based organizations are any criterion, testimonial dinners are increasing in tempo. In fact, the latest rage is typically Jewish: why go retail when you can do them wholesale? A totally new concept: wholesale testimonials; that is, citations not to one person per dinner, but to several awardees per dinner—an average of one awardee for every course served.

Let us thumb through a recent issue of a New York Jewish newspaper. On page 8, American Friends of Kiryat Zanz Hospital announces a testimonial dinner for the board chairman of a New York City bank. In addition, they will give the Tzedakah Award to a "Noted Philanthropist and Industrialist."

Page 9: The Board of Governors and the National Dinner Committee of the Torah Schools for Israel will honor two people with their Keser Torah ("Crown of the Torah") Award. And there will be seven (7) communal leaders who will receive the Chasan Torah ("Groom of the Torah") Award. Grand total of honorees: nine. (This may be a new world's record, but let us read on.)

Page 15: Yeshiva Be'er Shmuel of Brooklyn, at its annual testimonial dinner, will honor "Friends and Benefactors." They list seven names.

The same page 15 announces the annual dinner of a national body of synagogues. The Keser Shem Tov ("Crown of the Good Name") Award will be featured. In addition, there is a National Distinguished Service Award, plus a National Rabbinic Leadership Award.

270

And, beyond this, they will also give out the Annual President's Award to certain selected individuals from around the country. How many? Eleven (11). Grand total of awardees for the evening: fourteen (14).

Page 16: Poale Agudas Israel of America will honor a husband and wife who are "Noted Philanthropists and Communal Leaders." In addition, there will be a recipient of the Keser Shem Tov Award; a Woman of the Year Award; Harbazas Torah ("Spreader of Torah") Award. Grand total: six (6) awardees. This is a good try, but it lags far behind the synagogue body's fourteen and Torah Schools' nine.

Page 19: Yeshiva Torah Vodaath will honor at its banquet the man who is Chairman of the Board, plus his wife, plus the recipients of the following honors: Amudas Hachesed ("Pillar of Kindness") Award; Ahavas Yisroel ("Lover of Israel") Award; Founders' Award; Lev Tov ("Good Heart") Award; Keser Torah Award; and a Torah Benefactor Award. Grand total: eight.

Page 26: Mirrer Yeshiva announces that its dinner will honor an "Outstanding Philanthropist and Supporter of Torah" and his wife. No other awardees. No other titles. And on page 28, Yeshivat Mikdash Melech will honor two people for "Dedicated Service." Again, no other recipients or titles. (One should investigate these two yeshivot: have they run out of people, or are they trying to turn Jewish chaos into mere bedlam?)

While the hallowed tradition of dispensing yearly *kavod* is being widely observed and even expanded, we dare not rest on our laurels. There are still many ways in which the annual testimonial sweepstakes can be enhanced. We therefore submit the following suggestions.

Firstly, it is clear that with only five million Jews in America, these multiple-award dinners will soon find us bereft of awardees. *A recent Ivy League study showed that if present trends of intermarriage, assimilation, and rich banquet foods continue, the American Jewish community one hundred years hence may have as little as one hundred and ten potential honorees left.* Thus, a sensible suggestion: since the names of the award recipients are not remembered from year to year, why not establish a computerized "Central Registry of Honorees." Using this Registry, organizations could share honorees with one another as the needs arise. Certainly, in times where a critical awardee shortage awaits us, we will simply have to cooperate with one another. Our future as a Jewish community is at stake.

Secondly, there is the problem of the names of the awards themselves. Clearly, there are already too many identical names. Both the synagogue body and Torah Schools for Israel are giving the "Crown of the Good Name" Award. And Yeshiva Torah Vadaath and Torah Schools for Israel each gives the "Crown of the Torah Award." New titles, new awards, and new crowns are desperately needed. In a spirit of communal cooperation, we humbly tender here several new suggestions: the Crown of Humility Award; the Tzaddik of the Year Award; the Biggest Contributor Award; the Man of the Century Award; the Greatest Jew in the World Award.

Thirdly, there should be a major Annual Award given to that organization which distributes the most awards at one dinner. Surely, fourteen awardees at one dinner—this year's world record— can be surpassed with a little creative ingenuity. By utilizing the two suggestions above, it should not be difficult for any self-respecting organization to break the award barrier and aim for at least a doubling of that figure. At a time such as this, with mounting deficits and dwindling income, it is time to bite the plaque and take bold, imaginative initiatives. If you will it, it is no dream. It goes without saying that an award will be presented to that organization which wins next year's contest. This brand-new award will be known as the Award Award.

Finally, we propose that all award recipients band together into a major new organization, open only to those who have received awards in the past. This group would meet at an annual banquet and would honor those members who had received the most awards in the previous twelve months. The new organization would be known as the Annual Winners of Awards and Recognitions Division, or AWARD. It has the potential of becoming the largest organization in America.

The Beit ha-Mikdash Campaign

A number of years ago, the local Jewish Community Center decided by majority vote of its board of directors to open up its facilities on Shabbat, despite the strong protests of the traditional community. Outmanned, outfinanced, and outpowered, the traditional community had little in its arsenal but the pen. The outcome of the struggle is not important here, but, if one can judge from the cries of "foul" which were heard afterwards, the following item was among the more effective broadsides hurled during the ensuing fray. While matters are somewhat exaggerated here, be assured that the comments and actions depicted are based on actual events, and are not completely figments of the writer's imagination.

News Item: The local Jewish Community Center has announced that its building will henceforth be open on Shabbat. The decision was endorsed by the JCC's Study Commission, which recommended that the opening should be done in the "spirit of Shabbat," that a vase of flowers should be in the lobby, that a sign should read "Shabbat Shalom" in order to create the proper atmosphere, and that the day should be "meaningful."

A NICE CHRISTIAN lady called me the other day and asked, "Now that the Jews have all of Jerusalem, there is talk that you people are going to rebuild the ancient Holy Temple."

"No," I replied, "Jewish tradition prescribes that the rebuilding of the Holy Temple—known as the *Beit ha-Mikdash*—can only take place at the 'end of days,' when the Messiah arrives."

After she hung up, it occurred to me that we are fortunate to have such a tradition. Otherwise, the following might take place:

The Knesset today declared a worldwide fundraising effort to rebuild the Beit ha-Mikdash in Jerusalem. The Prime Minister extended personal invitations to the world's Jewish leaders (those who had given $25,000 and up to the UJA) to go up to Jerusalem on a special mission to discuss the situation with him personally. At the meeting, a goal of $1 billion was set for the campaign. In an emotional speech, the Minister of Interior declared, "We have been waiting for this event for two thousand years. This will mean ten million additional tourists in the next decade."

In Atlanta, the Jewish community was mobilized. A citywide Beit ha-Mikdash Committee was formed. In order to begin the campaign on a high note, the steering committee planned a Beit ha-Mikdash Kickoff Dinner Dance to take place at one of the posh nonkosher country clubs on a Friday night.

Shock waves were immediately felt throughout the Jewish community. The traditional Jews denounced the event as a religious affront; newspaper ads pleaded that it was a matter of conscience; rabbis declared that it was hypocrisy to rebuild a House of God by violating God's laws and recalled that in a democracy the voice of a minority must also be heeded.

But the steering committee was adamant. We must have it on Friday night, they said, in order to ensure the success of the campaign; we have taken a vote and majority rules; we will not be dictated to by a small group; besides, who keeps Shabbat and kashruth these days anyway? For those who want it, a fruit plate will be served. Finally, the committee chairman declared emotionally, "The Community Calendar has been cleared for this event; how can we change it now?"

But in an effort to heal the breach in the community, the committee formed a study commission to review the entire problem. After a number of meetings, the commission noted that Shabbat was a good thing. They also endorsed the Friday night Dinner Dance. However, the commission proposed new guidelines for future Friday night Dinner Dances:

1. The treifa food should be eaten in a spirit of kashruth.
2. The violations of Shabbat should be done in a spirit of Shabbat.
3. The affair should begin late enough on Friday night to allow everyone to go to services first.

4. Fruit plates should be available.
5. A Shabbat atmosphere should be created.
6. A bowl of flowers and a sign reading "Shabbat Shalom" should be placed in the middle of the dance floor.
7. All wines should be Israeli.
8. Everything that is done should be meaningful.

The steering committee approved the study commission's guidelines by an overwhelming majority, and the Beit ha-Mikdash Dinner Dance went on as scheduled on the appointed Friday night. Miss Israel of 5746 was a special guest, and received a standing ovation. The main speaker was a prominent figure in the Israeli Foreign Office, who spoke of the significance of the Beit ha-Mikdash. "Christians have their Vatican, Moslems have their Mecca," he said emotionally. "Why shouldn't Jews have their Beit ha-Mikdash in Jerusalem?" He received a standing ovation. He continued: "This building can be the final answer to Israel's economy. It will bring in millions of dollars to the country." The chairman of the steering committee then announced that the Beit ha-Mikdash would have a special "Atlanta Room," with a large bronze plaque on which would be inscribed the names of all those who contributed $5,000 and up on a five-year basis. "This is the first time in the history of the Beit ha-Mikdash," he declared, "that an Atlanta Room has been established." He received a standing ovation.

The evening was a huge success. Three million dollars were raised. "We are proud of you," said the chairman. "Because of your dedication and sacrificial giving, the Holy Temple will once again be a reality, as in days of yore. The Messiah is just around the corner!"

That year, American Jews raised almost a billion dollars towards the Beit ha-Mikdash campaign. But somehow, the building was never put up. Nor did the Messiah ever appear.

No one knows exactly why.

How to Be a Successful Rabbi

Our intrepid spies have just intercepted a piece of top-sacred information in the form of a memo sent by our rabbi to his rabbinical colleagues in the field (at this writing we have been unable to determine precisely the location of the field), sharing his secrets on how to be a successful rabbi. This exclusive, copyrighted story is for the eyes of Beth Jacob's members only (paid up, including Building Fund). Any other use, through photocopying, or electronic equipment, or plain plagiarism, is expressly forbidden.

MEMO TO MY colleagues the world over. I am deeply flattered to be asked to share with you my never-before-revealed secrets of rabbinic success. There are a number of factors that go into a successful rabbinic career:

1.) *Make-up and lighting.* I have known wonderful and promising rabbis whose careers have been dashed to the ground because their lighting and make-up on Friday night and Shabbat were not just right. These are the *sine qua non* before every sermon and religious service, probably the most important weapon in a rabbi's spiritual arsenal. It is beyond me how any rabbi can hope to influence his congregation to return to God, Torah, and mitzvot unless he uses lighting and make-up properly. I have known blond rabbis with blue eyes who ruined their ideal rabbinic look by the wrong make-up. In my own congregation, the plans for our new edifice call for special lighting booths and make-up alcoves right above the Ark. This is in keeping with the spirit of the old adage which was taught to me by my mentors, and which I always keep on my desk as an eternal reminder of what my true goals are: "Lighting is vital, but make-up takes the cake."

2.) *Robes.* Being a successful rabbi is a full-time job. Unless you are willing to give the necessary time and make the necessary sacrifices, all your years of study may turn out to be wasted. This is why robes are so vital. Proper selection of robes, in terms of fabric, color, and fit, can make or break a rabbinic career. Furthermore, the best lighting and make-up can be undone by poor robe selection. It is important to select the robes that present a picture of respectability, solemnity, and seriousness. Remember to bear in mind that on the High Holidays (those are the days when the synagogue is usually crowded even though there is no Bar Mitzvah; they invariably come towards the end of the summer vacation) it is best to wear white robes. Since on Yom Kippur (which usually falls about a week after Rosh Hashanah, the Jewish New Year) one usually does not eat, there is little problem of having these pristine white robes stained by food. On ordinary Sabbaths, black is *de rigeur*, since *Kiddush* can play havoc with robing. For very significant events, one can special-order velvet trimming for your robes. For weddings, for example, the latest fashion is a magnificent and awe-inspiring red. (It is advisable to check with the wedding families to make certain that wedding robes coordinate properly with the dresses, tuxedos, and gowns of the wedding party.) Hint: my own career has been greatly enhanced by the role of my personal wardrobe consultant, who has helped me across the many delicate and dangerous pitfalls which are endemic to the rabbinate. He also selects the right ties. (Occasionally, the wardrobe consultant can double as a media adviser as well.)

3.) *Prayer-shawls.* The prayer-shawl, worn on holy days and on Sabbaths, is a necessary part of the accountrement of the successful rabbinic ensemble. Warning: prayer-shawls come in all sizes, lengths, and materials. Woolen ones are to be avoided, since they are very uncomfortable in the summer, and they suggest an Old World effect, which is to be avoided at all costs if we want to attract large congregations. It is best to wear a prayer-shawl that is no wider than six inches, to keep it from obscuring the robe; it should preferably be of silk or rayon, or one of the exciting new polyester mixes. Vitally important: always coordinate these colors with your robe, your lighting, and your make-up for that particular day. Important note: the prayer-shawl is worn on the shoulders and not on the head or arms. These are not to be confused with phylacteries, also known as "tefillin," which are no longer worn by successful rabbis, since the Orthodox tefillin manufacturers insist that phylacteries must be all black, thus stifling creativity and innovation.

4.) *Sermon.* The sermon is often the downfall of an otherwise successful career. This is because the purpose of the sermon is not fully understood, even by rabbis. As I have stressed many times to my colleagues in the field, the primary function of the sermon is to provide an opportunity to set off the make-up and the lighting, and to view the robe. Once this is kept in mind, one can avoid the pitfall of delivering sermons that are thoughtful, controversial, learned, or inspirational. Such sermons do nothing more than distract the congregation from their essential role: seeing how you look. As the Torah itself says: when Moses descended Sinai, his face shone so brightly that the people could not gaze upon him because it was as bright as the sun. As a result, Moses had to put a mask over his face. (Some say that the bright light caused his make-up to melt, and this is why he had to cover his face with a mask.) In any case, this radical step by Moses could easily have been avoided had he provided himself with a proper lighting consultant. It is clear from the commentaries on this text that Moses' lighting consultant overdid it. Fortunately, we have learned from Moses never to repeat this mistake again. To my knowledge, no rabbi since the time of Moses has ever had to cover his face with a mask. This is ample proof that a good rabbi continuously looks to Moses as a shining example.

If Judaism is to have any future at all, it will be because we rabbis finally realize that it is up to us to provide the bricks for the highway which bridges the fields of old and the technology of the new, and which transforms both into a ladder going from that highway up towards heaven, where the radiance of the splendor above casts down a beam of light which will make up for the darkness which robes the universe when there is no faith, vision, hope, or media consultants. I therefore close by reminding all of you of the cardinal teaching of our wise leaders of old: "It is not who you are, it is what you wear; it is not what you think, it is what you look like that makes the difference."

A Sitting Ovation

ONCE UPON A time the routine was universally accepted. The speaker would finish his talk, he would sit down, the audience would applaud. It was as simple as ABC. But we live in inflationary times, and simple applause will no longer do. When a speaker concludes his remarks these days, anything short of a standing ovation is almost an insult. It matters not how nondescript the speaker or how dull-witted his talk, once he sits down he can rest assured that the audience will stand up. (And every speaker knows that a standing ovation, like any overused cliché, is today without meaning or significance.)

Recently in Atlanta the ultimate in Jewish standing ovations took place. The speaker was former Secretary of State Dean Rusk. During his remarks he came out in favor of the internationalization of Jerusalem. Most Jews know that this proposal—as favored by the USSR, the Vatican, and others—can only wreak havoc on a Jerusalem in which the holy places of all religions are respected, and Jew and Arab live peacefully side by side. But no matter. When Mr. Rusk sat down after making this proposal to his Jewish listeners, the audience applauded and, as if by a Pavlovian signal, sprang to their collective feet in standing ovation.

Poor Mr. Rusk, expecting a rather frigid reaction for his speech, must have been confused by all this. He may never know that his audience didn't necessarily agree with him and that they are simply Jewish victims of inflation.

I am told, by the way, that in that audience of hundreds there were six courageous souls who did not rise. More power to them. Having sat grimly through standing ovations for scores of politicians, hundreds of committee chairmen, and dozens of men-of-the-year, I know that lonely feeling well. Personally, I prefer the guide given to us by the *Shulḥan Arukh*. You rise for your teacher of Torah, for your mother or father, for a wise scholar of Torah, for an aged man, and perhaps for heads of state. Next time you hear a speaker, try the *Shulḥan Arukh*'s guidelines. And, occasionally, try a sitting ovation.

In Any Image Createth He Them

THE NIEMAN-MARCUS STORES have long been famous for their annual His and Her gifts. There have been His and Her camels, His and Her yachts, His and Her airplanes. For this year they offer something very special: His and Her people: full-dimensional, life-size facsimiles of—yourself. A life-size model will be done of you (you can specify the sitting or standing model), and you can have him (or her) as a constant companion. The model can be programmed to respond vocally at your beck and call. If you like appreciative listeners, she/he/it will laugh as long as you like at your jokes; or if you are the authoritative type, the model will say "Yes, sir" at the touch of a remote-control button. And when it runs down and gets tired, you simply plug in the accompanying cord to charge it up again. All this for only $3,000. (Clothes and sculptor's air fare are extra.)

The idea has infinite possibilities. For a rabbi—if he could afford it—it might well be worth the $3,000.

For example, I have often wished I could be two people. Now I can. When Organization X wants me to sit at the dais for their annual banquet and I would rather be elsewhere, I can now be elsewhere and send my $3,000 facsimile to the dinner. When I have to be present at a meeting when I'd rather be doing something else, I can send my double and do something else. When I am expected at an interminable cocktail party, my counterpart (the standing model) can go and smile affably, while I relax. Certainly it would be the kind of spiritual leader who offends no one: a true model rabbi.

The possibilities are dizzying: I could purchase a few models of synagogue officers and program them to say, "Yes, Rabbi," and all my requests for new projects and ideas would pass without a dissenting vote.

Or perhaps I should order a few dozen synagogue worshippers and place them strategically throughout the congregation on Shabbat. I would have them sculpted with eyes wide open, mouths closed, understanding looks in their eyes, expressions of sheer delight and joy on their faces as the rabbi delivers his sermon. They could even be programmed to say, "You didn't speak long enough."

But then again, things would probably soon get very dull with all those robots around. Genuine people are much more exciting, cost much less (at least initially), and come in many more interesting models. They are preprogrammed to speak softly or loudly, politely or rudely, honestly or deceptively. They have built-in souls, minds, characters—which even Nieman-Marcus cannot provide—and they come with various degrees of integrity, ethics, and morality. They do need an occasional recharge, and there is no handy cord to plug into the nearest socket—but there is always Shabbat, which is much more effective.

The live model does not always laugh at your jokes, occasionally says no, opens his mouth when it should be closed, closes his eyes when they should be open, and sometimes tells you that you spoke too long. They can be very vexing, these live models, but they are much more fascinating.

No, this year I'll have to pass up the His and Hers gift. Yachts, yes; camels, yes; airplanes, yes; but people facsimiles? Not just yet.

At least not until Nieman-Marcus develops a model which can be counted towards a minyan.

Space-Age Shopping For the Religious Jew

In my travels around the world, I have been able to pick up a variety of unusual and clever little gadgets which fit the lifestyle of the members of our congregation. After many years of collecting these gadgets, our members have importuned me to share these unusual one-of-a-kind collector's items with our readers. No synagogue member should be without them. Presented below are these satisfaction-guaranteed items, specially selected for the Purim season.

MICRO–MATIC SIDDUR. Trim, slim, ultra-light weight micromatic Siddur is also a pocket calculator, microwave toaster and daily prayer book all in one. Ingenious function lets you punch up *Shaharit* or *Minhah* when you are too busy to daven. Press a button and it plays *Adon Olam* and *Yigdal.* Also recites *Ha-Motzi* while instant microwave oven toasts 3″ × 4″ piece of bread. Ideal for the devout, frum man on the go. Tasteful carrying case with shoulder strap. Only . . . .$99.95.

BJ SCANNER XXI. Time-saving Torah-learning device actually studies Bible, Mishnah, and Talmud for you while you sleep. Silent, all transistorized, fits easily in briefcase or under pillow. Just set it and forget it—devours 500 pages per day. Light flashes when finished, reloads in seconds. Handles any size book from large Talmud size to mini-Bible. Gone are the days when knowledge of Torah meant a lifetime of study. With this scholarly aid, you can finish the Talmud in one night, while you have a full night's sleep. . . .$99.95.

SERMON NAP–SACK: Slip this fashion-styled European NAP–SACK over your head for restful sleep during long and arduous sermons. Double-stitched seams, reinforced ear and nose pockets, heavy-duty breathing grille. Comes in handy tote bag. Indispensable for those long Shabbat morning announcements. . . . .$99.95.

A companion item to the SERMON NAP–SACK is the BJ SERMON DETECTORANGE XLX. Futuristic device focuses rays on rabbi's face during sermons, and determines to the exact second how long sermon will last. Heavy-duty attachment available for Rosh Hashanah and Yom Kippur.

TEFILLIN AUTO-WIND. Attach this space-age wonder to your tefillin and watch the amazing results. Simply place tefillin on your forearm, press the button, and presto—the tefillin wind themselves around your arm and fingers in the proper halakhic manner. Why waste needless energy in tedious winding when this is so handy? Sephardic and Ashkenazic models available. . . . .$69.95.

BJ DAVENING VIDEO DISCS. Sensational new discovery allows you to stay in bed and enjoy services the way they were meant to be enjoyed. Why go to shul in the cold and rain when these full-color high-fidelity discs allow you to enjoy an inspirational service in the comfort of your own home? Fast-forward device speeds up rabbi's sermons and cantorial arias. Rewind feature allows you to hear rare jokes and witticisms again. Editing feature allows you to delete portions of services which are too long. Splice, edit, and tailor yourself the kind of davening which you alone deserve. Discs available for every Shabbat of the year. High Holiday attachment available soon. . . . .$89.95.

BJ WATER–MIK 2000XL. Designed on the famous blimp principle, the WATER–MIK inflatable mikvah stands on any flat surface. Blows up in seconds into a 6' × 9' tiled mikvah complete with shower, bath, hot and cold water, hair dryer, throw-away towels, and paper slippers. Completely waterproof. Solve your mikvah problems with one breath of air. No more waiting in line. Deflates to handkerchief size in seconds. Complete with rainwater starter kit. Comes in his and hers models . . . .$159.95.

THE BJ PREPPY BOOK. A Beth Jacob Preppy always wears a black-and-white striped tallis . . . never misses putting on his tefillin, and his tefillin boxes are never anything but square and pure black . . . always wears a black kipah . . . Preppies never wear velvet yarmulkas, how tacky . . . black homburg hats are in, colored kippahs are on their way out . . . a Preppy always asks for Hagbah or Gelilah, never for Shlishi or Maftir . . . always contributes a minimum of twice Chai to BJ . . . never looks at a book during sermons no matter how bad the sermon, no matter how good the book . . . never misses a shul function, and when he is out of town, always sends a check . . . makes certain that his tallis has pleats in the rear, plus a button-down front . . . these and other choice tidbits are all there in the BJ Preppy Book . . . .$5.95.

As you can see, when your rabbi travels out of town, he always has YOU in mind and heart, and is always on the lookout for items which will make your religious life easier and pleasanter. After all, God is good, and surely He in His infinite wisdom did not mean for us to strain ourselves in any way in the performance of His sacred tasks. During this coming year, I pledge my sacred honor to continue looking for those religious items which can make Beth Jacob the preeminent Orthodox synagogue in the world. Have a wonderful Purim. (And, if you have trouble drinking schnapps or eating hamantaschen, give me a call: I have a little Purim Drinkomatic item which allows you to eat and drink all you want, even after you are completely full.)

More Space-Age Shopping

NO ONE APPRECIATES more than your rabbi that it is not a simple matter to be a true-believing and practicing Jew, and I am happy to present to you these satisfaction-guaranteed items which can make life a bit easier for you. Last year's collection was such a phenomenal success that, at the urging of myriads of people, I present here—in honor of Purim—an updated list of the latest in sophisticated twenty-first-century wizardry. No Jew should be without them.

DIAL–A–GOSSIP XL100. A sensational time-saver for people who love to gossip but just do not have the time. Dial one number and get a prerecorded gossip message. Juicy, meaty stories about your neighbors, relatives, and friends, hot off the press. Special optional attachments feature fascinating gossip about the rabbi, assistant rabbi, cantor, executive director, and synagogue secretaries. Special: custom-made gossip about anyone you want $95.95

THE CIRCLE U AUTO KASHRUTH DEVICE 999. Trim, slim, ultra-lightweight, circle U stamp quickly and easily solves all your kashruth problems and avoids guilt at the same time. Ingenious device places kosher insignia on any food item in the supermarket. No longer necessary to waste precious time looking for the tiny circle U on your foods when you can do the imprinting with this space-age discovery. Foolproof. Turns any food delicacy into a kosher-approved item in a flash. Ideal for the modern Jewish woman. Indispensable for the balanced diet. Fits easily into your purse. Greatest contribution to kashruth since Sinai . . . . .A steal at $69.95.

SHABBAT LASER SHADOW BJ 84. This amazing precision instrument makes it possible for you to do what you like and strictly observe Shabbat at the same time. Futuristic invention allows you to be in two places at once. Spectacular laser device casts true-to-life shadow of yourself in your synagogue seat on Friday nights and

Shabbat mornings, while the real you is at home watching basketball. The Laser Shadow does all the right things: turns the Siddur pages, mumbles Hebrew words, says "good Shabbat," stands, sits, sways, bows, answers Amen, talks to your neighbor, sings off key, and takes naps during sermons—while all the time the real you is out shopping, visiting the barber, watching sports events, going to parties, and generally living it up. Ideal for the devout man on the go. Heavy-duty Rosh Hashanah and Yom Kippur models available . . . .$295.00.

THE PARLIAMENTARY DISC XLV101. This handy item slips into any television set and plays back famous parliamentary ploys, great parliamentary maneuvers, and points of order. One sensational section features history's most exciting motions to adjourn. Complete with diagrams, maps, strategies, and illustrations. For the synagogue board member or officer in your life. Wonderful for those long, lonely nights when there is no meeting anywhere in town to attend. Vicarious enjoyment for less than the price of a movie. Autographed by Robert Rules, this is the ideal gift for the synagogue board member or officer .special at $99.95.

ELECTRONIC SERMON SCORE CARD ESS98. Not a gadget or toy, but an expensive precision-made instrument which allows you to keep an accurate score sheet of 1001 sermons. In one carefully crafted instrument you can perform several functions simultaneously: checks length of sermon to the split second and records it for future reference; gives automatic rating of sermons on scale of 1 to 10; rates on content, delivery, depth, interest, relevance, and boredom; takes and summarizes every sermon into twenty-five words or less, saving you time and energy. No serious shul-goer can afford to be without one. Batteries extra. . . . . .Special at $89.50.

THE TALLIS AUTO–WIND. An indispensable companion piece to last year's popular Tefillin Auto-Wind. Attach this space-age wonder to your tallis and watch the amazing results. Simply place device on your folded tallis, press the button, and immediately the tallis climbs by itself to your shoulders and drapes itself around your body in the proper halakhic manner. No fuss, no bother, no falling edges. Press a second button and it recites the tallis berakhah while added function opens your Siddur to the proper page. Why waste needless energy in tedious attempts to keep tallis in place when this is so handy? End backsliding problems forever. When services are over, the Auto-Wind removes tallis from your shoulders, and neatly folds and stores it in tallis bag while you talk to your friends . . . .$75.00.

The Question of Questions

YOUR RABBI WISHES to make himself available to the members of the congregation in order to answer all of their questions in as efficient a manner as possible.

In order to implement this, your rabbi and his media consultants have worked out the following new policy and guidelines.

New Policy on Questions to the Rabbi

1. Effective immediately, questions to the rabbi which begin with the letter *W* will no longer be considered. This includes words such as "What, Why, When, Where, Who."

2. Any questions which begin with the word "rabbi" will no longer be considered. (Please note that questions which begin with the words, "Rabbi, why—" are a double violation of these new rules, and can result in immediate revocation of membership.)

3. Questions containing the following phrases will no longer be considered: "May I eat—"; "Is it true that—"; "I read that—"; "Where is it written that—"; "Is (name of any food) kosher?"

4. Telephoned questions can no longer be accepted. The telephone is an impersonal medium, and the rabbi wants to be close to his people when he answers their questions. At the same time, face-to-face questions are somewhat undignified and are therefore also no longer acceptable. Written questions, however, will be accepted when the following guidelines are followed: (a) all inquiries shall be typed on an Apple IIe word processor; (b) all questions must be triple-spaced; (c) three copies of each question must be submitted; (d) stamped self-addressed envelope must be enclosed. (In cases of urgent questions, where there is a time factor, two instead of three copies will be accepted.)

5. In order that the rabbi's time be utilized as efficiently as

288

possible, there will no longer be any Shabbat morning sermons. And, until further notice, no adult classes, youth classes, or discussion groups will be conducted by the rabbi. Instead, the rabbi's media advisers will present a brief weekly press briefing. (See below.) These will contain all the essential teachings which the rabbi wishes to impart to his members.

6. Your cooperation with these new guidelines is urgently requested. Its immediate implementation will give the rabbi more time to think, meditate, concentrate, cogitate, and ponder such imponderables as the state of world Jewry, the future of American Jewish life, and the problems of his backhand—always with the ultimate goal in mind that he should be able to serve you better and to answer all of your questions in as efficient and as meaningful a way as possible.

We close with this quotation from our beloved rabbi: "Judaism is a religion of questions. The Talmud is composed of questions. Constant questioning is a sign of questing and seeking. I want to encourage all my people constantly to ask, to question, to probe, to seek out, because only by asking the right questions can we learn the truths of the Torah. As is written in *Pirkei Avot* (Ethics of the Fathers), *lo ha-baishan lamed*, 'He who is shy (who never asks questions) will never learn.' "

It is in the spirit of this philosophy that our beloved and revered rabbi has requested that these new guidelines be instituted. As long as each question meets the guidelines in paragraphs 1 through 4 above, all questions will be answered with care and loving concern.

As a small example of the profundities of which our rabbi is capable once he is given the time to think, we are proud to present this advance copy of the first press briefing of the new season:

1. The rabbi has concluded that the Jewish people have a long history.

2. He stated that, after long and careful consideration, he thinks the Torah is really great.

3. He added that he feels that the commandments are great.

4. Finally, in keeping with his reputation as a rabbi who always calls the shots as he sees them, he has come out openly with the following declaration: God is also great.